Hunter's Guide to
Shotguns for Upland Game

Terry Boyer

STACKPOLE
BOOKS

Copyright © 2007 by Stackpole Books

Published by
STACKPOLE BOOKS
5067 Ritter Road
Mechanicsburg, PA 17055
www.stackpolebooks.com

Printed in China

First edition

10 9 8 7 6 5 4 3 2 1

Cover design by Wendy A. Reynolds
Cover photo courtesy of Winchester Arms

Photographs by the author, except where otherwise noted

Library of Congress Cataloging-in-Publication Data

Boyer, Terry.
  Hunter's guide to shotguns for upland game / Terry Boyer.
     p. cm.
  Includes index.
  ISBN-13: 978-0-8117-3358-8
  ISBN-10: 0-8117-3358-0
  1. Shotguns. 2. Small game hunting—Equipment and supplies. 3. Upland game bird shooting—Equipment and supplies.   I. Title.
  SK274.5.B69 2007
  799.2'02834—dc22

                          2006027038

*This book is dedicated to my
late Brittany, Dee Dee,
who for thirteen years found
and retrieved the birds.*

Contents

Foreword

Terry Boyer loves to hunt upland game. So do I, which is why it was a pleasure for me to read this book on upland shotguns. Although any old shotgun can be used in the uplands, Terry makes it clear what distinguishes a true upland gun from, say, a target gun, a waterfowl gun, or a turkey gun (although upland shotguns can also be used on targets, ducks, and gobblers). He further refines his definition to suggest guns (along with chokes and loads) for various species of upland game. You can hunt pheasants in open country and woodcock in the thick stuff with the same gun, but Terry will tell you why there are probably better, more specific choices in both cases.

I enjoy writers who aren't afraid to express their opinions. The late Jack O'Connor, to whom Terry refers a few times, was such a writer. And although Terry promises not to get up on his soapbox too often, he's not hesitant to do so when he deems it important to his readers. For example: "American shooters: wouldn't you like to know more about the shells that you are spending *your* money on than some outdated ritualistic formula?" He then proceeds to tell you what you really need to know about shotshells—and why.

On pheasant loads, he writes: "I personally believe that if you think you need a 3-inch load to hunt pheasants that what you need to do is get your gun out of the closet in the off season and practice shooting. That will help you take more pheasants than the heaviest 3-inch shell." I've lived in Iowa most of my life, hunted pheasants since the 1950s, and have never used a 3-inch shell to kill a rooster. Amen, Terry!

Whether you're a beginning upland hunter or a seasoned veteran, you'll learn something—probably a lot—from this book. Terry covers everything from gauges (still a mystery to many people), action types, currently available upland guns and shotshells, how to "customize" your shotgun from butt to muzzle (and your loads), how to clean, transport, and store guns, and the value of off-season practice.

He also makes the very logical point, which all too many hunters seem to ignore, that in choosing a gun/choke/load combination, you have to consider not only what you hunt, but how you hunt. Pheasants, for example: you'll likely have very different shots if you're involved in one of the large-group, block-and-drive operations in the Dakotas, as compared to hunting alone or maybe with just one other buddy, behind a good dog or two.

And Terry talks about other factors involved in upland hunting, including gear (such as boots and clothing) that will allow you to pursue your sport in greater comfort. On the subject of boots, for example, he points out that there are boots that give protection and support without excessive weight. The less weight on your feet, the longer you can walk—and upland hunting involves a lot more walking than it does shooting. (The late Bill Bowerman, track coach at the University of Oregon where he coached many national champions and American record-holders, made the same observation about his runners and their shoes. He felt reduced weight was so important that he started making shoes for his runners. One of the results of his fixation on shoe weight was the birth of a company you may have heard of: Nike). Upland hunters should have the same fixation.

Terry does have a few quirks some readers may find unorthodox. For example, he's a big fan of the 16-gauge, prefers over-and-unders to side-by-sides, and doesn't like double triggers. Whichever of those you find sensible as opposed to eccentric, Terry will give you solid reasons for his choices. And he'll also point out that what works best for him may not be what works best for you, all the while giving you information that will guide you through the complex world of today's upland shotgun.

While this book is thorough, it's not so long that reading it will seem a daunting undertaking. And when you've absorbed what Terry has to say, you may very well find that he's helped you choose a gun or load that's better suited to the game of upland hunting as you play it. That, in turn, may mean more birds in the bag and a more enjoyable time afield—because it can be frustrating when you're saddled with the wrong tool for the task at hand. I enjoyed it and learned from it, and I'm sure you will, too.

Larry Brown
Garden City, Iowa

Acknowledgments

This book came about from a conversation at the 2005 SHOT Show in Las Vegas. I want to thank Don Gulbrandsen, my editor from Stackpole Books, for all of his help, encouragement, and advice.

I also wish to thank Frank Kodl and Johnny Cantu from *Shotgun Sports Magazine* for their encouragement of my writing career for many years. A big thanks to Jeff, Tye, David, Danny, Steve, Terry, Don, and all the others I have had the privilege to chase birds with over the years. Thanks for all of the hunts, the fun, the experiences, and the camaraderie.

Thanks to Smoky, Gypsy, Daisy, and Dee Dee. They are gone but not forgotten. And to Dolly and Missy who share the bird fields with me today.

Above all, thanks go to my father, William C. Boyer, for introducing me to birds and guns so many years ago.

Thank you all.

1

What is an Upland Shotgun?

The successful bird hunter must be knowledgeable about many things, but in the end it comes down to this: He must know his birds, his dogs, and his guns.

—Geoffrey Norman, The Orvis Book of Upland Bird Shooting

The simplest definition of an upland shotgun is that it is any shotgun that is used to take upland birds and game. Of course, if we stayed with that description, there would be no reason for me to write this book!

Any shotgun is a smoothbore weapon that fires shot charges and is used to take birds and game, both large and small. The fine matched pair of English doubles used by a Lord of the Realm on a driven bird shoot is a shotgun. The smooth bore, pot-metal muzzleloader used by an African or Indian tribesman to provide meat for his family—and maybe cash from larger animals—is also a shotgun. Although there is a vast difference in the two guns and how they are used, they both meet the requirements of the simple definition above.

So what really is an upland shotgun? The upland shotgun is a key. It is a key to years of pleasant

There are lots of different options for an upland gun.

1

and memorable experiences. It is a source of joy and fellowship. It is a key to hours that add up to days that turn into years spent with good friends, both canine and human.

There is an old saying that politics makes for strange bedfellows. This may be true, but upland hunting makes for an even stranger mix of friends and companions. I have been knocking around chasing upland birds for over forty years. In that time, I have enjoyed the companionship and camaraderie of captains of industry, insurance salesmen, delivery drivers, mechanics, roofers, farmers, cowboys, and college professors, just to name a few. Among my current group of hunting companions are a surgeon, a defense attorney, an oilfield worker, a veterinarian, a judge, a youth counselor, and a real estate appraiser. The things we have all had in common are a love of bird hunting, shotguns, hunting dogs, and the outdoors.

The upland shotgun is your key to being in the outdoors in the glorious days of autumn and the short dark days of winter. It is a key to the world of hunters, a part of the eternal relationship of predator and prey.

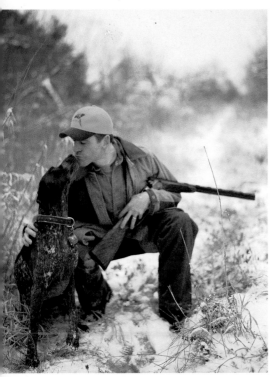

Fresh snow, a fine hunting dog, and your trusted over-and-under—ingredients for the perfect day in the field. BROWNING ARMS

Yes, in the most simplistic terms, the upland shotgun is merely metal and wood crafted together to launch a load of shot at a rising bird or a running rabbit. As it comes from the factory, the upland shotgun is nothing more, nothing less. It is the hunter that adds life to a shotgun. It becomes a part of the hunter and he becomes a part of the gun. It becomes a keeper of memories, a trusted companion, and adds life to the hunter just as the hunter adds life to it.

In World War II, Rear Admiral Daniel V. Gallery commanded a task force built around the escort carrier *Guadalcanal*. His group captured the German submarine *U-505* on the high seas. It was the first enemy vessel captured on the high seas during warfare since 1814. When speaking of his success, Admiral Gallery said, "Ships are just metal boxes. Some ships never 'come alive' no matter

Remington's Model 870 Wingmaster (here in 16 gauge) is a classic pump-action upland gun.
REMINGTON ARMS

how many crews serve on them. Other ships 'come alive' the first day and sail into history. The *Guadalcanal* was such a ship."

The upland gunner who has spent any time in the field will experience guns that "come alive" for him. They will hold a promise when he first picks them up, and they will grant that promise over months and years in the field. This book is for you, the hunter. I want you to be able to find and enjoy that particular gun that comes alive and becomes a part of you whether you are new to the sport or an experienced hunter (which is how I refer to myself instead of "old").

I can give you hints and ideas about what to look for when you're searching for your perfect gun. Is there a special gun out there for you? Yes, there is one, or more, for everyone. I have used many shotguns in many different environments and on many different types of game over the years. I have been fortunate to have several guns that fit the criteria of a special gun. What works for me won't necessarily work for you, but we have a common bond with our guns, even though they are different.

Forty-five hunting seasons ago, as a young boy using a borrowed 16-gauge single shot, I took a pheasant rooster while hunting with my dad. Since then, I have spent as much time as I could spare (and some I couldn't) chasing upland birds and game. I've learned from experience what works for me and even more about what does not. I've had custom guns made to order that I couldn't shoot worth a darn and off-the-rack guns that earned a special place.

Despite what others may think, right now is the golden age of shotguns. There are more makes, models, action types, and gauges being produced today than at any time in history. Modern computers and computer-operated machinery have eliminated much of the hand fitting that was required in the past for a gunmaker to turn out a high-quality weapon. Shotshell companies

Jon Uhart likes the weak-hand carry so that he can use his strong hand to give signals to his dog, Sage.

have spent huge amounts of money in recent years on research and development. This gives the shooter of today a cornucopia of gauges, loads, and shells that weren't even dreamed of just twenty or even ten years ago.

There is a whole industry of aftermarket accessories that can be added or done to a shotgun to increase its performance, fit, functioning, and looks. Today's consumer can custom-tailor his gun and the ammunition for it in a way that was only available to the very wealthy and very knowledgeable just a generation ago.

But before we go any further, I want to clear up a very important point. I retired after thirty years as a cop. During my tenure in law enforcement, I was classified as an "expert witness" in many fields and in many different courts. I *hate* the word "expert"! I may be a serious student of the subject, but I don't consider myself an expert. My dictionary defines an expert as: "One with special skill or knowledge representing mastery of a particular subject; or having, involving, or displaying special skill or knowledge derived from training or experience." Yes, I have lots of training and years of experience, but I am still just a student of the subject. I still learn on a regular basis about shotguns, birds, loads, hunting techniques, and other topics related to my preferred sport. And I intend to keep learning until about three days before my ashes are scattered over a favorite bird cover.

In any book like this there is a certain amount of technical information required to understand the subject. I will try very hard not to give you more than you need or can handle. Also, I will try not to get on my soapbox too often. When I do, please just bear with me. Having said that, I hope you will continue along as we look at upland shotguns in the twenty-first century. Whether you are a novice who picked up this book to get some ideas for your first gun or an experienced hunter who wants a reason to buy a new gun, this book will be for you.

So pour your beverage of choice, get comfortable in your favorite chair, and let's go hunting!

2 Upland Game

I was talking to a friend of mine about this chapter while pondering how I could describe upland game. His explanation was simple: "If you can carry it in a game bag, it is an upland bird or game animal. If it won't fit in a game bag, it ain't!"

That makes sense to me. Rabbits and squirrels are the upland game most often taken with a shotgun, and they can be carried in a game bag. All of the upland birds can be carried in a game bag, although some, such as sage grouse, can make for quite a load. Some writers consider the wild turkey an upland bird, but turkey hunting is done in a much different manner than hunting for upland birds. Camouflage, calls, and decoys make turkey hunting a separate sport closer to waterfowling. The guns and gear used are very different from the common upland gun, so in this book we will not consider the wild turkey an upland bird. Besides, a turkey won't fit in a game bag! That being said, let's take a look at the different upland animals and birds and the conditions in which they are hunted.

RABBITS AND HARES

The most common game animal taken with a shotgun is the cottontail rabbit. He is a fast and tricky target, relatively easy to kill, and excellent table fare. For many hunters, the first game they ever took was a cottontail.

Jackrabbit. U.S. FISH & WILDLIFE SERVICE

Hunting cottontails in thick cover—or in the snow with a beagle or two on the chase—is a joyful experience. I must confess, however, that I haven't shot a cottontail in over twenty years for two reasons. First of all, I hunt with bird dogs, and there is a cardinal rule of not shooting anything on the ground when hunting with bird dogs. This rule is in place not only to help with the dog's training but to also prevent any shooting accidents. My dogs are a part of my family and a part of me. You wouldn't want a member of your family injured or killed, and I don't want that to happen to my dogs.

My other reason for not shooting cottontails involves an experience in college. One year I lived in an old farmhouse that had been converted into student apartments. It was outside the city limits and the driveway was a two-track dirt road that ran three quarters of a mile from the highway. Beside the forty acres of grown-over cropland around the farmhouse, there was also an abandoned railroad track that ran across the property. It was cottontail heaven. The rabbit season was three months long and the limit was ten per day. I hunted several days a week with shotgun or .22 and usually limited out. Since I was a poor college student on the GI bill, rabbit became a primary meat source. During that year, I think I ate rabbit at least three times a week. I don't care how exquisitely you prepare rabbit, I still can't eat it, and I don't like to kill game animals I don't eat.

Snowshoe hares can provide great fun in the states where they are available. When I lived in Colorado, we would often come across them during our winter coyote hunts. I never hunted them there with a shotgun, but I have hunted them while armed with a shotgun—with and without dogs—in other states and have found them quite challenging to hunt.

Here in the West, jackrabbits can be an enjoyable hunt with a shotgun. The speed, maneuverability, and evasive tactics can make for a real challenge. I had a friend from the Northeast down for a few days of quail hunting several years ago. Jackrabbits kept jumping out right next to him and startling him. One morning as we were heading out to hunt, he asked if we could leave the dogs in the truck and hunt jackrabbits instead. I took him to a pasture that was overrun with these long-eared varmints. He was happier than a kid in a candy store and went through several boxes of shells shooting rabbits that morning.

QUAIL

I took my first bobwhite when I was about twelve years old. That's not the first time I had hunted them, but it was the first time I was able to hit one. Now, over forty years later, I still shoot holes in the air on covey rises and shake my head in wonder when I miss an easy single. Yes, I have had the privilege of hunting bobwhites when they behave like gentlemen and are hunted accordingly. I have also had to run like a sprinter to keep up with my dogs that were

Male and female Gambels and Mearns quail.

trying to keep up with a covey that ran because they couldn't fly that fast!

On the opening day of our Texas quail season last year, hunting buddy Jeff McVay and I took our limit of fifteen quail each in about six hours of hunting. What was unusual is that even though there are both bobwhites and scaled (blue) quail in the area we hunted (about 3,000 acres of pastureland near Sundown, Texas), our limits that day consisted of the faster-flying, harder-

California quail. U.S. FISH & WILDLIFE SERVICE

running blue quail. After seven years of drought, we finally had a year with above-average rainfall and the quail rebounded. During the course of the season, we usually manage a mixed bag of bobs and blues. Now I have read for years that the bobwhite is a gentleman of a bird that will hold for both dogs and hunters. That's not the case when he lives in mesquite and prickly pear country around scaled quail! The bobwhite learns how to run with the scalies and becomes a Texas redneck just like them.

Gambels, Mearns, valley (or California) and mountain quail are some of the most underhunted game birds in the United States. Having hunted all but the California quail, I can say that I enjoy pursuing all of them, but consider-

Gambels quail. ©ISTOCKPHOTO.COM/CAY-UWE KULZER

Sharp-tailed grouse. ©ISTOCKPHOTO.COM/LAWRENCE
SAWYER

ing the terrain, temperatures, and fauna of the western areas of the United States they inhabit, maybe the bobwhite really is a gentleman. He is at least easier to hunt over his range, which extends from the eastern seaboard west into Texas and north into Iowa and Minnesota.

GROUSE

Mention grouse to a hunter who lives east of the Mississippi River and they think only of the ruffed grouse, which has been called "King of the upland game birds" by a number of writers over the years. Most often hunted in the East and Northeast, ruffed grouse are challenging birds to find and are often hunted in very thick and dense cover. And those who hunt them are some of the most fanatical and dedicated bird hunters you can find. Mention grouse to a western hunter and he is liable to think of a half-dozen other species, all of which are usually found in varying habitat and hunted in different ways.

There are the greater and lesser prairie chickens, which can be hunted in the traditional way with dogs but are often shot as they fly in to feed in the morning or evening. These birds were once as plentiful as the buffalo on the western plains, but habitat loss and market hunting (not normal hunting) have made them very scarce throughout their range. Another resident of the plains is the sharp-tailed grouse. This bird inhabits the "wide-open spaces" but is hunted in cover you would swear could not hide a field mouse.

The mountains of the western and coastal states are also home to the blue grouse and the spruce grouse. Although seldom hunted in the more traditional manner of following a dog, these birds can provide an interesting and exciting hunt for the upland shotgunner with or without a dog.

Blue grouse. ©ISTOCKPHOTO.COM/SASCHA BURKHARD

Our largest upland bird, the sage grouse, is also currently suffering from habitat loss due to overgrazing and farming. Several states have closed or limited their seasons on this majestic game bird. Although they appear to be as big as a B-52 bomber and as slow as cold molasses, these birds are challenging targets for the shotgunner. Also, two sage grouse will easily weigh over ten pounds, and believe me, that can become a real burden in your game bag when you are two miles from the truck on a 70-degree Wyoming day!

PARTRIDGE

Although many types of grouse are locally known as partridge, or in that lovely northern accent as "pa'tridge," there is a difference in the species. There is the Hungarian partridge of the northern plains. These birds are often found in similar habitat and in the same areas as sharptail grouse. They can be tough to locate sometimes, but they're a fast and often difficult target when found.

While challenging enough when pen-raised on hunting preserves, in the wild, the chukar partridge is a bird that gives a new twist (and other aches, pains, bumps, and bruises) to the term "bird hunting." They are found in some of the roughest and wildest country in the West. When hunted in their natural habitat, chukars have you wishing by the end of your first day that it were legal to scan the hillsides for them and shoot them with a scoped varmint rifle rather than having to hike after them to shoot them with a shotgun.

Although it is often referred to as a grouse, the ptarmigan is actually a subspecies of the partridge. Found in Canada and Alaska, they are seldom hunted in the traditional way of using dogs and a shotgun. A guide friend from Alaska told me that most ptarmigan he has seen harvested were taken while sitting with a .22 or a 410 shotgun.

DOVES

The most commonly harvested game bird in the United States is the mourning dove. Hunters take millions every year, and a dove on the wing—especially if he is riding a tailwind—is one of the most, if not *the* most, challenging targets that can be taken with a shotgun. I have a good friend who is a retired aeronautical engineer. He worked on the designs of many of our fighter aircraft and also on the space shuttle. He has told me that man will probably never be able to design an aircraft that can maneuver like a dove. He then went into a long discussion about wing loading, velocities, wing and surface pressures, etc. Like the bumblebee that cannot fly according to the experts, the dove cannot maneuver the way it does, but it does! I have heard the dove aptly described as "a small bird surrounded by all of the sky." That statement about sums it up.

Besides the mourning dove, whitewing doves are found in the West and Southwest. They are larger than a mourning dove but are faster flyers and just as tricky and demanding to shoot.

A new dove that has immigrated to the United States in the last few years is the Asian collared dove. A native of the steppes of Siberia, it has become quite plentiful in the U.S. Some states have included it as a game species, while others, including my home state of Texas, have not yet protected it as a game bird. About half again as large as a mourning dove and slightly smaller than a whitewing, it is also a difficult and tricky target on the wing.

In a few western states, there are open seasons on band-tailed pigeons. These large members of the dove family are found in the high mountains and valleys and are usually hunted as they come in to water in the morning or evening.

Mourning dove. ©ISTOCKPHOTO.COM/C. PAQUIN

WOODCOCK

Known by a number of names, this charming and delightful bird is usually found east of the Mississippi River. I have also found them in Iowa. They are an excellent bird to hunt with a dog, as they will hold very tight and flush fast, straight up, and *very close!* I was visiting with one of my readers at the SHOT (Shooting, Hunting, and Outdoor Trade) Show in Las Vegas one year. He had hunted woodcock for the first time that year and had already developed that "glazed eye, drooling mouth" look of the woodcock hunter. He was telling me that in the terrain and cover he hunted, the shots were measured in feet, not yards, and he had yet to retrieve enough of a woodcock to enjoy a whole bird or even a whole breast of one. We talked guns and loads and I gave him some suggestions on available 28-gauge shotguns and some of my favorite loads. A 28-gauge over-and-under with special spreader chokes and light loads had him tasting the delightful flesh of woodcock that fall. Although I usually prefer white meat from my game birds, I must admit I have a special fondness for the dark, exquisite meat of the woodcock when sautéed in butter with portabella mushrooms.

PHEASANTS

I admit to being a rabid pheasant hunter. Although I love hunting any type of game bird that can be taken with dogs and a shotgun, I have a special love of pheasant hunting. My first ever game animal, taken when I was eight years old, was a rooster pheasant, and I have been addicted to these birds ever since.

The late and great Jack O'Connor, who was often called the "Dean of the Outdoor Writers," described the rooster pheasant as the "trophy whitetail buck of the upland birds." Jack didn't kill his first pheasant until he was middle-aged, and by that time he had killed many trophy

Ring-necked pheasant. ©ISTOCKPHOTO.COM

whitetail deer and hundreds of other trophy game animals.

There are as many ways to hunt pheasants as there are hunters. The classic English driven bird shoot is seldom seen or done in the United States, but it is available on some game preserves on a limited basis and at a very high price.

The author's dog, Dee Dee, brings in a rooster.

Many hunters prefer the large group drive-and-block for hunting pheasants. I have seen as many as thirty hunters in one field using this technique. Dogs may or may not be used. Many, many roosters are killed this way every year, but the pheasant is a smart and wily opponent that could teach evasive tactics at West Point. Even after a large group goes through a patch of cover, a hunter with a good dog can often find birds in the same field. I have done this many times over the years with my Brits and a friend or two. One year a friend and I watched a group of about twenty hunters sweep a half section of CRP grass. They had a number of birds get up and fly off unharmed. They also managed to bag about ten birds. There were probably a total of fifty hens and roosters that were flushed by the large group. After they got back into their vehicles and left, we loaded our guns and set the dogs loose. We needed three birds to fill our limits for the day. Within twenty minutes we had flushed four roosters, had taken three of them, and had headed the 150 yards back to the truck. These were birds that had either laid low and let the group walk right by them or had sneaked back behind and through the line of hunters.

Last year a friend of mine from Tennessee met me in Kansas for a middle-of-the-season hunt. At the motel where we were staying was a group of twenty-four that was hunting without dogs. They were gone well before sunrise every morning and returned long after dark. Steve, my friend's young nephew, and I headed out about 8 or 9 A.M. every morning and were usually back by 5 P.M. or so. We may not have limited out with four birds apiece, but we usually had eight birds or so. We also had tired Brittanies that put in long days covering miles of ground and finding lots of birds. One night we got to talk with several of the fellows from the large group. They told us that the twenty-four of them were averaging about thirty birds a day. One of them told me that you couldn't hunt the big fields without a big group. I was also told by several of the hunters that you couldn't find a dog that would hunt roosters. Fact is, we had taken all of our roosters in large blocks of public CRP land, and most were taken over points from our dogs. One year I was able to spend nine days hunting pheasants in three different states on one trip. In those nine days, over sixty roosters were taken over points from my Brits or the other pointing dogs that my friends were hunting. We never had more than four hunters and worked mostly large fields of cover.

Jeff McVay used his Benelli Super Black Eagle for this limit of Kansas pheasants.

3 Shotgun Gauges

With rifles and pistols, the size of the bore is given in inches or millimeters. This is the caliber of the weapon and usually a part of the name of the cartridge. For example, a .243 Winchester and a 6mm Remington both fire a bullet with a diameter of .243 inches (6mm). A 7mm Remington fires a bullet with a diameter of .284 inches, or 7 millimeters. A 308 caliber is .308 inches in diameter (or if given in millimeters is 7.62mm).

The gauge of a shotgun indicates the bore size of the gun as well, but a different measuring system is used. Shotguns are sized (or gauged) by a system developed in England in the 1700s. The gauge of a shotgun is the number of lead balls of the bore's diameter required to make a pound. Ten lead balls meant the gun was a 10 gauge. If twenty lead balls were required, the gun was a 20 gauge. Since the bore of a shotgun does not have rifling (lands and grooves), all shotguns are smoothbores.

The most common gauges in the United States today are the 10, 12, 16, 20, and 28 gauges. There is also the 410 gauge, but the 410 is actually a 67 gauge. The bore diameter of a 410 is approximately 45 caliber. It was derived from the

All of the gauges of shotshells.

shot cartridges provided to U.S. Army troopers during the late 1800s. Designed for use in the standard .45-70 caliber rifle, they enabled a trooper to pot a prairie chicken or sage grouse for dinner without tearing up the bird with a single 405-grain lead bullet. Later on, there were special smoothbores designed on the rifle actions. These "foraging" arms used an all-brass shell that contained the powder, shot, and wadding in a shotshell. Several commercial companies began making variations of these cartridges and guns. The earliest reference I have been able to find to the 410 shotshell is a 1911 Remington catalog listing it as a loaded round for the various single-shot guns developed from these foraging arms. The first reference I can find for a manufacturer is a Marble "Game Getter" manufactured about 1910. By the 1920s, all of the gun and loading companies had guns and ammunition in the 410 gauge.

Shotgun Gauge Diameters

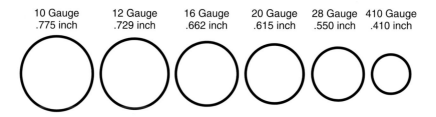

10 Gauge	12 Gauge	16 Gauge	20 Gauge	28 Gauge	410 Gauge
.775 inch	.729 inch	.662 inch	.615 inch	.550 inch	.410 inch

Other gauges have been manufactured and loaded over the years. Back in the days of blackpowder, 8-gauge shotguns were popular, and there were also 2, 4, and 6 gauges. Prior to the time of the American Civil War, rifles had lands and grooves and fired a ball that engaged the lands and grooves and caused the projectile to spin. Many of the weapons issued to the regular troops were smooth bore muskets. The way to increase the energy of the bullet was to increase the size of the bore. Since anything over 50 caliber (0.50 inches) was getting into the size of shotgun bores, most of these muskets were in effect very large-bore shotguns, but they were used with single projectiles.

Many of the famous explorers and ivory hunters of the early 1800s used such weapons. Sir Samuel Baker, who explored most of Africa and discovered Lake Victoria among many other places, used a 2-gauge smoothbore with an explosive shell as his weapon for elephants and other dangerous game. The gun weighed over thirty pounds and used 6 to 8 *ounces* of blackpowder as a propellant. Baker wrote the gun always spun him around three or four times and gave him a frightful headache and a severe nosebleed. It was usually two or three days before he could shoot this gun again, and he would rely on his smaller rifles (6 and 8 gauges) during the period of recovery.

Imagine firing a weapon like this. The lead bullet weighed a half-pound and the recoil would be absolutely punishing. I recall reading an article a number of years ago where the author tested a 4-gauge elephant rifle for recoil. This fired a 4-ounce ball with 4 ounces of blackpowder used as the propellant charge. The machine he used to measure recoil recorded it in foot-pounds of energy and had the ability to measure up to 200 foot-pounds of recoil. The first shot with the 4 gauge was so far over 200 foot-pounds that it broke the machine! In contrast, a modern 12-gauge 3-inch magnum shell in a 7-pound gun gives about 45 foot-pounds of recoil!

Fortunately, we do not have to concern ourselves with monsters such as this today. Modern shotguns and shotshells are much more efficient than these blackpowder cannons were. The guns and shells of today provide the shooter with velocities, shot amounts, and levels of efficiency unheard of even twenty years ago. Let's take a look at the different gauges available to today's hunter and check out the advantages and disadvantages of each.

10 GAUGE

When I was a kid growing up in the 1950s and 1960s, the 10 gauge was almost obsolete. I recall seeing a few in the collections of acquaintances of my father, but the only 10 gauge I ever saw in use was by a guide on the Eastern Shore of the Chesapeake around 1970. He had a foreign double with 32-inch barrels choked full and full. This behemoth weighed about 10 1/2 pounds and fired the 3 1/2-inch 10-gauge magnum load with a full 2 ounces of shot.

The 10 gauge had just about faded into oblivion when the restric-

10-gauge shell.

tions on the use of lead shot for waterfowl brought it back. The early nontoxic shells were not as effective as hunters were used to with lead loads. There was a resurgence of interest in the 10 gauge so those hunters could have the same shot weights (1 1/4 and 1 1/2 ounces) they were used to in the 12 gauge. The first company to take advantage of this new interest was Ithaca/SKB, which brought out their Mag-10 in 1975. Until then, shooters wishing to own a 10 gauge were limited to imported doubles and single shots.

Other manufacturers jumped on the 10-gauge bandwagon. Remington introduced their 1100/11-87 variation, the SP (Special Purpose) 10, in 1989 and Browning introduced their BPS-10 (Browning Pump Shotgun) in 1989 and their 10-gauge "Gold Hunter" semi-auto in 1994. The resurgence of the 10 gauge was brief. The Mag-10 was discontinued in 1996, and although Remington and Browning still offer their various 10-gauge models, most are being eclipsed by the 12 gauge chambered for the $3^{1}/_{2}$-inch magnum shell. Ten-gauge guns and ammunition are still available for the waterfowl or turkey hunter who wants the effectiveness of this big gauge. There are a number of choices in models, finishes, and barrels.

12-gauge shell.

12 GAUGE

The most popular shotgun in the United States and in the world is the 12 gauge. I have been told by the rep of a major ammunition manufacturer that in their product line, which is marketed all over the world, the 12 gauge outsells any other gauge by a 7 to 1 margin. Twelve-gauge shells can be found anywhere ammunition is sold, from the shelves of a "megamart" in the U.S. to the counter of a small trading post in the African bush.

The most common 12-gauge shell is $2^{3}/_{4}$ inches in length but it's also available in 2-, $2^{1}/_{2}$-, 3-, and $3^{1}/_{2}$-inch lengths. Please note that these are the dimensions of a fired shell. A loaded, crimped round is shorter. This means that a loaded 3-inch shell will fit in the chamber of a gun chambered for the $2^{3}/_{4}$-inch shell. Firing the longer shell in the shorter chamber will raise pressures to a dangerous level that will most likely damage the gun and possibly even injure or kill the shooter. This will be discussed more in the chapter on shotgun shells, but the hunter should always make sure he has the correct shell for the gun being used.

Prior to the 1980s, most 12-gauge guns available in this country were chambered for the standard $2^{3}/_{4}$-inch shell. Guns with the 3-inch magnum chamber were usually specialty items used by waterfowl and turkey hunters. Again, the requirement of using steel or nontoxic shot changed this. Prior to the ban on lead shot, a hunter equipped with a 12 gauge with a $2^{3}/_{4}$-inch chamber could use loads containing up to $1^{1}/_{2}$ ounces of lead shot. Due to the

On the left, 1½ ounces of copper-plated lead No. 4 shot (210 pellets); on the right, 1⅛ ounces of steel No. 4 (205 pellets).

difference in weight versus mass of steel and lead, most early 12-gauge steel loads in the 2¾-inch length were loaded with 1 to 1⅛ ounces of steel pellets.

In addition to being traditionalists, hunters in the U.S. also have a creed that if "big is good, bigger is better." I was actively involved with the Colorado Division of Wildlife demonstrating and informing hunters on this new shot. There are approximately 216 No. 4 steel pellets in a 12-gauge, 1⅛-ounce, 2¾-inch shell and approximately 204 No. 4 lead pellets in a 12-gauge, 1½-ounce, 2¾-inch shell. Over a two-year period, I was called a liar, a politician, and much worse when I tried to convince shooters of this. They had been using lead shot for years, and to them, if there were 1⅛ ounces of shot, it had to have fewer pellets, and therefore be less efficient, than 1½ ounces of shot pellets. I had containers with both lead and steel pellets and a scale with which to weigh them. Even after seeing the weights on the scale and counting the pellets out for themselves, many shooters still could not be convinced.

Gun manufacturers found that more and more shooters wanted guns that had 3-inch chambers and were capable of handling both 2¾- and 3-inch shells. This was easy to do in pumps and double barrels, but it required new research and development in both gas and recoil-operated semi-autos. Prior to this, most semi-autos capable of taking the 3-inch shell were regulated for the heavier recoil and pressures of these shells and would not function with lighter 2¾-inch loads. I owned one semi-auto during this transition period with an adjustable valve in the forend that was turned and set for light or heavy loads. Others either had to be completely revamped or a new design and gun had to be made. The excellent Remington 11-87 is one gun that came out during this period. The Remington 1100, while a fine weapon, had a gas system that couldn't be adapted to the various loads. Remington engineers

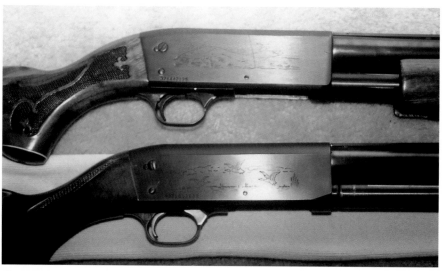

Size comparison of 12 gauge and 16 gauge receivers.

redesigned the gas system and implemented some other upgrades to the entire action and brought out the 11-87, which will function, without adjustment, with the lightest target loads to the heaviest magnum loads.

Now in the first decade of the twenty-first century, the standard chamber length in most guns is 3 inches. The shorter 2³/₄-inch-only chamber is found only in specialty guns. My favorite competition shotgun is a Browning Gold Sporting Clays model, and it only has a 2³/₄-inch chamber. The standard Gold Hunter is available with a 3-inch chamber.

In 1988, a new kid showed up on the 12-gauge block. O. F. Mossberg & Sons began marketing a strengthened version of their Model 500 pump shotgun and named it the Model 835. This new kid on the block was chambered for a 12-gauge 3¹/₂-inch shell. This new shell gave turkey and waterfowl hunters heavier loads that were previously available only in the 10 gauge, and this new chambering was soon available from a number of different manufacturers. The 3¹/₂-inch 12-gauge guns have surpassed the 10-gauge guns in sales. Not only does the hunter or shooter have adequate firepower when needed, but he can also use light 2³/₄-inch loads or 3-inch magnums in the same gun.

This new 3¹/₂-inch chambering does have some drawbacks. In a pump or double, of course, any 12-gauge shell can be fired. Because of the strength of the system for the massive 3¹/₂-inch shells, most semi-autos chambered for this round are limited to the lightest load that can be fired in them and still function normally. Most of the manufacturers recommend at least a 1¹/₈-ounce load at a velocity of at least 1,200 feet per second (fps) for reliable functioning.

I have extensive experience in load testing on several $3\frac{1}{2}$-inch semi-autos and have found the manufacturer recommendations are correct. But I have also found individual guns that would function with lighter loads. It is a trial-and-error method, and if you own one of these guns, you just need to see what the limits are on your specific gun.

This next topic will be covered more in another chapter, but I need to first bring it up here. Many shooters or hunters who are thinking of buying just one gun for all of their hunting think they need a gun with a $3\frac{1}{2}$-inch chamber. This is seldom the case. Most often these guns are considerably heavier than the equivalent 3-inch model to help tame the recoil of this Roman candle of a shell. When used as an everyday gun, they are often too heavy for carrying in the field and can cause the new shooter to forget hunting and take up golf instead. I know a number of 12 gauge owners whose guns will chamber the $3\frac{1}{2}$-inch shell. However, even for waterfowl

How 12-gauge (bottom) and 16-gauge (top) receivers fit in the typical hunter's hand.

and turkeys, most use 3-inch shells. I have one friend who bought one of the first $3\frac{1}{2}$-inch semi-autos to come out. He has had the gun for about six years, and I don't think he has ever fired a $3\frac{1}{2}$-inch shell in it.

16 GAUGE

I took my first pheasant in 1960 using a single shot 16 gauge with an exposed hammer and a load of No. 6 shot. Two years later, my Dad presented me with a 16-gauge double barrel as a birthday present. I used that gun on into high school but then succumbed to the siren song of a 12 gauge. Next was a long affair with a 20 gauge. Then it was back to the 12 gauge. In the last few years, however, I have found myself hunting upland birds more and more with a 16 gauge.

Up until World War II, the 16 gauge was the second most popular gauge in the United States and the most popular gauge in Europe. After World War II, the 12 gauge became the most popular and the 3-inch chambering was developed in the 20 gauge. Also, new gun models made of lighter weight alloys were coming out, and many companies found it was much more cost effective to gear up to make just two frame sizes instead of three. Prior to WWII, most 16 gauges were built on a frame size proportionate to the gauge. Most of the guns manufactured since then are built on 12-gauge frames, which makes a 16-gauge gun actually heavier than the same model in a 12 gauge. This defeats the handling characteristics that make a true 16 much livelier than a 12 gauge. I have a 16-gauge semi-auto that was one of the last built by a major company. Built on a 20-gauge frame, it is a joy to handle and shoot.

Pheasants taken with a 16 gauge over-and-under and a pump shotgun.

I don't know how many articles I have read over the years where the authors were writing an obituary for the 16 gauge. There has been an equal number of articles that explain why the 16 stays around. I can always tell if the writer has had any experience actually using a 16 gauge in the field. If he hasn't, he sounds the death toll; if he has, he knows why the 16 remains a popular gun among hardcore upland hunters.

Now the 16 is again having a revival in popularity. Several gun manufacturers that haven't made a 16 gauge in years have reintroduced 16-gauge guns, and there are a number of firms marketing guns made on true 16-gauge frames. A 16 in the right package is a real joy. It is light to carry, quick to handle, and with the proper loads will handle about 80 percent of all upland hunting. I have been using a 16 for most of my upland hunting the past few years, and I don't know why I stopped using one in the first place. Yes, I do. I was young and stupid! Now I am older—and hopefully wiser—and I have rediscovered the joy of the 16 gauge.

A word of caution: The 16 gauge was the last gauge to be standardized with a 2³/₄-inch chamber. It was the late 1930s in the United States and after World War II in Europe before the 16 adapted this standard

16-gauge shells.

chamber length. Many fine old 16s are found with 2¹/₂- or 2⁹/₁₆-inch chambers. Firing modern 2³/₄-inch ammunition in one of these short chambers is a recipe for disaster.

One of my uncles brought back a beautiful 16-gauge double from Europe after WWII. He didn't hunt much and I remember him saying that the few times he fired this gun, the gun would open on its own and the forend would come off. Years later, I was able to examine this gun and determined that it had a 2¹/₂-inch chamber. I've been trying to convince my uncle to let me have this gun (a Ferlach) ever since.

20 GAUGE

For years, the 20 gauge was considered a good gun for kids and women. The man who hunted with one was usually viewed as anywhere from mildly eccentric to absolutely crazy. Ironically, two of the most popular shotguns ever made, the Winchester Model 12 and the Ruger Red Label, were both introduced as 20 gauges. When the Model 12 was first introduced in 1912, it had a 2¹/₂-inch chamber. An old rancher friend of mine had one of these and he swore it was the best quail gun ever made. The 20 gauge

20-gauge shells.

was standardized with a 2³/₄-inch chamber in the 1930s. Around the same time, some of the executives with Winchester began developing the idea of a

3-inch-chambered 20 gauge. Some of these were made in the Model 21 double on special order. After WWII, Winchester again picked up on the idea of the 3-inch chamber in the 20 gauge. By this time, the standard 20-gauge round was loaded with a maximum of 1 ounce of shot. The new 3-inch model was first loaded with $1\frac{1}{8}$ ounces, then $1\frac{3}{16}$ ounces, and finally with the current loading of $1\frac{1}{4}$ ounces of shot.

This was a real boost to the popularity of the 20 gauge. Companies touted 12-gauge performance in a gun that weighed less. Almost every manufacturer of shotguns jumped on the wagon and began offering 20 gauges with 3-inch chambers. I was a gun-crazy kid and worked from dawn to dusk all one summer cutting trees and clearing brush on an uncle's farm to buy my first 20 gauge. It was a dressed-up version of the basic Stevens Model 311 but was marketed under the Fox name. This little jewel had a vent rib, 26-inch barrels choked Improved Cylinder and Modified, automatic ejectors, and a single trigger. Best of all, it was chambered for the 3-inch magnum shell. If I remember correctly, I paid $125 for it.

Suddenly I discovered that I could actually hit bobwhite quail instead of just shooting holes in the air. Of course, I was using a $6\frac{1}{2}$-pound gun instead of the 8-pound 12 gauge I had been using. Years later I discovered that this is a key element in being able to hit anything with a shotgun. This was the beginning of a love affair with the 20 gauge that lasted for almost 30 years. I was a convert! I could relate the advantages of the 20 gauge over any other gauge any day of the week. I had seen the light and it was in a lightweight, fast-handling 20 gauge.

I kept that little double for about eight years, had a brief fling with a 20-gauge semi-auto, and then bought an over-and-under 20 gauge with 26-inch barrels choked Improved Cylinder and Modified. I have no idea how many birds were taken with that little Ithaca/SKB, but I know that I killed everything from woodcocks to geese with it. That gun traveled many, many miles through the Midwest and the East. It was only when I started getting involved in testing shotguns and started hunting in the wide open and windy plains of the West that I began to realize the limitations of the 20 gauge.

There are times when the 20 gauge is in its element and is an excellent gauge to use. When dealing with longer-range shots and prairie winds, the shot string of the 20 gauge is affected more than the same shot charge out of a 16 or 12 gauge. This affects the striking power of the 20 gauge, and I lost too many birds due to my affection for the 20. For quail, the 20 gauge is fine, but when hunting larger birds, I found the 20 gauge was not the most efficient load to use.

I still have that little Ithaca. The bluing is worn on the receiver and barrels, and the checkering on the buttstock and forend has been rounded off and almost worn off in several places. I rarely use this gun anymore, but when I watch Lance, my three-year-old grandson, running around, I can just picture him and Grandpa hunting quail together a few years down the road. This will be a perfect gun for me to pass on to him.

Most 20 gauges manufactured today come with the 3-inch magnum chamber as the standard. Shooters buying a used gun should check because some makes and models didn't start chambering for the 3-inch shell until the 1980s; there are still a lot of short-chambered 20 gauges out there. The $2\frac{3}{4}$-inch chamber does not limit the use of a 20 gauge as much as a 12 gauge. And as we will see in the chapter on shotshells, the 3-inch magnum 20-gauge shell is not quite the performer that it has been hyped up to be.

28 GAUGE

Ah, the 28 gauge! For anyone married to his 12 gauge, the 28 gauge will always be his mistress! Back in the 1960s, there was a television program on ABC called *The American Sportsman*. It featured celebrities hunting and fishing all over the world. Two celebrities regularly featured hunting upland birds in various locales were Bing Crosby and Phil Harris. Phil Harris did all of his hunting on the program with a 28 gauge. This was my first exposure to the 28. When I started shooting skeet a few years later, I was made

28-gauge shells.

aware of the 28 gauge for skeet shooting. I was a poor college student and was lucky to come up with enough money for entry fees and shells for one gauge, yet alone something as exotic as the 28. The few times I had a chance to shoot a 28 gauge it was instant love. But it was also like being in love with a movie star because getting together with one just wasn't going to happen.

A few years after that, my buddy Jerry showed up on one of our annual get-together hunts with a 28-gauge Remington Model 870 pump. Jerry and I had been hunting together since we were kids, and we had both talked about someday owning a 28 gauge. Jerry had used a Browning Auto-5 in 12 gauge for years, and although he was fast with it, I could usually beat him with my 20 gauge. Not that we were ever competitive about things like that!

About 100 yards from the truck, my Brittany locked up on the edge of some woods. When we walked in, a covey of quail flushed at such an angle that I had the better shot at them. As my gun came up, I heard Jerry shoot and the bird I was tracking folded. As I swung on another bird, I again heard Jerry shoot and that bird folded! I quickly learned what the expression "green with envy" meant, although my face was more likely beet red! Jerry and I had hunted together enough over the years that we often knew which bird the other would shoot at, and Jerry used this opportunity to rub my face in the speed of handling his 28 gauge.

A couple of years later, I swapped an M-1 carbine for a Remington Model 11-48 in 28 gauge. This little gun had the promise of being a supreme quail gun. The first time I took it quail hunting, I was able to get a triple on a covey rise. Needless to say, I was hooked!

When I first started studying ballistics years ago, I learned that the first law is to always expect the unexpected. A physics professor friend of mine tells me that it is impossible to break the basic laws of physics, but ballistics will certainly bend some of those laws to the point where you can hear them twanging under the strain. The 28 gauge definitely bends the laws! How else would you explain that $3/4$ of an ounce of shot moving at 1,200 fps appears to break a clay target on the skeet range with more authority than $1^1/8$ ounces at 1,200 fps from a 12 gauge?

First, the 28 gauge and the one-ounce 16-gauge load are considered ballistically equal or "square" loads. In these, the height and width of the shot column (bore diameter) are very comparable and almost equal. This reduces shot deformation and the disrupting of the shot column as it goes through the forcing cone and the choke.

The 28 gauge and the words "quail gun" are synonymous in my vocabulary. I have used the 28 all over the United States on various types of quail and it has performed very well in every environment. As a dove, woodland grouse, or woodcock gun, it has to be the king of the gauges. The 28 is also an excellent beginner's gun. It has a much better pattern than a 410 and even in lightweight field guns, it has less felt recoil than a 20 gauge. I have started numerous women and young shooters on the 28 gauge; the lack of recoil helps them overcome their apprehension about the gun and they are better able to concentrate on the target.

A good friend of mine, David Guinn, had never shot a 28 gauge until several years ago. One day at the skeet range, he tried my little Franchi 48 AL in 28 gauge. Now he owns several different 28s and has started all three of his boys shooting with a 28 gauge. David is a defense attorney by trade and one day he made an interesting comment about the 28. He said that every drug user he had ever defended got addicted because someone "gave them a taste" for free and they were soon hooked. He commented that after he got his first taste of the 28 gauge, it was not long before he was hooked. Talk with anyone who shoots a 28 on a regular basis, and I can almost guarantee the comment you are most likely to hear is: "Man, I love shooting that little gauge!"

410 GAUGE

As a gun-crazy kid growing up and even today as a gun-crazy adult, one of my favorite authors is the late Jack O'Connor. Many times he has transported me to far-off and exotic places in *Outdoor Life* or *Petersen's Hunting* magazines. Although primarily known as a rifleman, Jack was a dedicated shotgunner most of his life and was as knowledgeable about shotguns as he was about rifles. In fact, his *The Shotgun Book,* although dated, is still an excellent resource today. The widow of a dear friend gave my personal copy to me and I cherish it not only for that reason, but also for the wealth of information it contains. Having said that,

.410-bore shells.

I am about to do something that I never thought I would do in this lifetime. I am going to dispute Jack O'Connor! In the chapter on shotgun gauges, Jack states: "The 410 is a kid's gun, a woman's gun, a pot gun for the farm and camping trip, a gun for small-bore and sub-small-bore skeet shooting and NOT a man's gun."

Sorry Jack, but you are wrong. I know of no better way to discourage a kid or woman than to try to get them to hit something with a 410. The small shot charge (half of an ounce in the 2½-inch shell) and the poor patterns that a 410 throws at even 20 yards make it a gun for the expert shooter, *not* the beginner.

Yes, I know, thousands of you started with a 410, and that's what you taught your kids on. We had a saying in one of the police departments where I once worked: "One hundred fifty years of tradition unimpeded by progress!" This is true of trying to use a 410 as a beginner's gun or on game. Of all of the thousands of hunters I know, there has been only one that was a good enough shot to consistently hunt quail with a 410, and even he limits himself to using it under ideal conditions.

The 410 is an absolute joy to shoot, but it is also very frustrating, even for the most experienced shooter. Watch the 410 event at a major skeet shoot and you will see shooters who have shot thousands of birds still shake their head in wonder when a shot doesn't break the target. Better yet, take that full-choke 410 out and shoot it on a pattern board at just 20 yards. There will be holes in the pattern you could throw a politician through!

These are the common gauges. There are others out there. I have in my shotshell collection loaded rounds in both 14 and 24 gauge. There is also a 32 gauge on the market and on occasion I get inquiries about these. Some reloading components are available through Ballistics Products, Inc. for these odd gauges. My personal experience with them is limited. I fired one round (twenty-five birds) of skeet with a 24 gauge over-and-under a couple of years ago. It was pleasant to shoot and use, but either a 20 or 28 gauge would do the same thing just as well. If I remember correctly, it fired a $^7/_8$-ounce load of shot—the same as a light 20-gauge load. The fellow who owned it told me that even with reloading, his costs were almost $1 per shell. In the 1960s, Winchester seriously considered marketing a 14-gauge shotgun, and I have seen several prototypes of both the gun and shell.

With all of the research and development going on in the field of shotguns and ammunition, I won't be surprised if my grandson has an even wider range of shotgun gauges to choose from.

1 Action Types

Although all guns made from the twelfth through the eighteenth century were smoothbores, the shotgun as we know it today did not become a viable weapon until the 1600s. Early ignition systems left much to be desired. It was not until the development of the flintlock that a reliable system was available for use on running and flying game.

With the introduction of the percussion cap, the shotgun as we know it today began to evolve. Most early shotguns were single shots, but some double barrels were made, especially after the invention of the percussion cap ignition system. As we saw in the chapter on shotgun gauges, these were smoothbores used either as shotguns with multiple projectiles or as rifles when fired with a single ball. The early guns were used for both purposes, and it was not until the development of the breech-loading weapon and rifled barrels that the two types of guns began to follow different lines of development. Eventually, the shotgun, firing multiple projectiles of either small shot (birdshot) or larger shot (buckshot), became a separate weapon.

As the concept of a breech-loading weapon containing the primer, powder charge, and projectile began to evolve in rifles and pistols, the same idea was applied to shotguns, and the shotgun shell was born. Various types of repeating shotguns were developed and tried, but the single and double barrels were the most common.

John Moses Browning was the most prolific firearms designer of all time. He had a close association with Winchester and developed Winchester's famous lever-action rifles, among others. In 1886, he adapted the lever-action design to handle shotgun shells. The Winchester Model 1887 was the first successful repeating shotgun. This model, which was made in both 10 and 12 gauge with either Damascus or steel barrels, was manufactured until 1900. A slightly improved version was introduced in 1901 (the Model 1901) and man-ufactured until 1920. I recently came into possession of both a Model 1887 and a Model 1901. These guns are big, ungainly, awkward, and so ugly that they are neat! Both of the models are 10 gauges. The Model 1887 has a Damascus (twist steel) barrel and the Model 1901 has a fluid steel barrel.

While these models were considered successes, John Browning wanted a more efficient shotgun, so in 1892 he designed the Model 1893 pump or slide-action shotgun. This gun had some refinements made to the original design and was introduced in 1897 as the famous Winchester Model 1897. These fine old guns were manufactured in various styles and configurations up until 1957. I have owned and shot a number of different Model 1897s over the years, and they have all performed flawlessly. An acquaintance of mine owns a very large collection of guns, but his favorite quail gun is an old Model 1897 in 16 gauge that was passed down to him by his father and grandfather.

The first successful self-loading or semi-automatic shotgun was also a John Browning design. It was also the gun that ended his long relationship with Winchester. Browning designed a self-loading shotgun in 1905, and he wanted a royalty on each gun instead of just the set fee that Winchester had been paying him for his designs. Winchester balked at this idea, so Browning took his design overseas to Belgium to the well-known European manufac-turer Fabrique Nationale, and the famous Browning Auto-5 shotgun was born.

This arrangement was to profit John Browning immensely in his later years, as he was now free to market his gun designs to other manufacturers. Some of his most famous designs were yet to come, and would eventually be produced by a variety of companies. This same decision cost Winchester dearly, and it was not until the late 1950s that Winchester was able to market a self-loading shotgun that didn't infringe on Browning's patents.

Browning sold the manufacturing rights of this design in the United States to Remington Arms Company, which brought out its Model 11 and later a redesigned and streamlined version called the Model 11-48. This gun was the mainstay of Remington's shotgun line until the introduction of their famous Model 1100 in the 1960s. The Browning A-5 is still manufactured by Browning Arms Company and is now made in Japan. Other companies still make variations of this grand old design that is now a hundred years old and still going strong.

The choice of an action type for a shotgun for upland game is often a per-sonal preference. Many hunters, including myself, use several different action types on a regular basis. We have our favorites, but we also recognize the strengths and limitations of the other types available. The most common action types in the United States are the semi-auto or self-loader, the pump or slide action, and double barrels, which are encountered in both side-by-side and over-and-under configurations. There are also the bolt actions, the single shots, the combination guns, and the blackpowder guns. Let's take a look at the strengths and weaknesses of these action types.

SEMI-AUTOS

The semi-auto or self-loading shotgun is just that. A shooter loads the gun by loading the magazine, which is usually under the barrel, and then placing a shell in the chamber. When the trigger is pulled, the action of the gun fires the shell in the chamber, ejects the empty shell, picks up the next live shell from the magazine, and loads it into the chamber. The gun is ready to fire when the trigger is pulled again. There are different methods used to operate the action. The most common seen today include the long-recoil action, the gas-operated action, and the inertia action. There are also designs that incorporate a short-recoil design.

The Browning A-5 and all of its variations are of a long-recoil design. The barrel recoils back into the breech as the gun is fired, ejecting the fired shell, cocking the gun, picking up a fresh shell from the magazine tube, and loading it into the barrel. Many people find the "double slam" of the recoil of the fired shell and the additional recoil of the operating action objection-

Long-recoil action shotguns.

able. These folks claim it actually increases the felt recoil when the weapon is fired. Having shot thousands of rounds of different gauges through a number of different guns of this design, I don't notice this double slam. To me, the recoil is equivalent to shooting a fixed-breech gun (double or pump) of the same gauge with the same load.

Winchester and several others experimented with a short-recoil design back in the 1950s. The Winchester Model 50 and Model 59 autoloaders are two

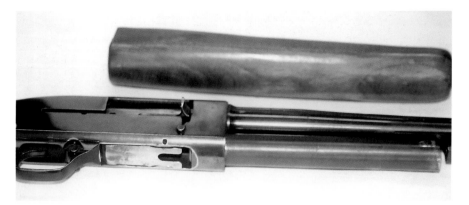

Winchester Model 50 short-action shotgun.

Different mechanisms on gas-operated semi-autos: (from left to right) Winchester 1400, Charles Daly, H&K, and Browning Gold.

versions of this design. Though popular in rifles, the short-recoil design never quite caught on in shotguns.

Although other designs came before it, the Remington Model 1100 was the first successful design to use a gas-operating system. In this type of action, some of the gas pushing the wad and shot charge down the barrel is bled off through a port in the barrel. This then moves a piston that operates the bolt and ejects the fired round, cocks the gun, picks up a fresh round from the magazine, and feeds it into the chamber. Many different companies make a variation of these gas-operated semi-autos. In most, the piston and action are contained in the forend of the weapon. They are reliable, efficient systems. A distinct advantage of the gas-operated semi-auto is that by using some of the pressure to work the action, the amount of recoil felt by the shooter is reduced. This makes for a very pleasant shooting gun. I shoot both an over-and-under and a gas-operated semi-auto in competitions. Although I am not recoil sensitive, I usually have a lot less discomfort by the end of a match if I use my semi-auto.

Another very efficient system for operating a semi-auto is the inertia system. The Benelli semi-autos and some others are the most common guns using this system. In this system, an inertia block recoils against the action, working both the bolt and the action. The inertia system has fewer moving parts and is simpler to maintain than the gas systems. In terms of felt recoil, it seems to be in between the long-recoil and the gas systems.

PUMPS

A pump or slide action uses a moving forend with attached machinery to eject the fired case, cock the weapon, and pick up and chamber a fresh round. Pumps are touted as being the most foolproof and functional of all the repeating action types and are supposed to be the most reliable and easy to maintain. I really disagree! In over twenty-five years of experience as a law enforcement firearm instructor, I saw more malfunctions with pump guns on the firing range than I have ever seen with semi-autos. Most often these malfunctions were directly related to human error rather than the gun.

The most common malfunction with a pump gun is called "short stroking" or "short pumping." The action of a pump gun requires that the action be moved all the way to the rear for the shell carrier to pick up another shell from the magazine and carry it to the chamber. Due to inexperience, haste, or just plain inattention, the shooter sometimes fails to take the slide all the way to the rear. When the slide is pushed forward, no round has been picked up to be placed in the chamber. When the shooter pulls the trigger the next time, they hear a click. I had a hunting buddy back in Indiana who, though an experienced pump shooter, would do this when he got excited while shooting at game. He did it so often that his nickname became "Click-Click"!

I was active in law enforcement training during the transition from revolvers to semi-auto pistols. At an NRA training program in 1981, another shooter and I were the only ones using semi-auto pistols. At the time, revolvers were being touted as more reliable and easier to use than semi-auto pistols. In reality, the opposite was true. I have seen semi-auto pistols, rifles, and shotguns fire under conditions that would lock up a manually activated action. In law enforcement, you always expect the unexpected and prepare for the worst-case scenario. I have had to use a weapon in extreme weather conditions and in times of extreme stress. Although I still enjoy hunting with and shooting a revolver and for approximately half of my law enforcement career was required to carry one, I still had an auto pistol readily available.

By the start of the twenty-first century, most law enforcement agencies had switched to semi-auto pistols. This same trend is starting to develop in shotguns for law enforcement. More and more agencies are discovering that semi-auto shotguns are easier to maintain and use than pump guns. They have also discovered that semi-autos are easier to shoot and that the line troop shoots better scores and are more comfortable and confident with the weapon. There are fewer malfunctions and when put in a lethal-force situation, the troops use their shotguns more often than they did in the past.

The pump gun is often considered an entry-level weapon for shotgunners. Many companies offer pump guns at prices appealing to the budget-minded shooter or hunter. Unfortunately, price has become a major selling point for the pump gun, and this has resulted in the demise of some famous pump guns. The Winchester Model 12, probably the most famous pump gun of all, was discontinued in 1964. Browning introduced some Japanese-made copies in the 1980s, but sales were limited. After discontinuing the Model 12, Winchester released a less expensive gun called the Model 1200. With some design changes from the original, the Model 1200 is now known as the Model 1300 and is still manufactured today.

The Remington 870 is probably the most common pump gun in the United States. First manufactured in 1950 and offered in almost limitless combinations of gauges, barrels, and finishes, it is still manufactured today. In 1987, Remington introduced their Express version of the 870 as a less expensive version. Although it has the same basic action, the gun is made with less expensive wood and metal finishes, and the price is comparable to other entry-level guns.

Remington Model 870 Wingmaster pump-action shotgun. REMINGTON ARMS

O. F. Mossberg and Sons has manufactured a good, reliable, entry-level pump since the 1960s. Their Model 500, which has been made in numerous variations, includes one feature that has always appealed to me: a tang-mounted safety that makes the gun more adaptable to left-handed shooters than the standard cross-bolt safety located in the trigger guard area. Although I use guns with both types of safeties on a regular basis, I prefer the tang-mounted safety to all others.

The Browning Pump Shotgun (BPS) currently being manufactured is a variation of the Remington Model 10. Manufactured in Japan, these are very nice, efficient, and popular guns. Although somewhat higher priced than the entry-level guns, they will provide a lifetime (and then some) of service.

Browning BPS pump-action shotgun. BROWNING ARMS

Another fine pump gun that has gone the way of the dodo bird is the Ithaca Model 37, which is also a variation of the Remington Model 10 design that has been manufactured since 1937. The company has had some ups and downs and has been in and out of business. As a result, the Model 37 is no longer being manufactured. This fine shotgun requires more hand fitting and consequentially has always commanded a higher price than other comparable guns. Back in the days of the Model 12 and the original Model 870, there was not that much of a price difference, but as more and more companies changed designs and produced guns overseas and by less expensive methods, the Model 37 became more and more expensive. I acquired one of Ithaca's 16-

Ithaca Model 37 pump shotgun.

gauge Model 37 Classics a few years ago. Built on a true 16-gauge frame, it has become one of my favorite upland guns. It is a well-balanced, fast-handling gun with a silky smooth action that has functioned perfectly for me from the very first day.

Although pump guns are reliable weapons, I disagree with the common belief that they are good beginner guns. For one, most pumps manufactured today have slim stocks with very sharp combs, which is the upper part of the buttstock where it comes into contact with the cheek. A sharp comb combines with a pump's lighter weight to increase the amount of felt recoil when the gun is fired. I shoot thousands of rounds of shotgun ammunition every year, yet every year for thirty years, there were twenty rounds of ammunition I dreaded having to shoot. This was during the semi-annual shotgun qualification in my police department. Magnum 00 Buck loads and 1-ounce slugs fired through a 6 1/2-pound 18-inch-barreled Model 870 Police produce more felt recoil to me than even a large-bore magnum rifle does. I've said before that I am not particularly recoil sensitive, but those rounds just flat out hurt!

The manipulation of the action on a pump can be a detriment to many new shooters. I recently introduced a neighbor's fiancée to shotgun shooting. She had shot his 12- and 20-gauge pump guns a few times in the past, but we used a gas-operated 28 gauge and then a gas-operated 12 gauge with light loads to introduce her to skeet shooting. Lindsey commented that she liked not having to worry about how to work the action and could just concentrate on shooting the target. Hitting the target is what it's all about, and Lindsey's comment summed it up very well.

BOLT ACTIONS

Although seldom seen today, there have been thousands of bolt-action shotguns manufactured and sold in the United States. They were relatively inexpensive to manufacture and sold at low prices. The size of a shotshell makes the actions on these guns rather large and bulky. Rather notorious for malfunctioning, they are also slow for follow-up shots. These factors led to their demise, and I am not aware of a bolt-action shotgun currently being manufactured as an upland gun.

The only bolt-action shotguns currently being manufactured are specialized guns for deer hunters who are required to use shotgun slugs for their deer hunting. With rifled barrels and scope mounts, these are actually rifle-style actions that have been modified to shoot shotgun slugs. When equipped with a scope sight, they are surprisingly accurate. I used one for some slug testing a couple of years ago. It shot fantastic groups at 100 yards and at 50 yards often made one large ragged hole in the target.

TWO-BARRELED GUNS

A double-barrel shotgun has two barrels that, when opened, swing down-ward on a hinge to expose the chambers, and the shells are then loaded or extracted. Doubles come in two different configurations. The barrels are side-by-side in a horizontal plane or stacked on top of each other in a vertical plane. A side-by-side is traditionally called either a side-by-side or a double gun. An over-and-under (or under-and-over as the English say) is seldom called anything but an over-and-under. Of course, some of my hunting buddies refer to it as a "two holer."

There are advantages common to both designs and to each individually. Either style can have longer barrels and still be a more compact package than a repeater. This is because neither type has the long action of the repeater. Two barrels offer a choice of two chokes, which can be a distinct advantage. Many a time I have hunted quail or pheasants with one barrel choked Skeet or Improved Cylinder and the other choked Improved Modified or even Full. This enables me to have the open barrel for close shots and the tighter barrel for longer shots on a second bird, or if I miss the bird close (which happens too often) and have to take it at a longer range.

Beretta Silver Pigeon over-and-under shotgun. BERETTA U.S.A.

Without the action of a repeater, the two-barreled gun is visually safer. With a pump or semi-auto, even if you can see that the action is open, you cannot tell if the gun has any shells in it without personally examining it. When a side-by-side or over-and-under is open, a glance at the breech tells even a bystander if the gun is loaded or empty. Safety is *always* the number one rule and concern. This visual confirmation is comforting when getting in and out of vehicles, crossing fences, or just meeting up with other shooters in the field or on the range.

The safety on either a side-by-side or over-and-under is usually located on the upper tang, just behind the opening lever. This is a very convenient place for a safety. The gun can be carried "on safe" with the shooter's thumb lightly resting on the safety. As the gun is moved to the shoulder and into a firing position, the safety is pushed off by the thumb as it moves to its firing position on the inside of the stock. The safety in this position is well placed and requires no changing for either a right- or left-handed shooter.

Often, the safety on a side-by-side or over-and-under is of a type called an automatic safety. With this type, the safety automatically moves to the "on safe" position when the action of the gun is opened. Some people, for whatever reason, have a problem with these automatic safeties and some even hate them with a passion usually reserved for bosses and ex-spouses. Sorry folks, but in our litigious society, you will be seeing more and more of these, and you will find fewer and fewer gunsmiths willing to convert them.

I have doubles with both types of safeties and I have no trouble with the automatic safeties. I am always aware of the position of the safety and unless my gun is coming up to the shoulder in the act of being fired, it is "on safe."

SIDE-BY-SIDE DOUBLES

I have no clue as to who first had the idea to place two barrels side-by-side to give the shooter two shots instead of one. I have seen a side-by-side double-barreled pistol that was manufactured in France in 1580. I have seen an illustration of hunters in the sixteenth century using side-by-side guns. No matter who invented it and when it first came into use, the side-by-side double is still a practical hunting weapon even in the twenty-first century.

Ruger Gold Label side-by-side shotgun.

The side-by-side double is a fine example of the gunmaker's art and is often considered the ultimate example. It is a fine-handling weapon and very pleasant to the eye. What is often considered "The Golden Age of Shotgunning" was a period between about 1880 and 1939. By 1880, more and more shotguns were using a self-contained shell. There was an abundance of birds and game in America and in Europe. This was the heyday of the British, German, and French empires, and custom-built guns were used in the homelands and in the far-off reaches of the empire. The side-by-side double was the gun of choice. Beautiful examples were made in England, France, Germany, and the United States, and many of these fine old guns are still available and in use today.

The compact length, balance, and lighter weight of a double barrel makes it a fine choice for the upland hunter. Many of the used double barrels on the market today have fixed chokes and barrels too thin to be threaded for adjustable chokes. With these, the shooter will often have to do a lot of experimenting with loads—either factory or handloads—to determine which ones offer the level of performance he desires. Older double guns made before 1970 and even some imported ones today have very tight barrels and very tight chokes. They were designed to give optimum performance with a certain load or even brand of shell. These shells had paper or felt wads, no protection for the shot, and often-inefficient crimps. Barrels were tighter to prevent the felt and paper wads from not forming a seal in the barrel and thus allowing the propellant gases to get past them to disrupt the shot charge.

Today's standard on the actual bore diameter of a 12-gauge shotgun is .729 inches. With a .729 bore, a choke that reduces the bore by .015 (15 thousandths or 15 degrees of choke) will give a pattern that should be in the midrange of Improved Cylinder (41 to 49 percent). I have seen side-by-sides manufactured in both the United States and Europe prior to World War II that had bores as tight as .718 inches.

I tested a side-by-side from a famous American maker for a friend last year. This gun was one level below the top-of-the-line gun and was manufactured in 1935. The bore measured .724 inches. The choke then measured .018 but was calibrated and marked as an Improved Cylinder. This means that as the shot charge entered the choke area, it was reduced by .018 inches to .706 inches. After managing to find some old-style wads and a roll crimping tool and using paper shells, this particular gun did manage low-end Improved Cylinder patterns averaging 41 percent. The other barrel was marked Modified. It also had a .724-inch bore. The choke on it reduced the diameter by .022, and it produced low-end Modified patterns, which averaged 54 percent. Both the Improved Cylinder and Modified barrel loads had large gaps in the patterns and many pellet strikes outside the 30-inch circle. This is indicative of shot deformation. The loads were $1^{1}/_{8}$ ounces of chilled lead No. 8 shot at a given velocity of 1,200 feet per second (fps) but which actually averaged 1,129 fps over my chronograph.

Now to put it mildly, loading forty rounds of this "old-timey" ammo was a word used to describe female dogs. It took me longer to load those forty rounds than it takes to load 200 rounds of modern ammo. Using modern ammo with one-piece plastic shotcup wads, hard shot, and very efficient powders in this same gun and bores, I shot patterns that averaged 61 percent (Improved Modified range) with the Improved Cylinder barrel and 78 percent (Full Choke range) with the Modified barrel. The fellow bought this gun for ruffed grouse. In the era it was made and with the loads for which it was designed, it would have been a dandy. Now, without some expensive barrel work, it would make a good open-field pheasant gun if modern loads were used with a larger shot size. If he tried using it with modern ammo on grouse, he will have a lot of misses or wing-tipped birds caught with just the edge of the pattern or by some of the deformed shot from the pattern. If he does catch a grouse with the full pattern at typical grouse ranges, he will be serving grouse hamburger or sausage instead of grouse breasts for dinner.

CZ Bobwhite side-by-side shotgun, manufactured by Huglu in Turkey. CZ-USA

Another factor with the side-by-side is the felt recoil. In most side-by-side guns, the more open barrel is the right barrel. When this barrel is fired, the recoil is to the left and directly into the face of a right-handed shooter. When the left barrel is fired, the recoil is away from the face. This difference in recoil can affect the shooter and his ability to hit with the gun. Most shooters will tell you that with comparable weight guns shooting the same load, they experience less felt recoil with an over-and-under than a side-by-side.

The wide muzzles of the side-by-side are also often touted as an advantage. Over-and-under shooters proclaim the advantage of the single sighting plane. In truth, when properly shooting a shotgun, the eye should be focused on the target, either feathered or clay, and the muzzle should be seen only in the peripheral vision. The wide muzzles of the double are a deterrent to those shooters who find their eye naturally drawn to these instead of the target. Some shooters have the same problem with the "humpback" of the Browning Auto-5 and similar semi-autos. Most of the time, this will cause the shooter to shoot below the target. A properly fitted stock can resolve this problem but can be an expensive project. Many shooters are not willing to spend the time or money to change a stock and they curse the gun instead.

The compact length, point of balance, and quick handling of a side-by-side double make it a fine gun for the upland hunter. If you are switching to a side-by-side from a different action type, you will need to practice extensively prior to the season. The side-by-side has a different balance point and will swing at a different speed than your other guns, and you must practice to master these. One of my quail hunting buddies has several different side-by-side doubles that he enjoys. Every year before the quail season, though, he brings them out to the skeet field and shoots until he is comfortable with the different handling characteristics and is confident that he can hit with them.

Side-by-side doubles are still popular, and there are currently manufactured but reasonably priced side-by-side guns available. Ruger has recently introduced their Gold Label side-by-side, which is modeled on the Dickson round action and is priced around $2,000. An original Dickson brings prices much, much higher.

Many of today's mass-produced side-by-side guns are looked down upon by some gun writers because, according to them, these new guns do not match the quality of the older guns. This is true in some, but not all, cases. The craftsmen that did the hand fitting on the old L. C. Smith, Ithaca, and Parker guns are long gone. Modern computerized manufacturing processes can produce tighter tolerances and guns that are actually better fitted than those created by even the master craftsmen of old. With modern production methods, these guns can be marketed at a price that is but a fraction of the cost of an older side-by-side in today's market.

I have a lovely old 20-gauge Ithaca Grade 3 that was owned by a great uncle of mine. He bought it new, on special order, in 1936 for I believe $73. It is a fine little shotgun, and he used it for many years as his grouse gun in western Pennsylvania and West Virginia. It has 28-inch barrels and is choked Improved Cylinder and Full. While delightful, I have seen modern side-by-sides just as well made and delightful to handle and are less expensive.

For years, the side-by-side double barrel has been championed as the ultimate upland gun by a number of writers. They have managed to convince the average Joe that unless you are using an English-made, double-triggered, straight-gripped side-by-side on upland birds you are not a true upland hunter. Many hunters shoot side-by-side doubles simply because they think they have to, even if they don't shoot them as well as another action type. One good friend and hunting companion swears by his side-by-sides even though he admits to shooting better with an over-and-under. I have owned and shot a number of side-by-side doubles over the years. I have had side-by-sides custom built to my measurements, and I found I didn't shoot them any better than other action types. In a couple of cases, I actually shot worse.

One of the advantages often touted with side-by-side doubles and double triggers is that the shooter has an instant choice of different chokes and can fire the tighter barrel on long shots. First, if the shooter is someone accustomed to shooting his birds inside of 25 yards, the lead and angles of a 35-yard shot will make it a difficult shot for him. Second, if the shooter has to think about changing hand and finger position to shoot with the rear trigger, this will interfere with his normal timing and swing. Third, there are a number of single-trigger doubles in both side-by-side and over-and-under configurations with the trigger selector part of the tang safety. The shooter can instantly decide which barrel to fire as the safety is thumbed off when the gun is raised to the firing position.

I have several friends who have been brainwashed into using double-triggered side-by-sides and have argued this point with me many a time over the years. For one whole season, I asked four of them to keep track of how many times they fired the tighter-choked barrel first on a flushed bird and how many times they actually hit the bird. Now, these are not novice or part-time hunters. Between the four of them, they probably spend over a thousand days afield each year hunting grouse, woodcock, quail, and pheasant. When the results were tallied, only twelve shots were fired with the tighter-choked barrel first and *only one* bird was hit!

I shoot an over-and-under quite often in the field. I have the ability to select the barrel in conjunction with the safety on several models. I find the most common situation where I will fire the tighter barrel first is when dove hunting and shooting incoming birds. I fire the tighter barrel first, as the birds are coming in, and the more open barrel when the birds are overhead. I set my barrel selector, and I don't have to think about changing hand or finger position as I shoot.

Yes, a hand-fitted side-by-side double is a beautiful example of the gunmaker's art. It is a fine handling weapon and very pleasing to the eye. It is *not*, however, the ultimate answer to a gunner's prayers, as too many gun writers have touted it to be. Cost is another factor. Side-by-side doubles that sold new prior to World War II for $30 are now worth hundreds, if not thousands, of dollars. It is not unusual to look through a catalog of fine side-by-side double guns and find five- and six-digit price tags. Sorry folks; even though I can appreciate a gun like this, that amount of money would have a lot of other uses in my household. I would rather enjoy twenty $1,000 hunting trips with an $800 gun than one hunting trip with a $20,000 gun.

OVER-AND-UNDERS

Probably the most popular style of double-barrel guns in the world today is the over-and-under, where the barrels are "stacked" vertically. The over-and-under has many of the same advantages of the side-by-side, in a package that is easier to shoot for many people.

Sporting clays is a clay target game that began in the 1980s and has blossomed all over the United States and the world. Many of the sporting clay shooters are recreational shooters who enjoy the game and the competition. Although sporting clays began as a game for hunters, it has evolved into much more. Many of today's shooters shoot sporting clays for recreation instead of playing golf or tennis.

Without a doubt, the most popular gun seen on any sporting clays course is an over-and-under. The choice of different chokes for different targets, the ease of shooting and handling, the visible open action for safety, the quick second shot, and the balance and fit of over-and-unders have made them the gun of choice. A very distant second is the semi-auto. Pumps and doubles are rarely seen, except in specialty shoots designed specifically for them.

For the upland hunter, the over-and-under is also an excellent choice. There is the option of two chokes and the similar advantages of ease of carry and handling found with the side-by-side. A definite bonus for the average hunter is the cost of an over-and-under in comparison with a side-by-side. The over-and-under costs much less in most cases. There are currently more makes and models of over-and-unders available today than at any time in history and new ones are being introduced every year.

Ruger Red Label over-and-under shotgun. STURM, RUGER

I have personally used over-and-unders in the field for many years, and if forced at gunpoint to admit what I would pick if I could only have one gun for upland hunting (God forbid!), I would probably pick an over-and-under. With the barrels in a vertical plane, when either barrel is fired, the force of recoil goes directly back into the shoulder of the shooter. Most experienced shooters will tell you they feel less felt recoil with a comparable weighted and loaded over-and-under than with a side-by-side.

The current trend in over-and-unders used in competition is long barrels (32 to 34 inches). These are fine on a competition gun that is carried a little and shot a lot but not on a field gun that is carried a lot and shot a little. Although the longer barrels swing easier and more consistently and give a longer sight plane, they can be a disadvantage in the field when trying to be shouldered and fired on a flushing bird or running rabbit. There is also the weight factor. The longer barrels weigh more, and although this can be a very positive factor during a 100-bird match, they can also become a real burden by the end of a long day afield. I regularly shoot an over-and-under with 30-inch barrels for skeet and sporting clays. With the 30-inch barrels in place, it weighs about 8 pounds. When I take this same gun pheasant or quail hunting, it has the 26-inch barrels on the receiver. With these, the gun weighs 7 pounds, 4 ounces.

Now 12 ounces of weight may not seem like much, but it can feel like 12 tons at the end of a long day. My shooting, which isn't flawless on good days, really suffers when the extra weight of a gun makes me fatigued.

Longer barrels can be an advantage in the smaller gauge guns. I have a beautiful little 28 gauge that weighs only 5 1/2 pounds with a 26-inch barrel. As much as I love to carry and use this little gun, the shorter lightweight barrel requires some serious thought when I am shooting at a bird. I have to remind myself to swing through or else I tend to stop my swing with the short light-

SigArms TT-45 over-and-under shotgun. SIGARMS

weight barrel. I am currently trying to decide between one of two over-and-unders for my next 28-gauge gun. Both balance very well with 30-inch barrels, and in the 28 gauge, there is only 4 ounces of weight difference. Until my experience with the other 28 gauge, I probably wouldn't even be considering 30-inch barrels, since I prefer 26-inch barrels on 12- and 20-gauge over-and-unders. This is a matter of personal preference, but many shooters I know find they shoot better with longer barrels in either a 20 or 28 gauge even on fast flushing game birds.

SINGLE SHOTS AND SPECIALTY GUNS

Single-shot guns can be as simple as a "behind the door" gun at a farmhouse or fishing cabin to as sophisticated as a custom-built gun used by a competitive trapshooter. There are also single shot combination guns where a single receiver can be used for either a rifle or shotgun barrel. Many of today's shooters started on a single-shot gun, and there are still single shots with either exposed or enclosed hammers available. It is an excellent beginner's gun when properly loaded. Most of these guns are very light in weight and if used with even standard skeet loads may generate more felt recoil than a 12 gauge with magnum loads.

The exposed hammer is a safety factor but can also be a very real danger. If teaching a youngster or another person with one of these, they should be able to demonstrate that they can release the cocked hammer under all conditions. This does not mean just on the range during shirtsleeve weather but also when wearing heavy gloves and when excited about being in the field. I know of too many accidental discharges of this type of weapon when an inexperienced or excited shooter was trying to lower the hammer. I have even been too close to a couple of them.

There are also combination guns that contain one or two rifle barrels in conjunction with one or two shotgun barrels on a single receiver. These guns are commonly called drillings (from the German word "drei" for three) and were very prevalent in Europe prior to World War II. Many were brought back by returning GIs. Most of the variations I have seen had side-by-side shotgun barrels with a single barrel for a large-caliber rifle underneath. I have also seen them with two rifle barrels and a single shotgun barrel underneath. The most unusual variation had two side-by-side 16-gauge shotgun barrels with a 9.3 x 57R rifle barrel underneath and a .22 Hornet barrel on top in the sighting rib between the shotgun barrels. Since the 16 gauge was the most popular shotgun gauge in Europe at this time, most of these guns are found in 16 gauge and very few in any other gauge. As stated in another chapter, the 16 gauge was the last gauge to be standardized with a $2^3/4$-inch chamber. If anyone is fortunate enough to have one of these fine old guns, a competent gunsmith should check the chamber length and barrel strength and construction before it is fired.

These guns were also made in over-and-under form with either the shotgun or rifle barrel on top and the other underneath. This particular configuration is familiar to many U.S. shooters because of the popularity of the Savage/Stevens Model 24 and its variations. In this unique gun, the most common chambering was a .22 Long Rifle barrel over a 410-shotgun barrel. I don't think I know a single shooter of my generation who didn't covet one of these growing up. The kid that had one was fortunate indeed and was the envy of all his friends.

Thousands of single-shot guns with and without exposed hammers have been built over the years. Various companies produced many as "private brands." Many were also built with long (36 inches or longer) barrels because consumers were under the impression those longer barrels "shot harder." In the days of blackpowder this was true, because a longer barrel was needed to provide adequate ignition for the coarser-grained blackpowder used in shotguns in order to reach the expected velocities. But after the velocity was achieved, there was no increase despite the length of the barrel. With smokeless powder—especially the ones available today—most of the powder is consumed and the required velocity is reached within 18 inches of barrel. A shotshell that propels the load at 1,200 fps will do so in either a barrel of 20 inches or a barrel 30 inches in length. The longer barrel does not increase velocity and in some cases with modern powders may actually decrease the velocity. I can't believe this old wives' tale is still around, but it is. I still hear from shooters that a longer barrel will "shoot harder"!

There is an entire subculture within the shooting public that enjoys shooting blackpowder muzzleloaders. Many do so because they are required by local regulations to use a blackpowder muzzleloader or a shotgun on deer and other big game. Others do it for fun and enjoy hunting and shooting more traditional rifles and shotguns. Although he enjoys all types of firearms, a good friend of mine prefers to do his elk, deer, and turkey hunting with traditional flintlock muzzleloaders. Walt is a preacher and I kid him that the smell of the sulfur and charcoal of blackpowder smoke gives him inspiration for "fire and brimstone" sermons.

Now I admit that I really enjoy shooting blackpowder, but I am naturally lazy and would rather clean and load in the comfort of my home than out in the field. Taking game with a traditional muzzleloading blackpowder shotgun is a lot of fun, and they can be surprisingly effective. I hunted with a friend who used a side-by-side blackpowder 10 gauge on a pheasant hunt one year. The first time he fired it on a rising bird my Brittany actually stopped in midstride and looked back with an expression that said, "What was that?" I also found it interesting that after shooting, my friend immediately ducked to a kneeling position so he could peek under the cloud of powder smoke to see if he hit the bird. So much for getting off a quick second shot.

In my limited experience with muzzleloading blackpowder shotguns, I have found the 12 and 10 gauges most common. Because of the design of the muzzleloader, most are pure cylinder chokes and require different wadding than do modern shotshells. This is also true if shooting blackpowder in a shotshell. Your shot size and shot amounts will remain similar, but everything else is so different that I am very uncomfortable giving any information. If you would like to try using a blackpowder shotgun on game, I suggest you meet and become involved with your local muzzleloading club, which will have people with much more experience to help you. There are also a number of online sites available that provide information.

Which of the many action types you choose or use is a matter of personal preference. Don't become locked into the idea that because you have used only one action type it is the only one that will work for you. You may find that you enjoy another just as much or even more. For example, if you enjoy shooting a pump but are bothered by recoil, switching to a gas-operated semiauto will reduce the felt recoil considerably, and the gun will be similar in size and weight to what you are used to. I own and shoot different action types on a regular basis, and while I have ones I prefer, I enjoy the fun and challenge of shooting all of them.

Choosing A Shotgun

What should the hunter looking for a new gun use as criteria for choosing a shotgun? There are a number of different factors to consider. What type of game will you be hunting? Is there an action type you prefer? What price range are you looking in? What type of features do you want on the gun? What other uses (clay target games, deer hunting, etc.) will you have for the gun? Do you have a particular gauge in mind? Do you hunt with a dog, and if so, is it a pointer or a flusher? Looking at these factors individually will hopefully help you decide which gun to purchase.

TYPE OF GAME

This can be a very influencing factor. It is also a great reason to have more than one gun. If you are hunting grouse, woodcock, or quail in heavy cover, you want a gun that is easy to carry in one hand as you use the other hand to force your way through the briars and brambles. Many of your shots will be less than 20 yards, so you will want a gun that is quick handling and comes to the shoulder easily.

Shorter barrels and open chokes will also be assets in this type of cover. In the grouse woods, seldom do you have a shot that requires a long fluid swing. Many of your shots will be fired as soon as the gun comes in contact with your shoulder and will be of the "point-and-shoot" type. We will cover this and other types of shooting styles more in another chapter.

If you only do this type of hunting, you will probably be considering a 20 or even a 28 gauge. The 12 and 16 both work fine for these birds, but 20s and 28s usually come in a lighter, handier package. In the past, the options were usually limited to either a 26-inch barrel on a double or a repeater, a fixed

Improved Cylinder choke on a repeater, or Improved Cylinder and Modified on a double or over-and-under. With the proliferation of screw-in choke tubes, the gunner of today can pick whatever choke he or she wants and needs for the conditions and in less than a minute have it installed in the barrel or barrels.

Several years ago, I was hunting grouse with a friend in Minnesota. The leaves were still on the trees and although shots were close, they often had to go through a canopy of leaves to get to the bird. I was using an over-and-under and a combination of a Skeet 1 choke (less than Improved Cylinder) and a Skeet 2 (between Improved Cylinder and Modified). It was a perfect setup. The Skeet 1 gave open-enough patterns for the very close shots, and the Skeet 2 gave sufficient pattern density to penetrate the leaves and still be open enough to take the bird at less than 25 yards. My hunting partner was using a repeater and his choke choice was an Improved Cylinder.

What if you are going to be using the gun on pheasants and quail in more open terrain? Then you might want a gun that has a slightly longer barrel and is longer overall. You still need to have a comfortable weight in order to carry and use the gun efficiently. Believe me, an extra pound of gun weight can feel like an extra ton by the end of a long day chasing pheasant and quail in big fields. The type of hunting you are doing here can influence your gun choice. Are you hunting big cornfields with a large group of other hunters in a classic pheasant drive? If so, you will probably want a 12 gauge and tighter chokes in a longer barrel that enable you to swing on a crossing rooster. If hunting alone or with one or two companions behind close-working pointing dogs, you might find that your grouse and woodcock gun works fine even on pheasant.

Will you be using the gun as a double- or triple-duty piece and hunting waterfowl or wild turkeys with it? If so, you will probably want a 12 gauge, and unless you are a card-carrying masochist, you will probably want a little more weight to help tame the recoil of the heavy loads used in this type of hunting.

ACTION TYPE

This is really a matter of personal preference, but it doesn't mean that because you have always used one type that you are limited to it. Back in my college days, I was limited to one shotgun. I had a little 20-gauge semi-auto one year, which turned out to be a year of record rainfall and of some of the best duck hunting ever experienced in that area. This was back in the lead shot days, and my 20 gauge worked fine on decoying ducks. I broke a part in the second weekend of the season, and while waiting for a replacement, I used a borrowed 20-gauge pump for a couple of weeks. Prior to the semi-auto, I had hunted with a single-trigger double for a number of years, so I was used to just pulling the trigger for follow-up shots. My hunting buddies got so tired of hearing me cussing the pump when I would forget to work the action that they started hollering "Pump!" every time they heard me shoot. Another good friend of mine had hunted most of his life with a Winchester Model 12 pump. One year, he bought a Benelli semi-auto and the first few times he took it dove hunting, he tried very hard after every shot to work the forend and cycle another shell!

A couple rounds of skeet, sporting clays, or even shooting doubles from a hand trap will get you accustomed to a new action type. This should be part of your practice routine anyway to help you become a better and more confident wing shot. Believe me, nothing will send a cold shiver down your spine quicker than hearing someone you are hunting with look at the gun in his hands and ask, "How's this thing work and how do you load it?"

Three favorite 28-gauge shotguns, in pump, semi-auto, and over-and-under actions.

PRICE RANGE

The price range for a gun will vary with each individual hunter. For some this may be under $300. For others it may be under $1,000 or $2,500 or higher. Whatever your price range, buy the best gun you can afford! If you like a gun that is outside of your price range, then shop the used market and you can probably find one that will fit your budget. Buying a used gun used to be limited to whatever was available in your area. Now with the Internet, there are many websites that sell guns. These may be Internet offers from a supplier or even come direct from the factory. There are also websites that offer guns of all categories for sale. The only one with which I am personally familiar is gunbroker.com, but there are many others. These will often even provide you with a listing of Federal Firearms License holders in your area that will handle the paperwork on the transfer of the firearms to you.

I said earlier that you should buy the best gun you can afford. This does not mean you have to buy the most expensive gun in your price range. I have seen shooters who had $2,500 to spend and who bought a gun for $1,200 and spent the other $1,300 on shells and clay target practice. Believe me, by the time the season rolled around they were better shots with their $1,200 gun than the fellow who spent the whole $2,500 on the gun.

One of my neighbors is a college student and a pretty good hunter. He spends so much time going out with me shooting and dog training that sometimes I think he's the son I never had. He's a fair shot with a shotgun and is willing to practice with his inexpensive pumps to make himself a better shot. A good friend of his is one of these people who think they can buy success. He never wants to go shooting with us during the off-season because he is such a poor shot that he embarrasses himself. Instead of practicing, he buys new guns. Last year, the week before the season, he spent $1,300 on an over-and-under to replace the $500 semi-auto he had been shooting. He still missed. Last week he showed up with a new $2,500 over-and-under. He's confident he will be able to hit birds this year, but he doesn't want to take the time to practice beforehand. Every successful competitor in any sport will tell you the equipment only helps you if you can get the use from the equipment.

A once-a-week golfer may have the same clubs Tiger Woods uses, but he won't have the same scores. My good friend and fellow writer Dave Holmes says it best: "Buy a $800 gun and shoot $1,200 worth of shells in it the first six months. You will be happier than if you bought the $2,000 gun!" I do not know of a single sport where money buys proficiency, but I know practice breeds proficiency in any sport.

FEATURES

What features do you want on your new gun? Do you like a wood or synthetic stock? Do you prefer a traditional blue finish or one of the new dull synthetic finishes? If you are going to use the gun for waterfowl or turkeys, you may want a camouflage version.

Most of today's guns come with standard features that were only available as expensive custom features just a short time ago. For years, if a hunter wanted to change the choke in the barrel, he would have to bear the expense of extra barrels or have an adjustable multi-choke installed on the gun. If he wanted to change the angle or the cast on the stock, he would first have to find a knowledgeable gunsmith and then have an extensive trial-and-error period.

As late as the 1980s, the hunter wishing to have a gun capable of firing both $2\frac{3}{4}$- and 3-inch shells would often have to have two different guns. His 3-inch-chambered double would be too heavy for a field gun and his 3-inch-chambered semi-auto would not work reliably with light $2\frac{3}{4}$-inch dove or quail loads. Today, most guns come with interchangeable choke tubes that can be changed in less than a minute. Many guns also include different shims that

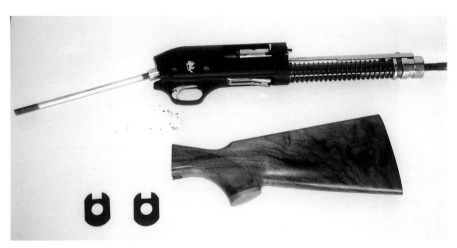

Factory-supplied stock adjusters.

can be easily replaced in the stock by the shooter to alter its height and angle. As we saw in the chapter on the shotgun gauges, 3-inch chambers are the most common chamber lengths today in both the 12 and 20 gauges.

Wood or synthetic stocks? Dull, glossy, or oil finishes? Blue, black, or camouflaged metal parts are often personal preferences. The black synthetic stocks and the dull metal finishes are often touted as being weather resistant, and it is implied that they are easier to take care of. Well, I have spent many a day afield in the rain or in a muddy field for ducks and geese. It still takes the same amount of energy and effort to clean the gun and keep it functioning whether it has a black stock and black parts or wood and blued parts.

Synthetic stocks have a real function with rifles. Being impervious to moisture, they don't swell and contract with moisture as wood stocks do. This will affect the point of impact of the bullet, sometimes dramatically. For seven years, I was an officer with a small department in the mountains of southwest Colorado. Every year we would open up our police rifle range to deer and elk hunters to sight-in their rifles. We were at almost 8,000 feet in elevation in a very dry climate. Many are the rifles I saw that came from high humidity areas that could be as much as a foot off, just from the drying out of the wood over a few days. Point of impact with a shotgun is not nearly as critical. When you are dealing with a 20- or 30-inch area of shot (pattern), 2 or 4 inches will not make a difference.

Also, shotgun stocks are designed differently than rifle stocks. A rifle stock presses against the barrel and action and strengthens it to keep the selected load shooting to the same place (zeroing). A shotgun stock does not have this requirement, and shotgun stocks are seldom a supporting part of the action. Rifle stocks, whether wood or synthetic, are one piece—either cut from the same stock blank or molded in the same mold. Most shotgun stocks are two pieces and may be separate pieces glued or molded together. I never really noticed this with wood stocks, but it was brought home to me rather painfully with a synthetic stock. I was testing some heavy ($1^3/_8$- and $1^1/_2$-ounce) 12-gauge pheasant loads. I was using my wood-stocked over-and-under, a wood-stocked semi-auto, and also my pheasant-hunting buddy's synthetic-stocked semi-auto. When pattern and velocity testing, the shotgun is held in a tight, stable position that enables you to center the patterns but also maximizes the recoil. I never really noticed the little seam on top of the synthetic stock until I saw blood dripping off my face. This little seam opened up a $2^1/_2$-inch gash on my right cheek that took two stitches to close. A couple of new shooters I have coached with this same model of weapon have also noticed discomfort from this seam.

One of my few ties with tradition is with blue steel and wood stocks. I just personally like the appearance of them, but I do own guns that have both black synthetic and camouflage stocks. If you are going to use your gun for a dual purpose and want the dull or camouflage finish for turkey or water-fowl hunting, make sure the whole gun is finished that way. Several years ago, I was in a goose field and there were three other hunters with a decoy spread about 200 yards west of us. It was a bright sunshiny morning and we could consistently see flashes as bright as a mirror coming from their blind. If we could see it, so could the geese, and these fellows had birds constantly flaring just out of range. After the morning flights, we were sitting outside our blind drinking coffee and two of these fellows walked over. They were relatively new goose hunters and wondered if we could check their decoy spread to see if we could figure out why the birds kept flaring. As we were walking back to their spread, we commented about the flashing light we kept seeing from their blind. They couldn't figure out what it was. Their decoy spread looked good, and I happened to glance at one of their shotguns. They were all shooting the same model and all had fully camouflaged stocks and metal parts. The problem turned out to be the shiny, polished, bright chrome bolt on each of the guns. Every time they moved, these chrome bolts flashed like neon signs. A few minutes of work with a black or dark brown marker pen will correct this but won't affect the functioning of the weapon.

The other features you pick for your gun will depend on your personal preferences. One valuable item would be a recoil pad, traditionally made of hard rubber and in styles more fitted to the trap gun or rifle than the field shotgun. The numerous new materials being used in recoil pads today are softer and absorb recoil better than the solid rubber. Two of my favorites are the Kick Eez and the LimbSaver. The design of pads has also changed because of the popularity of sporting clays. Many sporting clay shooters mount their guns as they call for birds, while some sporting clay disciplines require the "low gun." Pads have been developed with smooth upper and lower coverings that slide along clothing and don't interfere with the mounting of the gun. A properly fitted gun with a good recoil pad makes for comfortable and better shooting.

GAUGE

As we discussed in the chapter on shotgun gauges, the most popular gauge in the world is the 12 gauge. If you will be hunting a variety of game birds and animals, the 12 gauge is probably your best bet. If you are hunting smaller birds such as grouse, woodcock, or bobwhite quail exclusively, you will probably prefer a 20 gauge or even a 28 gauge. Of course, a 16 gauge is also a perfect upland gun.

Limbsaver prefit recoil pad on a Browning Gold shotgun.

Although it will be discussed further in the chapter on shotshells, more and more areas are being designated nontoxic-shot zones. Although there have been great strides in the effectiveness of nontoxic shot since it was first introduced, there are not vast options of loads available for upland hunting as there is with lead shot. If you are forced to hunt in areas where nontoxic shot is required, you will probably want a 12 gauge. This is simply because there are more nontoxic loads available in the 12 gauge than all of the other gauges combined.

12 and 28 gauge over-and-under shotguns.

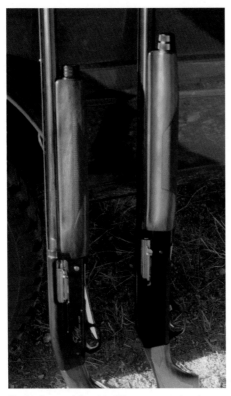

Browning and Beretta 12-gauge semi-autos.

This benefit of using a 12 gauge for nontoxic shot was brought home to me on a pheasant hunt last year. I was hunting in three states on this trip, and when I arrived in Nebraska, the local fellow I was hunting with advised me that on some of the state land we would be hunting, nontoxic shot was required. Of course I had a whole case of various nontoxic loads for the 12 and 16 gauges I had along; the problem was, it was sitting in my "War Room" back in Texas. All I could find at the local Wal-Mart were 3-inch shells in the preferred shot size. Fortunately, I had a 12 gauge with a 3-inch chamber along. To really add insult to injury, when I got home from this trip, waiting for me was a case of a new nontoxic shell in 16 gauge sent for field-testing by the manufacturer, and they were in the shot size I prefer for pheasants!

Many hunters prefer a 20 gauge. As stated earlier, I was a disciple of the 20 gauge for a number of years. I had too many lost birds when shooting western pheasants and grouse with the 20 gauge, however. Some of the first load testing I ever did was with 20-gauge 3-inch shells. Despite the choke, the patterns were too patchy and full of holes to satisfy my requirement for a pheasant gun. I still enjoy shooting the 20 gauge, especially on smaller birds (quail and doves), and if you prefer it, go for it. Of course, if you ever shoot a 28 gauge, you will soon find that the 28 beats the 20 at the same game!

I was at a very large Texas ranch this past year. This ranch is world famous for the quality of quail hunting found there. There were two racks of shotguns for guests that were paying up to $1,000 a day to hunt birds. Of the forty guns in the rack, thirty of them were 20 gauges and twenty of these were semi-autos. The other ten were over-and-unders. On a three-day hunt, we averaged thirty coveys of birds a day, so guests were presented with lots of opportunities to take birds. I talked with one of the guides about this, and he said they have found just about any hunter can handle a 20 gauge and that with the excellent dogs on the ranch, most shots on coveys are inside of 20 yards. He said the 20 gauge fits their needs the best. Of course, there are vast differences in the shell-to-bird ratio among the shooters he sees every year.

LENGTH AND WEIGHT

When you get into your vehicle, you have the seat and the steering wheel adjusted for your personal preference. If you are like me, when someone else has driven your vehicle, you will adjust both even if the other person has made an attempt to put them back where they were. You wouldn't think of driving with the seat too far back or too far forward.

The shotgun you choose should also fit your physique. We will talk more about the actual fitting of the gun in another chapter, but for now let's just consider the length and weight of the gun. I stand 5 feet, 9 inches tall and weigh in the vicinity of 180 pounds. I happen to have broad shoulders, a barrel chest, and short arms and legs. Several years ago, I measured and weighed all of my guns to see what the average length and weight was. It was not surprising to discover that one of the guns I shoot best was right on that average. What works best for my physique may not work well for you.

I am most comfortable with an upland gun that weighs between 6 1/2 and 7 pounds, and in the past I would have recommended this weight for just about everyone. However, I have hunted with several 2-XL people who are just as comfortable with an 8-pound gun. For them, a 6 1/2- or 7-pound gun is too light and they have a tendency to stop the swing. Also, for me, a gun of about 46 inches in overall length fits my physique and my short arms very well. I have several friends who stand over 6 feet, 4 inches and have very long arms. They find that a longer gun, even up to 50 or 52 inches, better matches their physique. They are uncomfortable with a shorter gun.

It is also very easy to have a gun that is too long. Several years ago, a friend of mine bought his dad a new gun for Christmas. It was a model his dad had wanted and was a beautiful weapon. The only problem was, with the 30-inch barrel on the gun, it was almost 50 inches in

Jeff McVay prefers his Benelli Super Black Eagle for pheasants.

length and weighed almost 8 pounds. His dad stood about 5 feet, 4 inches tall and had short arms. As much as his Dad loved the new gun, it was just too big for him. When he purchased a 22-inch barrel for the gun and put it on, the gun felt comfortable to him and he became an excellent shot with it. This is a very important consideration when outfitting a young shooter or a woman with a gun. If they are comfortable with the fit and handling of the gun, they will become more confident and capable with it. If it is too long or too heavy, they will be uncomfortable with it and will not enjoy shooting.

I wish there were a magic formula I could tell you to determine what length and weight is right for you. Unfortunately, there is not. It sounds like a cliché, but if your dream gun feels right in the store, it will *probably* feel right in the field. If it feels too long or too heavy in the store, I will guarantee you that it *will* be too long and too heavy for you to shoot effectively in the field.

HUNTING WITH OR WITHOUT A DOG

Why would hunting with or without a dog influence the gun that you pick? If you are hunting with a trained dog, you will find that you will be taking birds at closer ranges than if you are hunting without a dog. Whether you are using a pointing dog or a flusher, the dog will tell you by its body language when it's scenting game and "getting birdy." This will enable you to be ready for the shot and not have to overcome the "surprise factor" of a bird or birds flushing unexpectedly. Experiencing the joy that a hunting dog brings to the field and into your life is also a reward that cannot be measured. When first hunting with a dog, many hunters become rather intimidated and don't know what to do when the dog goes on point. There are a number of things that hunting with a dog requires, but the most important is to remember that the dog is telling you there is a bird close and you need to be ready to shoot it.

Many people think you have to walk up directly behind the dog when on point. Most dog handlers will tell you, however, that they prefer you walk in to one side or the other so that the dog can see you and so that you can see the dog's head and face. This will give you an idea where the birds are and in what direction they may flush. Also, a dog scents the bird on the wind. In most cases, the bird will be upwind of the dog. If the bird is moving, the dog's body language and position will give this away. When exposing a new hunter to my dogs, I always tell him to move in from the side and move quickly into the wind. This can make the difference between having an easy 15-yard shot or a difficult 30-yard shot.

I love to hunt upland birds, but I also love hunting them with my dogs. I have hunted birds without dogs, but now my dogs are as much a part of the enjoyment of the hunt as the birds are. If you are hunting with dogs, no matter what the breed or the birds, you will usually find you are getting closer shots that you are better prepared to take than if hunting without a dog. This can influence your choice of shotgun, choke, and load.

Whatever shotgun you choose, get out and enjoy it. We will talk about off-season practice in a later chapter, but to be a good wing shot, you need to be familiar with your shotgun. Sticking the gun in the closet and only taking it out the morning you are going hunting will cause much frustration when you miss birds because the gun feels alien to you. Even if you don't get the opportunity to shoot your gun as often as you want, spending some time handling it every week, or better yet, every day, will help you to become a better shot. If you spend five or ten minutes a day mounting your gun, taking the safety off as you mount, and swinging the gun as

A proper retrieve.

though you were swinging at a bird, you are developing the "muscle memory" needed to be proficient with the gun.

USED GUNS

I want to touch on one other subject before we close this chapter—buying a used gun. Guns are designed for years of use, and I know very few shooters who have ever shot a gun so much that it required rebuilding. Neglect or misuse causes most problems with a gun. Talk to any gunsmith and he will tell you that 85 to 90 percent of the malfunctioning guns brought in just need a good thorough cleaning to get them working again.

When you are buying a used car, as any consumer is aware, there can be many hidden faults and problems that only a detailed check by a trained mechanic can locate. This is not true with guns. Even someone with limited experience can usually tell if a gun has been abused or neglected or how much it has been used.

First, check the barrel, both inside and out. Rust spots on the barrel or bright places that indicate where rust has been polished off may indicate the gun has been stored improperly or has not been taken care of. A few minor spots are usually nothing to worry about, but it will pay to check the action to see if there is any rust down inside. This will seriously affect functioning and may require a costly repair job. Is the bluing worn in places where the gun would be carried in the hand or does it show wear in places where it may have hung in a gun rack or sat in a safe? A normal amount of wear is expected, but if there are areas that are worn bright, it can indicate much use or abuse.

Check the bolt face. If the gun has been fired very little, there will often be no or very little wear on the face of the bolt. If the gun has been fired a lot, there will usually be a round area of wear on the bolt face indicating the constant contact with the base of a shotgun shell. This is not necessarily a bad thing since most guns will stand up to more rounds than many shooters will ever fire in their lifetimes, but it may give you a bargaining tool on the price of the weapon.

These buttstock scratches represent normal wear and tear for a field-used shotgun.

Has the gun been reblued or refinished? This may indicate there was extensive rust or damage done to the gun. Rebluing may not be immediately obvious, but look at the markings on the receiver and barrel. Are the letters and numbers distinct or do they show some rounding and blending, which indicates they were rounded off by the polishing required to take the gun down to bare metal before being reblued?

A good friend of mine owned a gun shop for many years. When someone was trying to sell or trade a gun to him, he would always hold it up to his face and take a strong sniff at the area where the wood and metal came together. I asked him one day why he did this. He told me it was a sure way to tell if a gun had ever been exposed to a fire. The wood would retain the smell of smoke, which could be smelled even if the gun had been reblued or refinished. I have had numerous chances to check this over the years and it is true. If a gun has been exposed to fire there will be a definite woodsmoke smell in the area, even if the gun has been refinished. This could potentially affect the gun's function and safety. If you smell smoke, it may be a very wise idea to pass on that gun.

Another area to check is where the buttstock joins with the metal of the action. Far too many gun owners over-lubricate their weapons. When the gun is stored in a muzzle-up position (the most common), oil and solvents run down into the stock area and may weaken the wood. A fellow skeet shooter always sprayed down and then wiped down his expensive over-and-under with a well-known name brand of aerosol gun oil after every time he shot. After several years of doing this, the wood fractured at the "wrist" where the buttstock and action came together. The interior of the wood literally oozed oil! What he had been doing to protect his gun actually damaged it. If the wood around where it joins the metal appears darker than the surrounding wood, it may be an indicator that this gun was over-lubricated.

Buying a used gun can result in some real bargains. I picked up a favorite 16 gauge in a pawnshop a few years ago for $135. After a good cleaning, it has performed flawlessly. Later I found out this gun was a rarity because it was built on a 20-gauge frame and was worth much more. If you are in the market for a used gun, you can find some real bargains and also some real turkeys out there. It may be to your advantage to take a knowledgeable friend or family member along on your shopping trip.

6 What's Out There?

As stated earlier, today is really the golden age for shotguns and the shotgun shooter. There are more manufacturers making guns, ammunition, and accessories than at any time in history. Often one of the determining factors in choosing a shotgun is money. I have often been guilty of having champagne tastes on a tap water budget. Like many of you, my money for guns came after all the bills were paid and I could squirrel a little away. Sometimes it was for a specific gun or model; other times I just went hunting for something new and different.

Guns are very similar to cars in some ways. Presentation-grade wood and elaborate engraving are nice to look at and have some prestige, but it is still the same basic gun whether it has grade five wood or just the basic walnut, and whether it has gold inlaid engravings of birds or just a blue receiver and barrels. Let's face it; we all like our possessions.

When this book was still in the proposal stage, Don Gulbrandsen, my editor, and I spent a lot of time discussing what we both wanted in this chapter. We agreed the easiest way to set parameters for this chapter was to set a dollar limit on it. The upper limit we agreed on was $2,500. There are guns out there that cost many times more than that, but there are also hundreds of guns that cost less that will perform just as well in the field.

I have said before that although I can appreciate the beauty of a well-finished gun with beautiful wood, I use my guns. I don't abuse them, but I hunt hard and in rugged terrain, and my guns show it. The guns are exposed and come in contact with fences, rocks, cactus, and brambles among other things and in all types of weather conditions. They get laid down in the field and get stepped on (or worse) by dogs and hunting companions. I have put scratches on the stocks and in the bluing on numerous occasions. I have even put a dent in a barrel or two. I sent a test gun back after one dove and quail season. It was a beautiful little double with exquisite wood, a beautiful finish to the metal, and some very nice engraving. The president of the company called me after he received it and asked me if I had dragged it behind a truck! I told him no; it was just six months of shooting doves and chasing quail in Texas and Arizona. Let's just say that by the end of that phone conversation we didn't part on a friendly basis, and I haven't had any other offers to field test guns for his company. I have a friend who gets absolutely ecstatic over good-looking wood on a shotgun. He also has a tendency to start crying when he picks up one of my guns with high-grade wood and sees all of the scratches, nicks, and dents in them. Of course when we hunt together, I am the one busting the cover and staying with the dogs, and he is the one walking in the plowed field or outside the cover waiting for a flush.

We will look at a number of different makers and models of guns in this chapter. It would take a much larger book to catalog all of the various makers and all of the models available. Some manufacturers will invariably be left out. This is not to say they don't make a good, serviceable gun; it just means there wasn't room to profile them. Rather than listing all of the guns by individual manufacturers, I have grouped them into action types and offer a fair sampling of the different models available in that action type.

PUMPS

Pumps or slide actions are often entry-level guns for many shooters and hunters. There has been a decline in the popularity of pumps in the clay target games over the last two decades. At one time, pump guns dominated the trap and skeet fields. Pumps are still popular with hunters, though. Here are some of the ones currently available.

Remington

There have been more Remington 870 shotguns made than any other pump gun. Remington has sold more than six million 870s since they were introduced in 1950. The gun has been offered in every gauge from 10 through 410 and in more than forty different variations and configurations. It is made today in twenty-five different models. The lower-cost Express has a parkerized finish and plain wood. In 12 gauge it weighs 7 1/2 pounds with a 28-inch barrel. The current manufacturer's suggested retail price (MSRP) for this model is $345. The Wingmaster is an upgraded model with bluing and nicely finished wood. The current MSRP for a Wingmaster is $629. Both models come with interchangeable choke tubes, ventilated ribs, and recoil pads. If you would like a 28 or 410 gauge pump, Remington has the Wingmaster LW Small-Bore at 6 pounds with a 25-inch barrel in both 28 and 410. The 28s have

Remington Model 870 Wingmaster pump-action shotgun, in 16 gauge. REMINGTON ARMS

Remington Model 870 Express pump-action shotgun. REMINGTON ARMS

choke tubes and the 410s have a fixed Modified choke. A Wingmaster LW Small-Bore will set you back $787 for a 28 gauge and $729 for a 410. You can see the full line of available 870s at www.remington.com.

Mossberg

Mossberg makes more than thirty different variations of its Model 500 pump gun. If you add in the Model 835, which is chambered for the $3\frac{1}{2}$-inch shell, the company has more than sixty variations available in a pump gun. The field model of the Model 500 is available in 12, 20, and .410 gauge. The gun comes with choke tubes and a recoil pad. A 12-gauge Model 500 weighs in at $7\frac{1}{2}$ pounds and has an MSRP of $316.

Mossberg Model 500 pump-action shotgun. MOSSBERG

A feature I have always enjoyed on the Model 500 is a tang-mounted safety. This makes the safety visible and easily accessible to either a right- or left-handed shooter. It is the most comfortable and accessible position for a safety and, as an old two-barrel shooter, it places the safety in the location I am used to.

Although the finish of the alloyed receiver and the not-too-fancy wood on a 500 make many think that they are "cheap," they are in fact very reliable and serviceable guns. I had two Model 500s that I used in law enforcement firearms training for a number of years. These guns had thousands of rounds of target ammo and full service (hard recoiling) slug and buckshot loads shot through them every year with minimal maintenance. Mossberg's web site is www.mossberg.com.

Benelli
Benelli makes a very unique pump shotgun. The Nova (3-inch) and Super-Nova (3 1/2 inch) is a new concept in metal finishing and stock design. It is definitely a twenty-first century gun with modern looks and extensive new engineering concepts, and is very popular with new and experienced shooters alike. The stock design and some very innovative technological advances

Benelli Nova pump-action shotgun. BENELLI U.S.A.

reduce felt recoil in this gun by an awesome degree. There are more than twelve models of the Nova and ten models of the Super-Nova currently available. A 12-gauge Nova with 26-inch barrel weighs in at 8 pounds and has an MSRP of $360. The web site at www.benelliusa.com has all of the various models listed.

Browning
BPS stands for Browning Pump Shotgun. Based on a silky-smooth pump action with bottom ejection and featuring a tang-mounted safety, the BPS is a fine choice for either a right- or left-handed shooter. (The very first gun my

Browning BPS pump-action shotgun. BROWNING ARMS

dad bought me was a Remington Nylon 66 .22 that had a tang-mounted safety. I have always wondered why this type of safety isn't used on more guns since it is so convenient and visible.)

The BPS is available in thirteen models and is offered in 12, 20, 28, and 410 gauge. All models come with interchangeable choke tubes. There is also an "Upland Special" model available with a 22-inch barrel and straight "English-style" stock in 12 and 20 gauge. A 12 gauge BPS weighs 7¾ pounds and has an MSRP of $509. Browning's web site is www.browning.com.

SEMI-AUTOS

I find it interesting that I still hear hunters speak ill of semi-auto shotguns. Comments calling them jamamatics, unreliable, too prone to malfunction, etc., are still heard, and often the speakers aren't old enough to have much experience with any shotgun, let alone several generations of semi-autos. I heard the same arguments against semi-auto pistols during my career in law enforcement, but you will be hard pressed to find any police agency in the United States today that still issues revolvers. If they are so unreliable, why has the Browning Auto-5 been around virtually unchanged in design for a hundred years? Why is the John Browning-designed Colt 1911 pistol still the most popular combat pistol in the world today? I know of two Texas Rangers who survived more gunfights and killed more men than most of the famous Old West gunfighters. Neither one of them would take anything but a semi-auto Colt pistol, a semi-auto Browning or Remington shotgun, or a semi- or full-automatic rifle into a dangerous situation. I have spoken with an old market hunter from the Chesapeake Bay area. I have held his Remington Model 11 with the ten-shot extended magazine—bluing and stock finish long gone from exposure to the salt air—and listened to his stories of killing hundreds of ducks in one day and thousands during the year. These were men who depended on their guns not only for a living, but also to keep them safe on a daily basis. The secret then, as now, is familiarity and proper maintenance, which will keep a semi-auto going long after manually operated actions have quit.

Granted, we don't often need the firepower of a market hunter or a Texas Ranger, but the reliability and user friendliness of the semi-auto is better today than it was in the models used by these men. In the chapter on action types, I discussed the difference in the operating systems used in the semi-auto shotguns of today. Let's look at some of the many different models that are available.

Browning

The Gold Hunter has been Browning's success story for a gas-operated semiauto that is as reliable and as popular as the venerable long-recoil action

Auto-5. The Gold Hunter is available in twenty-five different models in 10, 12, and 20 gauge. Do you want a factory ported barrel? A camouflage finish? Factory installed high-visibility sights? The Browning Gold has all of these options available and more. I have used a Browning Gold Hunter Sporting Clays model as my competition gun for a number of years. It has performed flawlessly. I also use this gun for a lot of load testing because its weight (8 1/2 pounds) and reduced recoil (due to the excellent gas-operated system) minimizes the results of hard-kicking loads on my tender body.

Browning Gold semi-auto shotgun. BROWNING ARMS

For the upland hunter, a 12-gauge Gold Hunter is a good all-around choice. A new one with interchangeable choke tubes, high-visibility sights and either a 3-inch or 3 1/2-half inch chamber weighs in at 7 pounds and has an MSRP of $1,083.

Beretta

Beretta semi-auto shotguns are favored by some of the top sporting clay shooters in the nation and are the most common semi-autos seen at any sporting clay match. Beretta has constantly improved, developed, and redesigned its guns over the last decade. The company's current model, the 391, is offered in more than twenty variations in 12 and 20 gauge. There are a variety of stock choices, finishes, chamber lengths, and barrel options available that will fit the desire of any upland hunter.

Beretta AL391 Teknys semi-auto shotgun. BERETTA U.S.A.

A Beretta 391 in 12 gauge with a synthetic stock and a 28-inch barrel with Beretta's Optima choke tubes weighs in at 7.3 pounds and has an MSRP of

$1,050. Check out all of the available semi-autos from Beretta at www.beretta usa.com.

Benelli

Benelli has been an innovative company for years. It was the first to introduce the unique inertia operating system and the first company to move from traditional wood stocks and blued metal parts with black synthetic stocks and flat black metal finishes. Without the additional weight of the gas systems of other guns or the springs of the older long-recoil designs, Benelli has some very lightweight field guns, especially in their wood-stocked Montefeltro series. The original Black Eagle is now known as the M-1 and M-2 models. The 3¹/₂-inch chambered field gun is known as the Super Black Eagle or SBE. I have several friends who hunt with various versions of the Benelli guns and have had excellent success with them.

Benelli Montefeltro semi-auto shotgun. BENELLI U.S.A.

The Benelli M-1s and M-2s are available with 24-, 26-, or 28-inch barrels at a weight of 7.2 pounds and with an MSRP of $1,515 with black metal and a black synthetic stock or $1,450 in the wood-stocked, blued Montefeltro version. Visit www.benelliusa.com to check out all of the different models.

Remington

Probably the most popular semi-auto shotgun ever made is the venerable Remington Model 1100. This was the first successful and accepted gas-operated shotgun and has been in production since 1963. Model 1100s have been made in numerous variations in 10, 12, 16, 20, 28, and 410 gauge. Although it was supposed to have been superceded by the upgraded and redesigned Model 11-87 in 1987, Remington has continued to manufacture the 1100 because of popular demand. Any variation of the 1100 or 11-87 will give a lifetime of use. Currently Remington offers fourteen different variations of the 11-87 in 12 and 20 gauge. A 12-gauge Model 11-87 with Rem-Chokes will weigh in at 7³/₄ pounds and set you back $907. The Model 1100 is currently offered in nine different models and in 12, 16, 20, 28, and .410 gauges. A 12-gauge Model 1100 weighs 7 pounds, 14 ounces with a 28-inch Rem-Choke barrel and has an MSRP of $875. Check out the full line at www.remington.com. The Remington guns will stand up to a lifetime of use.

Last year a friend called me well after the bird season had ended and asked me if I wanted to come shoot some pest birds around his company warehouses. He works for a large seed company, and when certain pest species migrate through, they can cause thousands of dollars in damage to the seeds. When I showed up, he pulled a pair of Remington 1100s in 410 out of his pickup, which had cases of 410 ammo stacked in the back. We each fired five cases (1,250 rounds) of ammo that afternoon, and the guns were so hot the

Remington Model 1100 Sporting 12 semi-auto shotgun. REMINGTON ARMS

Remington Model 11-87 Upland Special semi-auto shotgun. REMINGTON ARMS

forends were literally smoking. When he had hauled out a bucket of water at the start of the shoot and told me it was to keep the guns from catching fire, I thought he was kidding. Several times during the afternoon when the forends got too hot to hold, we took them off, immersed them in water and put them back on the guns and kept shooting. He told me the guns belonged to the company and that this type of shooting was done about ten times a year. Not many guns would hold up to this type of use but these little Remingtons had been doing it for the five years he had worked there.

Franchi

Once known only for its line of lightweight aluminum-framed shotguns, Franchi has expanded their line of semi-autos dramatically. Franchi is owned by Benelli, which in turn is owned by Beretta. Under this agreement, Franchi has introduced a line of semi-auto shotguns that include gas operation, inertia operation, and the old long-recoil design. The inertia mechanism is on the 712 (12 gauge) and 720 (20 gauge). The 912 is a gas-operated semi-auto.

The Model 48 AL is the classic long-recoil design that is currently offered only in 20 and 28 gauge. These are beautiful little grouse, quail, and dove guns. I have used one of the Model 48 ALs in 28 gauge for a number of years. At a little more than 5 pounds with a 26-inch barrel, it is an absolute delight to carry on long days in the field. It is also an excellent beginner's gun with the light weight and the low recoil of the 28-gauge shell. I've taught a number

Franchi 720 semi-auto shotgun. BENELLI U.S.A.

Franchi 912 semi-auto shotgun. BENELLI U.S.A.

Franchi Raptor semi-auto shotgun. BENELLI U.S.A.

of young people and ladies to shoot with this little gun. The 48 AL is available in 20 gauge with your choice of 24-, 26-, or 28-inch barrels with choke tubes. This delightful little gun weighs 5.6 pounds and has a current MSRP of $749. The 28-gauge version is available with only a 26-inch interchangeable choke tube barreled version and a weight of 5.4 pounds. The current price is $850.

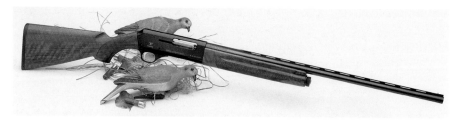

Franchi's venerable 48 AL semi-auto, in 28 gauge. BENELLI U.S.A.

To check out the latest Franchi has to offer, go to www.franchiusa.com.

Mossberg

Mossberg has made several variations of semi-auto guns over the years. A factory representative from Mossberg told me that they discontinued the previous lines because they did not have the reliability and dependability that Mossberg has been famous for with the Model 500 line of pump shotguns. The company's latest semi-auto offering is the best to date. The Model 930 is available in 12 gauge with a number of variations of stock length, barrel lengths, and finishes. Mossberg's guns come standard with some features that are only

Mossberg Model 930 Field semi-auto shotgun. MOSSBERG

available as aftermarket work on other guns, including ported barrels to reduce barrel rise and fiber optic sights. The Mossberg Model 935 is a semi-auto designed for the powerful 3½-inch 12 gauge shell. Mossberg was the first company to make a gun for this shell and still continues to design a gun from the ground up for this shell rather than just adapting an existing design for it.

CZ-USA

CZ-USA imports a line of semi-auto shotguns made to its specifications in Turkey. The CZ 712, CZ 720, and CZ 712 Magnum are gas-operated 12-gauge, 20-gauge, and 3½-inch 12-gauge shotguns, respectively. They are well-made and dependable guns at a very good price. Check out the full line at www.cz-usa.com.

CZ Mallard over-and-under shotgun. cz-usa

There are lots of other semi-autos available from other makers that I didn't have the room to cover. The annual *Gun Digest* carries a complete list of guns currently available and for someone looking for a new gun, it is a good investment since it lists *everything* that is available. I sometimes think that the *Gun Digest* should be printed on water-resistant paper to prevent the drool from taking its toll on the pages during the course of a year.

SIDE-BY-SIDES

As has been discussed previously, the prices on either American made or imported side-by-side double barrel guns can be unbelievably high. There are side-by-sides out there that cost more than my truck and even more than my house. The good news is that there are also a number of reasonably priced side-by-sides currently available for the hunter who wishes to own and use one without having to get a second mortgage or a divorce.

Ruger

The late Bill Ruger of Ruger Firearms was a very innovative and knowledgeable man. Beginning in the 1940s, he introduced new guns to the American market that were unique and different. Bill always held the philosophy that if he liked using a gun others probably would, too. An inexpensive semi-auto .22 pistol, various single-action pistols,

Ruger Gold Label side-by-side shotgun.

a classic designed bolt-action rifle, and a single-shot centerfire rifle were among many of the designs Bill introduced. Despite the prediction of the nay-sayers that there wasn't a market for these designs, Bill was a marketing genius. Every gun he introduced became immensely popular. Before his death, Bill was working on a design for a side-by-side double based on the English Dickson round-action game guns. Taking a handmade design and developing it to modern production methods took several years longer than expected, and the Ruger Gold Label side-by-side did not reach full production until after Bill's death. It is yet another example of his genius. It has the petite and classic designs of the original Dickson but with modern stainless and blue steel and oil-finished wood. This was another gun I was privileged to test for *Shotgun Sports Magazine,* and although I didn't get to keep the one I tested, there will be a Ruger Gold Label in my gun safe soon. Yes, this is coming from the same person who wrote his not-so-glowing opinions of side-by-sides in an earlier chapter. What can I say? I liked the gun and shot well with it, and at 6 pounds, 5 ounces, it makes for an excellent carry gun in 12 gauge. With an MSRP of $2,050, it is even affordable for a starving writer. You can view the Gold Label on the Ruger web site at www.ruger.com.

CZ-USA

CZ-USA imports a fine line of side-by-side doubles made by Huglu in Turkey. The Ringneck is a Prince of Wales-gripped side-by-side with a single trigger and extractors. The 12 gauge weighs in at 7.3 pounds and is available with a 26- or 28-inch barrel at an MSRP of $912. The other Ringneck models are built on dedicated frame sizes. This means that the 16 gauge, the 20 gauge, the 28

CZ Ringneck side-by-side shotgun. CZ-USA

gauge, and the .410 are all built on a frame size comparable to the gauge—there are not 16-gauge barrels on a 12-gauge frame and 28 or .410 barrels on a 20-gauge frame. This doesn't sound like a big deal, but it makes a drastic dif-ference in the carry and handling characteristics of the guns. The 16 gauge with 28-inch barrels weighs 6.8 pounds and will set you back $1,095. The 20 gauge weighs 6.3 pounds and costs the same as the 12 gauge. A 28 gauge will weigh in at 5.9 pounds and costs $1,095, and the .410 costs $1,045 and weighs in at a petite 5 1/2 pounds.

For the purist, like my friend Larry Brown, who thinks that a double should have a straight grip, double triggers, and extractors, CZ-USA offers the Bobwhite series in 12, 16, 20, 28, and .410. Again, these are all made on dedicated frame sizes. The 12- and 20-gauge Bobwhites weigh 7 and 6 pounds respectively. The current cost is $695. A 16-gauge Bobwhite weighs 6.6 pounds and costs $869. A 28 gauge weighs in at 6.2 pounds, and a .410 at a miniscule 5.2 pounds. The price on both the 28 and .410 is $869. Check out all of the CZ-USA guns at www.cz-usa.com.

TriStar

Another company that imports a nice line of reasonably priced side-by-sides is TriStar. The Brittany model is a straight grip, single-trigger (sorry Larry) ejector gun that is available in all of the gauges. A 12 gauge Brittany weighs in at 7.4 pounds with a 28-inch barrel and has an MSRP of $1,050. The 16 gauge weighs the same, and the 20 gauge weighs in at 6.9 pounds. Both share the 12-gauge Brittany price of $1,050. A 28-gauge Brittany weighs 6.4 pounds, and the 410 model weighs 6.2 pounds. Both have an MSRP of $1,069.

The York model is for those who prefer a pistol-grip stock and extractors. Available in 12 and 20 gauge with a 28-inch barrel weighing 7.4 and 6.8 pounds, respectively, the York has a very reasonable price of $609.

A slightly more dressed-up version with a pistol grip and extractors is the Gentry, which is available in 12, 16, 20, 28, and .410. The Gentry has an MSRP of $929 in 12, 16, and 20 gauge and an MSRP of $945 in 28 and .410. The full line of TriStar guns is viewable at www.tristarsportingarms.com.

Marlin

The Marlin Firearms Company is importing a reproduction of the famous L. C. Smith double guns. One of the most famous and beloved of the American made doubles, this Italian-made reproduction is a faithful copy of the great Elsies once made here in the United States. Currently available in 12 and 20 gauge with either pistol-grip or straight stocks and an MSRP of $1,499, these nicely made, serviceable doubles. At 6 1/4 pounds for the 12 gauge and 6 pounds in the 20 gauge, they make excellent upland guns. You can look at these fine reproductions at www.marlinfirearms.com.

OVER-AND-UNDERS

There are more over-and-under shotguns made and imported today than any other style. To keep this portion of this chapter shorter than the entire book, I will be mentioning just a few of the hundreds of different ones out there.

Browning

Browning started it all with the Superposed models back in the 1930s. Today Browning has continued their tradition of over-and-unders with its extensive line of Citori models. There are currently twenty-eight variations in the Citori line. There are far too many to attempt to catalog here. For the upland hunter, a good choice in the Citori line is the Classic Lightning Feather. With an MSRP of \$1,991 and a weight of 7 pounds in the 12 gauge and $6^{1}/_{4}$ pounds in 20 gauge, the CLF carries and performs well in the field.

Browning Cynergy over-and-under shotgun. BROWNING ARMS

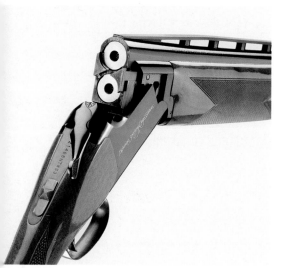

Browning Citori Sporting Clays Edition over-and-under shotgun. BROWNING ARMS

If you would like a Citori in 28 or 410 gauge, the Lightning model is available for \$1,743 in either gauge. The Citori line also offers two- and four-barreled sets for the hunter/shooter who wants one gun to do it all. Go to www.browning .com to view the full line. I'll give you a hint, though—have a large towel handy to mop up the drool so it doesn't damage your computer.

In 2004 Browning introduced its line of Cynergy guns with twenty-first century innovations in design, appearance, and options. These guns are too radical-looking for many shooters, but the innovations and design changes make them truly user-friendly guns in felt recoil reduction and handling. I am sure that many shooters in the 1930s thought the original Superposeds were radical-looking, too. There are twelve models of the Cynergy currently available in field and target versions. The Field Composite in 12 gauge has stainless steel action and barrels and a black composite stock. It weighs in at $7^{1}/_{4}$ pounds with a 26-inch barrel and costs \$1,986. If a lot of your upland season is spent in misty mornings and drizzling rain, this might be a good gun to consider since it will require less maintenance than a traditional blue and brown gun. If you prefer blue and brown and would like a 12, 20, or 28 gauge Cynergy, they are available with 28-inch barrels and cost $2,048 for the 12 gauge and $2,062 for the 20 or 28. At 6¼ pounds, both the 20 and the 28 are good field guns. The Browning web site has pictures and specifications for all of the Cynergy guns.

Traditions
Being a fan of the 16 gauge, I always enjoy using a 16 gauge that is built on a 16-gauge frame instead of having 16-gauge barrels on a 12-gauge frame. That is why I have enjoyed using a Traditions Real 16 while researching this book. Built by Stefano Fausti, this gun has proven itself in the pheasant and quail fields of Iowa, Kansas, and Texas. The model I have is the Real 16 Gold, and it weighs 7 pounds with its 26-inch barrels. It has a retail price of $1,599. I also enjoy it because I get into interesting conversations when I show up at the skeet field with a 16 gauge over-and-under! Traditions has an extensive line of side by sides and over-and-unders that are excellent guns at reasonable prices. Check out the complete line at www.traditionsfirearms.com.

Ruger
The Ruger Red Label is a very popular over-and-under. Ruger offers twelve different models of the Red Label in 12, 20, and 28 gauge. These guns are available with 26- and 28-inch barrels in the field models and have an MSRP of $1,702. Check them out at www.ruger.com.

Ruger Red Label over-and-under shotgun. STURM, RUGER

TriStar
In addition to its side-by-sides, TriStar also has an extensive line of reasonably priced over-and-under shotguns. Of particular interest to the upland hunter who carries a lot and shoots a little is the Hunter Lite model in 12 and 20 gauge. With a 28-inch barrel, the 12-gauge version weighs in at only 6 pounds! The 20 gauge weighs a mere 5.4 pounds. An expenditure of $499 gives you a single trigger, extractor-equipped gun with choke tubes. TriStar also offers

Ejectors or Extractors?

When purchasing a side-by-side or over-and-under, you'll have to decide if you want ejectors or just extractors. When the action is opened, ejectors raise the unfired shells up where they can be removed with the fingers. Fired shells are ejected out of the action, usually over the shoulder of the shooter.

With extractors, the shell is raised up whether it is a fired or unfired shell. The shooter must then remove fired shells by hand and replace them with unfired shells. I often read that extractors are preferred by handloaders so that they can retain the fired case. Of course, the writers who champion extractors are also the ones that usually champion hunting with *only* English-made side-by-side doubles.

I have been shooting side-by-sides and over-and-unders for years, and I am a handloader and a proponent of *always* picking up your empty shell cases—but I find extractors to be a royal pain in the rear. Trying to extract a fired shell with your fingers while on the move requires you to look down at your gun and be unable to mark the place where your bird went down. This can mean a lost bird. With ejectors, I can keep my eye on the location where the bird went down and start towards it while calling the dog in for the retrieve if it didn't see the bird fall. I catch the fired case, stick it in the pocket of my vest, and load a new round in the chamber. I can do all of this while moving, and I don't even have to look at my gun.

I frequently hunt the high plains of the Midwest, Southwest, and the West. In the dry, dusty conditions in these parts of the country, an air-

the Hunter version with a traditional steel receiver at $459 or the top-of-the-line Silver II version in 12, 16, and 20 gauge with single trigger, auto ejectors, choke tubes, and schnabel forend at a cost of only $915. Look them over at www.tristarsportingarms.com.

CZ-USA

CZ-USA has a line of over-and-under shotguns with the features any hunter will want—from the very plain to the very fancy. If you like double triggers and extractors, then the Mallard model at $487 will suit your needs. If you like extractors but prefer a single trigger, then upgrade to the Canvasback model at $708. The Redhead model comes with a single trigger, ejectors, and an MSRP of $836. I picked up a Redhead model at the CZ-USA distribution center washed bird that takes off running can leave very little scent for a dog to follow. A rooster or quail that has the smallest bit of life left will try to hide after it hits the ground. There will be a brief period, usually of fifteen to thirty seconds, that it will lay there before running off. Dealing with extractors can cause enough delay so that a bird has sufficient time to make a run for it before a hunter locates where it fell.

If you are wearing gloves, the delay caused by dealing with extractors can be even greater. I wore gloves on the street as a cop and wear them all the time in the field. (I favored Browning shooting gloves for a number of years. My current choices are the Bob Allen uninsulated shooting gloves, the Cabela's brand of shotgun gloves, or GripSwell gloves.) They protect my hands from mesquite thorns and stickers during warm weather and also protect my hands from wind and cold. They are very flexible, thin, and strong—but I still can't extract fired cases from extractors with them on.

How much do I hate extractors? Several years ago, I had a beautiful, custom-built, 28-gauge side-by-side. It had gorgeous wood, a beautiful finish, engraving, custom checkering, and a straight English-style grip. It had 28-inch barrels with screw-in choke tubes. It was without a doubt the finest (and costliest) new shotgun I have ever owned. This particular maker did not offer the option of ejectors on its 28-gauge guns, so I had to do with just extractors. This gun was an absolute jewel that fit me very well and I shot it very well—but I hated it from the first day because of those extractors and got rid of it within four months!

in Kansas City during a three-state pheasant hunting trip last fall while en route from Iowa to Kansas. Although the 7.9-pound weight with the 28-inch barrels was considerably heavier than I am used to, it really helped the gun swing through those Kansas roosters. Of the five chokes supplied, I used the Cylinder and Improved Cylinder chokes. When combined with Remington's

CZ Canvasback over-and-under shotgun. cz-usa

CZ Redhead over-and-under shotgun. CZ-USA

excellent Nitro-Pheasant loads of 1¼ ounce of copper-plated shot at 1,400 fps, twenty one birds were taken with twenty-three shots. Not only did I impress my hunting buddies with this gun, hell, I impressed myself! Since then I have used this gun in a couple of competitions instead of my normal competition gun. I usually tweaked out a few more birds than my average with this gun.

CZ-USA's top-of-the-line Woodcock model is one gorgeous shotgun. Available in 12, 20, 28, and 410 with beautiful wood, exquisite case hardening, and a single trigger and auto ejectors, it shoots as good as it looks. The 12 gauge weighs 7.9 pounds, and the 20 weighs in at 6.9 pounds. They share an MSRP of $1,078. The 28 weighs 6.3 pounds, and the 410 version tops the scale at a mere 6 pounds. Shelling out $1,152 will equip you with a delightful quail, dove, or woodcock gun that will look better than your hunting buddies. Again, all of the CZ-USA guns can be viewed at www.cz-usa.com.

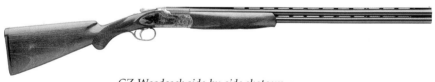

CZ Woodcock side-by-side shotgun. CZ-USA

Mossberg

Mossberg has also begun importing a Turkish-made line of over-and-unders that sell at very reasonable prices. Dave Holmes, my friend and fellow staff writer at *Shotgun Sports Magazine,* did a review of the Mossberg Silver Reserve

Mossberg Silver Reserve over-and-under shotgun. MOSSBERG

in the magazine. Dave is not an easy person to please when it comes to guns, but he was favorably impressed with Mossberg's entry into the over-and-under field. It is available in 12, 20, 28, and 410 gauges and carries an MSRP of $631.

Beretta

Last, but certainly not least in our overview of over-and-unders is Beretta, which offers an extensive line of over-and-unders for any clay target sport or upland game. There are six models of the White Onyx in series in 12, 20, and 28 gauge with an MSRP of $1,875. The Onyx Pro with a traditional blued receiver also has an MSRP of $1,875 with eight models available in 12, 20, and 28 gauge. The fancier Silver Pigeon line in 12, 20, 28, and .410 has eight models and a price tag of $2,150. Of interest to the upland hunter who prefers 12-gauge performance without 12-gauge weight is the Ultralite. Weighing only 5³/₄ pounds with a 28-inch barrel, this is a great gun to carry on long days afield with lots of walking in-between shots. I think I would recommend this as the perfect legal gun for chukar partridges if you prefer a 12 gauge. The MSRP is $1,975. You can check out all of the extensive line of Beretta guns at www.berettausa.com.

Beretta Onyx Pro over-and-under shotgun. BERETTA U.S.A.

Beretta Ultralight over-and-under shotgun. BERETTA U.S.A.

OTHER MAKERS

Again, please do not get the idea that the guns mentioned here are all that are available. There are many fine makers of guns that could not be included due to space. Verona, B Rizzini, Rizzini USA, F.A.I.R., Fausti, Savage Arms, and Stoeger are just a few that I wish I had the room to tell you about.

Stoeger Condor over-and-under shotgun. STOEGER

One final piece of wisdom I would offer. Never buy a gun because someone else recommended it, even if it was a glowing recommendation from a gun writer. Buy the gun because it is what *you* want and because it is what works for you.

Can One Gun Do it All?

"Never bet against the man with just one gun."
—Anonymous

In the previous chapters we have looked at all the various gauges, action types, and a few of the different models available from different manufacturers. I hope you have felt like a kid in a candy store through those chapters and have constantly been saying to yourself, "I really need one of those." I know I said it to myself while writing those chapters!

A chapter on buying only one gun is both an easy and a difficult chapter for me to write. It is easy because I have always enjoyed using and experimenting with different guns all of my life, and I enjoy sharing the knowledge I have picked up with other shooters. It is difficult because I would really hate to be limited to just one gun for my bird hunting.

To me, bird hunting is so much more than just putting birds in the bag. It is more than just a hobby or a recreation. Yes, as an outdoors and gun writer it is part of my job, but it is so much more. It is good friends, great memories, good dogs, and favorite guns. It is great shots and easy misses. It is experiencing the beauty of an autumn or winter morning and the companionship of good friends and good dogs. It is the heart-stopping rush of an exploding covey of quail, the cackling rise of a rooster pheasant, or the thundering flush of a grouse.

Countless hunters choose pump actions as the ultimate style of upland shotguns. WINCHESTER

It is passing on the heritage to a new hunter, regardless of age. It is seeing the joy and excitement on their faces as they walk in on their first point, take their first shot at a game bird, and experience the thrill of their first kill. It is in the hours of discussion on trips while driving and around the campfire or motel rooms after the dogs are fed and groomed, the birds and guns are cleaned, and a little bit of snakebite medicine has been poured and tasted.

Yes, it is also the guns. It is the thrill of rewarding all of the dog's hard work, your physical exertion, and the tactics used that brought you to the flush. Then, when walking in, you know you have the right tools in your gun and ammunition to produce a quick, humane kill of the animal.

I have been a fan of the John Browning–designed Colt 1911 pistol in .45 caliber ever since I first shot one at the age of ten. When I moved to Colorado and became the Firearm Training Officer for my small department, I couldn't wait to convert everyone on the department to the .45 Auto. I have made few mistakes in my life that were greater than that and a lot that were less. The .45 Auto is a fantastic weapon and in the hands of an experienced shooter, probably the best combat pistol ever made. The key words in that sentence are "experienced shooter." Although there were only four officers besides me on the department, I quickly learned that the .45 was too much gun for three of them. These were all fine officers, but they weren't "gun nuts" and experienced shooters. To them, the pistol on the right side of their belt was just another tool of the profession, like the radio on the left side. I spent eighteen more years in law enforcement after that and was a firearms instructor the whole time. During those years, the auto pistol became the weapon of choice for law enforcement. These autos were of a less complicated design that was easier for the average officer to use than the .45. By the way, the fourth officer on my department was an active reserve Army Special Forces officer and was one of the best shots with a rifle and pistol I have ever known. He had been in combat and knew the importance of being able to use a weapon under conditions of extreme stress, and how vital it is under combat conditions to be able to hit your target.

I realize that very few hunters and even very few competition shotgun shooters are "gun nuts." They may study different styles and mod-

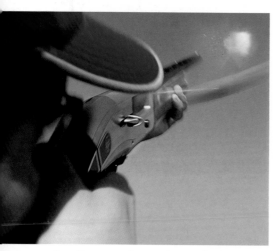

Spending some time on the trap field is a great way to get familiar with different shotgun models. BERETTA U.S.A.

els when choosing a new gun or try different loads for their hunting or shooting, but most are content to find what works for them and then stick with it.

There have been times in my life when financial conditions limited me to just one gun for all of my bird hunting. Fortunately, I have been able to quickly remedy that situation. For others, though, when they buy one gun, it is the gun they will be using for everything because that is what they prefer. My veterinarian, Carl, a good friend and fellow bird hunter, is one of these people. He has one 12-gauge shotgun that he uses for everything, and he is perfectly happy with this decision. Even after a number of years hunting with only this one gun, he hasn't changed his mind. We have an arrangement. When one of my dogs runs afoul of barbed wire or stray metal in the field, Carl stitches them up, usually after hours. Then sometime during the bird seasons and at the end of the seasons, I take his gun completely apart and clean and lubricate it for him.

When I was a kid, one of my hunting mentors was a neighbor and friend of my maternal grandfather. Mr. Kilgore was a fine old gentleman but somewhat cranky and opinionated at times. In many excursions over a number of years with him, I only saw him shoot one gun and one load. He had a Browning Auto-5 Sweet 16 in 16 gauge. This gun had a 26-inch barrel and a fixed Improved Cylinder choke. The *only* load I ever saw him use in it were Winchester Super-X loads of $1\frac{1}{8}$ ounces of shot. The *only* shot size he ever used was No. $7\frac{1}{2}$. It was not uncommon to bring home rabbits, quail, pheasant, ducks, woodcock, or even a goose or two when out for a day with Mr. Kilgore. It didn't matter to him. He shot any and all of them with the same gun and the same load. I had a 16-gauge double-barrel side-by-side that I used during those years. One day I got in the truck and was very excited to show Mr. Kilgore the new

The best upland gun is the one that makes you confident—and successful—in the field.
WINCHESTER

plastic shotgun shells that were made by Remington in 16 gauge. I will never forget his response. He told me those new plastic shells might be okay but that I should put those green (Remington) shells on the dashboard of the truck and wait until they ripened to red (Winchester) before I used them. Talk about brand loyalty!

This brings up a question I get asked often. A reader or acquaintance will ask me what I would recommend they buy for an all-around shotgun. Yes, there are guns available that will perform well in multiple hunting situations and can be used on all types of game birds and animals. What you need to understand is that, although they perform well at all of these, they are seldom the best choice for any. I liken this to vehicles. I have driven what are now called sport utility vehicles, or SUVs, with four-wheel drive for three decades. These have always been my choice because they provided enough room for me, my companions, the dogs, and all of our gear and clothing. They are comfortable and the four-wheel-drive option enables me to get in and out of hunting areas in inclement weather and poor road conditions. They are perfect for me during the hunting seasons. During the other six months of the year, they are still comfortable and pleasant to drive, but I have no need for the extra room and the four-wheel drive. I pay extra all year in gas, insurance, and maintenance for what I actually use only part of those six months of the bird seasons. For me though, the SUV is perfect for what I need, when I need it. The same is true when using one gun for everything. There will be times that it is almost—if not *the*—perfect weapon, but there will be other situations when you make do with it because it is what you have. So if you are just going to buy one gun, what should you get?

The choice of what gauge is easy. Although each gauge has definite advantages and disadvantages, if the gun is to be used for everything, it should be a 12 gauge. There are more loads available in the 12 gauge than any other. The 12-gauge shooter can shoot lead loads from $^7/_8$-ounce to $1^1/_2$ ounces in $2^3/_4$-inch shells or to $1^7/_8$ ounces in a 3-inch chamber. There are more non-toxic loads available in 12 gauge than in all of the other gauges combined. This will be an advantage when using the gun for waterfowl or even on upland birds in an area where lead shot is not allowed.

For years, a pump gun was recommended as a good beginner's gun. As we have seen in other chapters, the pump may not be the best choice. The recoil and having to manually work the action will inhibit the new shooter. Believe me, the pain from using a 3-inch magnum shell in a 7-pound pump gun will definitely get your attention!

What about a double barrel in either a side-by-side or over-and-under configuration as your one gun? A double-barrel side-by-side is a good choice. It gives you the option of different chokes; it is a handy and compact weapon.

Remington's Model 870 Express pump gun is a versatile and affordable general-purpose shotgun. REMINGTON ARMS

Three factors would limit my choice of a side-by-side as an all-around gun, however. The first is recoil. I own and shoot double barrels as upland guns on a regular basis. I notice the difference in recoil, however, when I use a side-by-side for just one round (twenty-five birds) of skeet.

The second is cost. A side-by-side double is usually more expensive than a comparable over-and-under and much higher than a repeater. I don't treat my guns rough, but I hunt hard. My gun will have scratches and a few dings on the wood and metal by the end of just one hunting season. This is a fact of life for me, and although it happens, I hate to take a nice gun with good wood out into the field.

The third factor is barrel length. Although a 26-inch-barreled side-by-side will function quite well in heavy cover, it may not be the barrel length of choice when a long fluid swing is needed. This is a personal preference, but I find that I shoot a longer barrel better on shots where I have to swing through and other shooters that I know have found the same thing.

What about an over-and-under? I said in one of the other chapters that if I was held at gunpoint and had to pick just one gun for my upland hunting, it

Some hunters think that an over-and-under—such as Franchi's Alcione—is the best choice for an all-around gun. BENELLI U.S.A.

would probably be an over-and-under. I have used them for years and shoot them well. What about barrel length? The 28-inch barrel is a good compromise. If I were choosing an over-and-under as my only weapon, I would probably go to the expense of having two sets of barrels with interchangeable chokes in each. One set would be 30 or 32 inches in length and the other set would be 26 inches in length. I actually have this combination with one over-and-under and it works very well. I use the 26-inch barrels for upland game and the 30-inch barrels for off-season practice, dove hunting, and waterfowl hunting. The gun has 3-inch chambers in both barrels, and I have a set of extended choke tubes in different chokes that fit both barrel sets.

While I was in the process of writing this book, my college student neighbor Chad came over one night. We poured some snakebite medicine and sat down to talk. Chad had been mulling over buying a new shotgun for the last year. He told me he had finally decided what to buy. I told him that would be a good choice. He also mentioned one of his professors had come up to him after class one day because Chad was wearing a T-shirt with the name of a gun company on it in class. His professor asked him if he was a hunter. During the ensuing conversation, his professor asked for Chad's advice on shotguns. Chad referred him to me.

The first time Dale called me, we spent over an hour on the phone talking about guns and hunting. We had several conversations over the next few weeks, and Dale's wife surprised him with a new shotgun for his birthday. It was just what he wanted and surprisingly was just what we had been discussing for an all-around gun. Dale's primary hunting would be for doves, quail, some ducks, and wild turkey. This new gun would be good for all of these.

So what do I recommend for an all-around gun? My recommendation would be for a 12-gauge semi-auto with a 3-inch chamber. I personally would recommend a gas-operated semi, but if your personal preference is for an inertia- or long-recoil operated, both will be fine, but neither will have the recoil reduction available with a gas-operated semi-auto.

What about barrel length? The most common barrel length is 28 inches. This is a matter of personal preference and will be determined by what length gun feels the most comfortable to you. With a 12-gauge semi-auto, I prefer a barrel length of 24 to 26 inches for an upland gun. With the length of the receiver, this makes the gun the same length as a side-by-side or over-and-under with 28- and 30-inch barrels. For me, the extra length of the receiver on a semi-auto and a shorter barrel make a good combination. Others may prefer a longer barrel.

I would also strongly suggest you buy a gun with interchangeable choke tubes. These are standard in most guns today. If the gun has a fixed choke,

choke tubes can probably be fitted to it by one of the aftermarket choke companies. This can be a bargaining tool on the price of a used gun.

A real advantage of a semi-auto is the cost of a new gun. The median manufacturer's suggested retail price (MSRP) for semi-autos is about $900. Of course, you can find others that cost a lot more and others that cost a lot less. Use the Internet and do a little searching. You can probably find your gun of choice at prices from $50 to $200 below the MSRP.

A 12-gauge semi-auto with a 26- or 28-inch barrel and chambered for the 3-inch magnum shell will enable you to successfully hunt any type of upland bird or game and still use the gun for turkey, waterfowl, or deer. It will provide you with years of service and be a pleasant and comfortable gun for any clay target games you wish to shoot in the off-season.

A word of caution: One of the "megamarts" in the United States often offers name-brand guns in models that are sold for much less than the MSRP of the gun. These will often be offered with a synthetic stock or lower-grade wood stock and will usually have a dull and rough finish on the metal parts. Yes, these are the same guns. Yes, the same manufacturer makes them. No, they are not of the same quality. Several gunsmiths I know have told me they see more malfunctions with these megamart guns than they ever see of the same make and model bought elsewhere. These gunsmiths also tell me the parts are not as well finished and there are a lot of rough edges on these guns. This causes problems that affect the reliability of the gun.

There is an old saying that the buyer should beware. I happened to be in a gunsmith's shop when he was working on one of these megamart guns. He was also putting a recoil pad on another gun of the same model that had been pur-

Gambels and Mearns quail with Beretta semi-auto.

chased elsewhere. Now as on many guns today, this gun uses a process called investment casting to mold the parts. My gunsmith friend showed me the parts from the two guns side by side. He told me the only way he could get the megamart gun to function the way it should was to polish and smooth the action so it was similar to the other gun. This was going to cost as much as the price difference between the guns, and the repair time would leave the customer without his gun for several weeks. His comments were interesting. He said even though both guns are made on the same machinery in the same factory, when the retail gun comes out of the mold, it is fitted and polished and then put together. His experience with the megamart guns is that when they come from the mold, they are put together, put in a box, and shipped.

In case you are wondering which guns my friends chose for their all-around guns, my veterinarian Carl shoots a Browning Gold Hunter with a 26-inch barrel; Dale bought a Remington Model 11-87 with a 28-inch barrel; and Chad bought a Winchester SX-2 with a 26-inch barrel. My primary hunting buddy Jeff McVay is also a real fan of the 12-gauge semi-auto. He currently has an old Remington Model 1100 Special Field with a 23-inch barrel, a Beretta Model 390 with a 28-inch barrel, a Benelli Montefeltro with a 26-inch barrel, and a Benelli Super Black Eagle with a 26-inch barrel. On all of the hunting trips we've taken together over the years, I have never seen Jeff use anything but a 12-gauge auto, even if he had something different at home.

Remington's Model 1100 semi-auto is one of the most popular shotguns ever made.
REMINGTON ARMS

8 Shotshells

*"The shell in the chamber can be more important to the perform-
ance of the gun than the choke in the barrel."*

—George Trulock, *Trulock Chokes*

Almost every maker of ammunition publishes a recommendation of shot sizes and loads to use for various game. These charts can be found in their catalogs or on their websites. They may also be found on the individual boxes of shells. Sometimes these charts will also give recommendations on the gauge and choke to be used.

These are usually good general indicators that give the new or inexperienced shooter a place to start. They are not the final word on which load and shot size to use, though. Experience, weather conditions, type of cover, the presence of other game, and many other factors will influence the type of shell and shot size to be used most effectively.

I grew up hunting in the upper Midwest. In many areas I hunted, quail and pheasant were found in the same covers. Much of the hunting was done on fencerows and along irrigation ditches, creek bottoms, and small woodlots. For years I hunted almost exclusively with a 20-gauge over-and-under. It had fixed Improved Cylinder and Modified Chokes. Even when pheasants were taken, the cover usually limited the range to 25 yards or less.

Smart hunters devote ample range time to testing shells and selecting the right loads for their guns and game choices. WINCHESTER

Since quail were the predominant species hunted, I used loads of No. 7 1/2 shot extensively.

In the 1980s I began to hunt in the West and Southwest. This was more open terrain and shots were generally longer. Wind was also a new factor to be considered on most days. Pheasants and prairie grouse were the predominant species, and quail were found in specific areas and not in all places hunted. I hate to lose a bird under any circumstances, and there were just too many times—and once is too many in a season for me—that I hit a bird with my faithful 20 gauge and watched the bird set its wings and drift off to the horizon. At first I started using heavier shot and then heavier loads, but I finally had to admit that in the areas I was hunting, I needed more gun. I changed to a larger gauge and more effective shells than I had been using. All of the gauge, load, and choke combinations I had been using were recommended by the ammunition makers, but they all had to be matched together correctly to be effective.

There are more shotshells and more loadings available today than ever before. Today's shooter has an unbelievable option of velocity, shot sizes, shot weight, and hull construction. Let's take a look at the basic shotgun shell from the inside out and bottom to top.

First is the case, which may be made out of paper or plastic. Inside the paper case will be a basewad of compressed paper. This will be in the bottom (the base) of the case. To manufacture paper shells, sheets of paper are cut to length and then treated with a wax process to make them water-resistant. The flat paper is then formed into a tube, which is joined to the metal case head. The base wad is then pressure-formed into the bottom of the case, now ready for loading.

A plastic shell is made by one of two different processes. The first is called compression forming. This case is made in one piece of compression-formed plastic with an integral basewad. The second type of plastic case is called a Reifenhauser case. This case is made in a process similar to that of the paper case. This type of shell will have a separate basewad—usually made of plastic but in some cases made of compressed paper—in the bottom of the case. The basic case, no matter how it was made, is now ready for the components to be loaded into it.

On the outside of the case is metal that forms the rim and the case head for the shotshell. Once almost exclusively made of brass, in today's shells it may still be made of brass, or steel, zinc, aluminum, or a number of other metals. On paper shotshells, this metal was needed to keep the paper from burning through when the case was fired, and it also provided strength to the case. This is why the older paper cases were considered either "high brass," with the metal extending almost half the length of the shell, or "low brass," after

Cutaway Shotshell

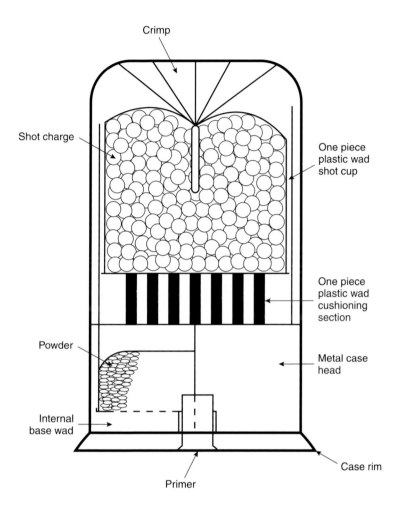

the shells were loaded to lower pressure with less powder and the added strength was not needed.

With today's shotshells, this metal is actually only decoration. The plastic in modern shotshells is strong enough to contain the pressures and not burn through. The plastic is also strong enough to form the rim of the case. In fact, several different companies have marketed all-plastic cases over the years. I have used these and they performed very well. None of these all-plastic cases ever caught on, though, because the American shooter is generally a tradition-alist, preferring the metal case heads.

Starting at the bottom of the case is the primer. The purpose of the primer is to be struck by the firing pin and ignite the load of powder inside the case. Prior to World War II, many shotshells were loaded with mercuric or corrosive primers. The residue from these primers attracted moisture and would cause rust to form in the bore within a short period of time. This is why so many older guns are found with rust or "pitting" in the barrels. Up until the 1980s there were two different sizes of primers. Remington and some other manufacturers used a primer that measured 0.157 inches. Other makers used a primer that measured 0.209 inches. Although there are some slight variations in the exact diameter, all primers loaded in commercial shotshells throughout the world today are loaded with the 0.209-inch or size 209 primer.

Next is the powder. There are hundreds of different powders manufactured today that are used in a variety of shotshell loads. I could write an entire book about modern shotgun powders, their different burning rates, pressure curves, and applications. For now, I will just say that the powders used in modern shotshells are well matched by the manufacturers to the specific loads and shells and their shot charges.

After the powder is the wad. A plastic one- or two-piece wad is the most common type used in today's shotshells. This plastic wad serves several functions. First, it provides a gas seal between the powder and the shot. The variations in the size of the bore in shotguns keeps the powder gases from blowing past the wad and disrupting the shot column, which was a common problem with cardboard and felt wads that allowed the seepage of gas around the wad. Not only did this disrupt the shot column and the patterns of the shot, it also affected velocity and pressure.

The plastic wad also protects the shot as it moves down the barrel, through the forcing cone and the choke. This keeps the shot from coming into contact with the steel of the barrel. The softer lead shot is deformed when it comes into contact with the harder steel surface of the gun barrel. These deformed pellets do not fly true and are lost out of the pattern at the normal

Cutaway shotshells showing interior components, including various wadding types.

ranges that birds are taken. This greatly reduces the effectiveness of the pattern and lengthens the shot string.

The plastic wad also contains the charge of shot. These small lead pellets are what makes the shotgun unique and makes it the weapon to use on small moving game or flying birds. Modern lead pellets come in sizes from No. 12 through No. 2. There are also the sizes of BB and BBB. Buckshot is also a lead pellet, but it is sized and named differently. Steel and nontoxic pellets are offered in sizes from No. 7 1/2 to BBB. There are also larger nontoxic shot pellets in sizes "F" and "T." We will discuss steel and other nontoxic shot options later in the chapter. For right now, let's just concentrate on lead shot.

The larger the shot size number, the smaller the diameter of the pellet and the greater number of them in a given weight of shot. No. 9 shot, which is used for skeet shooting and some upland bird hunting, has a diameter of 0.08 inches, and there are approximately 585 individual pellets in an ounce. No. 5 shot, which is an excellent choice for pheasants and other large upland birds, has a diameter of 0.12 inches. There are approximately 170 No. 5 lead pellets in an ounce.

SHOT SIZES		
Shot size	**Diameter**	**Number per ounce**
● – No. 9	.08 inch	585
● – No. 8 1/2	.085 inch	480
● – No. 8	.09 inch	410
● – No. 7 1/2	.095 inch	345
● – No. 7	.10 inch	300
● – No. 6	.11 inch	225
● – No. 5	.12 inch	170
● – No. 4	.13 inch	136
● – No. 2	.15 inch	88

The pellets themselves are made of lead, but an alloy called antimony is added to the lead to increase the hardness of the shot. This resists deformation of the shot as it passes through the barrel and comes into contact with the steel of the barrel. Up to a point, the higher the antimony content, the harder the shot. There is a point where too much antimony makes the lead too brittle, and pellets that come into contact with the barrel during the firing process will literally disintegrate. Antimony was first added to shot not to increase the hardness but to make the shot easier to manufacture.

Modern shot is produced by pouring melted lead through a sieve of the proper size at the top of a tower. As the pellets fall through the air, they are formed into round lead pellets by aerodynamic forces. The pellets fall into a tub of water that chills the shot and hardens it into a lead sphere. All lead shot produced in the United States today has some amount of antimony in it. Up until the 1950s, pure lead or soft shot was available in some factory loads and to reloaders. Many hunters believed that soft pure lead shot pellets deformed when they struck a bird and that these pellets transmitted additional hydrostatic shot to a bird in much the same way an expanding rifle or pistol bullet does. This is why many claimed that soft shot was a better killer than harder shot. When they cleaned birds and found deformed pellets, they believed these pellets had deformed *after* striking the bird. They were wrong. The pellets had been deformed during the firing process, and the bird happened to be struck with some of the deformed pellets on the fringe of the pattern. Yes, in some instances, soft shot was a better killer, but only in the hands of a bad shot.

I came across a quantity of pure lead shot a few years ago and ran some tests on it. When fired in a modern shell with a one-piece plastic wad and an open choke tube, it gave acceptable performances out to about 25 yards. When fired in a paper shell or in a shell with the old style paper and fiber wads, which offer no protection to the shot, the performance dropped dramatically. At 25 yards I was getting weak Improved Cylinder patterns from Full choke tubes, and the patterns were very poor and full of holes. This is one of the reasons that many older guns were choked much tighter than the guns of today.

The most common shot in the United States today is chilled shot. This shot has a small amount of antimony (usually around 2 percent) mixed in with the lead. This antimony makes the shot flow better. Chilled shot is found in most loads manufactured today. I would guess that probably 95 percent of the shot fired at upland game and birds during the year is chilled shot.

The next type of shot is hard shot. This may be marketed as magnum or tournament-grade shot. This shot usually contains between 4 and 7 percent antimony. This is the type of shot found in the high-grade target ammunition made by various companies. Hard shot resists deformation and provides denser, more uniform patterns with few out-of-round pellets. In his excellent book, *Shotgunning: The Art and Science,* Bob Brister replaced the chilled shot in several factory loads with hard target shot taken from target loads. His patterns increased dramatically in both quality and quantity. I have found this to be true as well with increases as high as 17 percent on the pattern board when using hard shot instead of chilled shot in a load.

Finally, there is plated shot. A standard lead pellet is plated with copper or nickel plating. Often the shot is relatively soft chilled prior to plating. Shooters often use this fact to argue that plated shot is not worth the extra expense. What they do not realize is that the copper or nickel plating is much harder than the lead and resists deformation in both the firing process and when it strikes a bird or game animal. These resistances to deformity will almost always not only increase the effectiveness of the pattern but will also increase the density in the center of the shot pattern, which increases the overall effectiveness of the load.

This nickel-plated shot was recovered from birds taken in the field.

I have a favorite 16-gauge semiauto that I use often as a pheasant gun. It has a fixed Improved Cylinder choke. Using identical components, if I load with chilled No. 5 shot, I get patterns of about 41 percent at 40 yards. About 40 percent of these will be in the 20-inch inner core. When I use hard or magnum No. 5 shot, my patterns jump to 50 percent and about 52 percent are in the inner core. When I put copperplated No. 5 shot in the load, the patterns increase to about 54 percent and about 54 percent are in the inner core. With nickel-plated No. 5s, the patterns run about 58 percent and 60 percent of those are in the

This copper-plated shot was recovered from birds taken in the field.

inner core. I effectively have four different chokes in this gun just by changing the shot used in the loading. I have used both copper- and nickel-plated shot in my pheasant loads for years. I have a bottle full of shot that has been recovered from birds. Even after breaking heavy wing and leg bones, this shot will be deformed dramatically less than unprotected lead shot.

The efficiency of the patterns and the shot can be seen in the field. When a bird is taken and there is a large cloud of feathers around the bird, it often means the bird is centered in the pattern and a number of shot have made contact. Often, though, there will be a large cloud of feathers and the bird still flies off. What has happened here is that the pellets have actually slid along the skin and cut feathers but have not penetrated into the vitals of the bird.

When you are cleaning a bird taken with chilled lead shot, you will often find feathers clumped around and in pellet holes in the skin. You will seldom find this with plated shot. The increased hardness and the increased viscosity of the plating enable the shot to penetrate through the feathers into the skin rather than sliding along the skin and cutting them.

Although hard shot for reloading or in factory shells costs a few dollars more than chilled shot—and plated shot costs even more—it is money well spent. I have had such good luck with plated shot that all of my pheasant and grouse loads contain plated shot, preferably nickel-plated. I even use plated shot in my quail loads. About the only birds I hunt on a regular basis without plated shot are doves. Even then, my dove loads are either premium target ammunition or handloads with high antimony (hard) lead shot. My practice and competition loads are of the same quality. The only chilled shot I load and shoot on a regular basis is No. 9 shot in my skeet practice loads.

The final part of the shotshell is the crimp. The most common crimp used today is the folded or "pie" crimp. The shell has six or eight indentations (points) that are folded down to meet in the middle and seal the shot inside the shell. Eight-point crimps are usually found on target ammunition. Most target cases are designed to be reloaded, and the eight-point crimp works easier and wears longer. Six-point crimps are found on most field ammunition and on all 28- and 410-gauge ammunition because there is not enough room to divide these dainty cases into eight "pieces of pie."

A variety of crimp styles, including roll crimp and six- and eight-point star crimps.

Prior to the development and almost universal acceptance of the folded crimp, many shotshells had a roll crimp where a cardboard or felt wad was placed over the shot and the case was then rolled down to crimp around this. This process gave more interior space in the shell and was often found on higher velocity or heavier shot weight loads. Often the shot weight, size, and velocity were stamped on the cardboard wad. When companies switched over from the rolled crimp to the folded crimp, many of these earlier loads had a piece of paper on top of the crimp with this same information. This was to appease shooters who were resistant to change and who still wanted the information on the crimp and not the side of the shell.

THE MYSTERY OF THE DRAM EQUIVALENT

A dram is a measurement of weight under the avoirdupois system. An avoirdupois dram weighs 27.344 grains. An avoirdupois ounce contains 437.5 grains. When shotshells were loaded with blackpowder, a required weight (drams) of shotgun blackpowder was required to obtain a certain velocity with a shot charge of a certain weight. Early smokeless powders for shotguns were designed to weigh and measure the same as blackpowder. These were the bulk powders. When smokeless powders began to be developed and became more efficient, the ammunition companies began using the phrase dram equivalent to tell shooters the relative power and velocity of the shells. Unfortunately, this phrase became like a government bureaucracy. Once it got started, it could never be stopped.

Dram equivalent is an ambiguous term that may have made sense to the shooters of a century ago, but it is antiquated, confusing, and unneeded today. The velocity of a dram equivalent is relative to the gauge of the shell and the weight of the shot charge. If you pick up a box of shells marked "2$^3/_4$ D.E./1$^1/_8$ ounce/7$^1/_2$," the only clear information is that these shells contain 1$^1/_8$ ounces of No. 7$^1/_2$ shot. If the shell in question is a 12 gauge, then the D.E. (dram equivalent) means the velocity of the shell is approximately 1,145 feet per second (fps). If it is a 16-gauge shell, the velocity is approximately 1,185 feet per second. If it is a 2$^3/_4$-inch 20-gauge shell, the velocity is approximately 1,110 feet per second, and if a 3-inch 20-gauge shell, the velocity is approximately 1,250 feet per second. Confusing and as clear as mud, isn't it?

More and more companies are starting to list the actual velocity of their shells on the box, but the old dram equivalent phrase still refuses to die. On Winchester's excellent line of AA shotshells, they still list the dram equivalent on their trap and skeet loads. They list the actual velocity on their Handicap and Super Sport sporting clays loads. Even though companies are starting to list the actual velocity of the shells on the box, it is often hard to find. On a box of 16-gauge Federal shells, for example, they are listed in large letters as being "2$^3/_4$ Dram Equivalent," but in smaller letters it tells you that the velocity of these shells is 1,185 feet per second (fps).

What about that other lovely term seen on so many shotshell boxes: "Max Dram Equivalent"? Unless you are a very knowledgeable shotgun shooter with a prolific memory, you would have to have a chart to tell what is "max" for any given charge weight. Even then, you would probably be wrong!

For example, many times you will find this designator on what I call seasonal shells. These are usually the promotional shells for a specific season or game and will often be called Dove and Quail, Heavy Dove, Rabbit and Squirrel, or Pheasant loads. Most of the time they will have pretty pictures on the box of the game that is supposed to be hunted. These loads are often specially priced and will sell for less than the higher-quality shells with the same amount of shot and velocity.

Let's take a 12 gauge with a load of $1\frac{1}{4}$ ounces of shot. The velocity of this load with $3\frac{1}{4}$ Dram Equivalent is approximately 1,220 feet per second. This is commonly marketed as a pigeon load, since it was very popular when live pigeon shooting was active in the United States. When this shell has a $3\frac{1}{2}$ dram equivalent with $1\frac{1}{4}$ ounces of shot, the velocity is approximately 1,275 feet per second. With a $3\frac{3}{4}$ dram equivalent, we are pushing this $1\frac{1}{4}$ ounces of shot at 1,330 feet per second. At one time this was considered the maximum velocity for this amount of shot, so this was the max dram equivalent. Developments in powders, wads, and primers over the years make it possible to push this same amount of shot out of a 12-gauge barrel at velocities up to 1,495 feet per second. I guess that max really isn't the maximum any more!

Listing velocity as max dram equivalent or any dram equivalent is a marketing tool that has been done for so long that many companies don't even know what it really means. One year at the annual Shooting, Hunting, and Outdoor Trade Show (SHOT Show) I asked the representatives from several ammunition companies to explain to me how dram equivalent related to velocity. Only one could adequately explain it, and he was the one who admitted to me that it was and is primarily a marketing tool!

American shooters: wouldn't you like to know more about the shells that you are spending *your* money on than some outdated ritualistic formula?

I rate modern shotshells into four categories. These are cheap, good, highgrade, and premium. In all cases (pun intended), you get what you pay for. It never ceases to amaze me the number of shooters who will brag about having a gun worth thousands of dollars. They will brag about how much money they paid for their dog and how much the trainers have cost them. They talk about how much money they spend on their hunting trips. They have specialized hunting vehicles in four-wheel drive with all of the extras and creature comforts. Then they brag about how cheap they bought their shotguns shells. Let's take a look at shells in each category and see what defines them.

Cheap loads are also the seasonal loads. These are made by most manufacturers to be sold during the bird seasons at the lowest possible price. The entire shell will reflect this. The case will be a thin two-piece plastic that will often jam in the magazine of pumps or semi-autos when the thin plastic bends or flexes. The case head will be steel or aluminum and may cause feeding problems in pumps and semi-autos or extraction problems in all types of guns. Inside the case will be soft shot, mediocre wadding, and little or no protection for the shot as it passes down the barrel. Cardboard or fiber wads will be used and they may not form a good gas seal, causing gas blow-by to disrupt the patterns. I have tested these loads in some Full-choke guns that were giving Cylinder patterns at 40 yards.

At the lower end of the price category of good shells are the all-around shells made for informal target shooting and hunting. These may be called universal or all-around or multi-purpose loads. In my experience, these are often very good performing shells with decent wads and uniform but soft chilled shot. Companies save money in the manufacturing process of these shells by using thin plastic for the case body and either a zinc or aluminum alloy for the case head. This case can be reloaded, but in the reloading process so many cases will be lost due to case or head failure that it is not economical to reload them. At the upper end of the good category are the shells designed for hunting. These will often bear a trademarked name by the manufacturer and are their most well-known loads. Designed for hunting, they usually have higher velocity and use good wadding, crimps, and uniform chilled-lead shot. They will have the name of the manufacturer and the specific trademarked name of the shell on the box. Seldom will you find pretty pictures of game birds or animals on the box.

All of the target ammunition made for the clay-bird shooters falls into the high-grade category. These shells are made for a demanding market and are

Too many shotgunners focus strictly on their guns and mistakenly treat shell selection as little more than an afterthought. WINCHESTER

the best for the clay-target games of trap, skeet, and sporting clays. The shooters in these games want consistency and uniformity shot after shot, and these shells are designed and manufactured to produce it. They have strong plastic cases that may be reloaded many times. They have the most efficient wads made by the manufacturer and contain high antimony, select-grade shot that is very hard and very uniform in its roundness and pellet diameter. These are also very effective field loads for dove, quail, grouse, rabbits, and even pheasants under some circumstances. An acquaintance of mine used to manage a pheasant hunting preserve. For twenty years, he had shooters of all levels of experience and knowledge come to hunt pheasants. Because the average shot of these pen-raised birds was often under 25 yards, his loaner guns were all 12-gauge skeet guns with open chokes. All he ever used for his loaner shells was a well-known target load in 12 gauge with $1^1/8$ ounces of No. $7^1/2$ shot at 1,200 fps velocity. This combination was deadly in the hands of experienced shooters and gave the new shooters an effective margin of error.

Premium loads are just that. They are often the best the maker has to offer and are designed for specific types of shooting or hunting. They will often contain plated shot that has been inspected closely by quality control for roundness, uniformity, and hardness. They will also often be buffered with a compound within the wad that fills in the air spaces around the shot and protects the shot from deformity during the firing process. You won't find these shells at the local megamart. They are available at various chain sporting goods stores throughout the United States and are often available on the Internet from distributors or even the manufacturer. The price on these will often be three to four times as much as the seasonal loads and often twice as much as even the manufacturer's well-known hunting loads. After years of using these loads in the field on various species of birds and animals, I can sum them up succinctly. They are worth the price.

As I am writing this chapter, it is in the middle of our two-month-long dove season. I have read that dove shooters account for over two-thirds of all the ammunition fired at game birds annually. A dove is a small bird surrounded by a lot of airspace and is a very challenging target. They are hard to hit but not that hard to kill. Shotshell companies know this and realize that if they name a shell a dove load, they will sell millions of them because shooters will see the word dove on the box and know that these are just what they need. Because of the number of shells expended by the average shooter, most shooters will buy the most inexpensive shell they can find. The ammunition companies know this as well, so the boxes at the lowest price with the pretty pictures of doves on the box will be the cheapest loads the company can make! I have tested these shells extensively over the years, and with very few exceptions, the less expensive a shell the less efficient it is. Some of these were

Target ammunition is perfect for use in the bird fields in addition to the range.

so bad that I think you would have had just as good a shell-to-bird ratio if you threw the shells like rocks instead of shooting them.

I lived in "enlightened" states that didn't allow dove hunting and where I didn't get a chance to go dove hunting until I was thirty-five years old. By that time, I had experience testing shotguns and loads, and the loads I continue to use are either high-grade target loads, if I am shooting factory ammo, or reloads made to the same efficiency level. Over the years I've kept track of my shell-to-bird ratios, and I have averaged 3.8 shells per bird on dove. Yes, there have been days when I killed a limit of birds with less than a box of shells. There have also been days like one this season when I fired thirty-eight shells and came home with six birds. I think if my dogs could have found a different way home that day, they would have taken it, choosing not to be seen in public with me. That day there was no problem with the shells I was using, it was with the shooter. There are times when the shell can cost you a bird. If you got a "great deal" on the shells, you probably won't have that "great a day" with them in the field.

The *only* way that you will know how your gun performs with a given load is to pattern the gun and load with the choke you are using at various distances. I suspect that since patterning is such a time-consuming process, less than 1 percent of all shotgunners actually do it. Even though patterning is an essential part of the research I must do as a writer, I must confess that too often I will put it off. This is especially true if I am testing a load or gun for an article and use it in the field before I get a chance to pattern it. If it performs well in the field, then I often put off the trip to the patterning boards. So far this year I have fired almost 1,200 patterns of various loads, chokes, and guns. I still have over a thousand waiting to be tested, however. Yes, it is time consuming. Yes, counting holes in paper can be boring. Yes, it requires very detailed record keeping. And yes, it is worth it!

Patterning will tell you how well a particular load is performing out of your gun. I have said it before and will say it again: in ballistics testing, one should always expect the unexpected. A load that performs very well out of your buddy's gun may not be worth a hoot out of your identical gun. Shooters will argue for hours about the effect that .005 inches of choke difference will make on targets. However very few will be able to tell you the exact difference it makes on the pattern board.

Detractors will often state that since the pattern board is two-dimensional it does not give an adequate representation of the shot, since the length of the shot string makes the pattern three dimensional. To me this is akin to arguing the different colors of white paint. If a given gun/load/choke combination does poorly in the two-dimensional arena of the pattern board, it will not magically increase when done in three dimensions. The late great Bob Brister proved this with his moving target tests in *Shotgunning: The Art and Science*, and it has also been proven by a number of computer programs.

The common distance to test patterns from 10-, 12-, 16-, 20-, and 28-gauge shotguns is 40 yards (410s are patterned at 25 yards). To be quite honest with you, I don't know how this 40-yard mark became the norm. I have read that when Fred Kimble, who was one of the first to develop the use of chokes in a shotgun, demonstrated his new idea of restricting the shotgun barrel (choking) he used a 40-yard distance. When others started choking shotgun barrels, they used this 40-yard distance and the percentages developed by Kimble to demonstrate their guns and loads.

I often hear shooters say they have never patterned their gun because they don't need to know what the gun does at 40 yards. This is like saying you should always drive your car at 120 miles per hour because that's what the speedometer goes up to. It is important to pattern your gun with the loads and chokes you use at the ranges that you will be taking your game. If you are hunting grouse in thick cover and a long shot is 20 yards, then test your grouse gun and loads at 15 and 20 yards. If you are goose hunting out of a field blind and your shots are at 45 to 50 yards, then test your goose gun and loads at those ranges.

Forty yards is as good a place to start as any when testing new loads. In shooting thousands of patterns, I have never found a pattern that performed

Premium loads result in fewer lost birds.

well at 40 yards that didn't perform well at lesser or greater ranges. I have also never found a pattern that performed poorly at 40 yards that became a great or even good pattern at lesser ranges.

Over the years I have dissected hundreds of shells and tested thousands more on pattern boards, clay and feathered targets, and over the chronograph. One year I fired over twelve cases of target loads for an article in a national magazine. I have found a few very consistent and definitive facts from all this testing:

1. The more uniform and harder the shot, the better the performance of the shell.

2. Good wads make for good performance. They protect the shot from deformation and keep gasses contained and pressures consistent throughout the firing process by providing good gas seals.

3. High-quality ammunition will be a consistent performer in velocity and patterns out of most guns.

4. High price does not necessarily mean high quality. I have tested some high-priced loads that were mediocre performers and some inexpensive loads that were outstanding performers. This is especially true today with shells being imported into the United States. Some of these will sell for less than American-made brands but will be high-quality performers. Some of these may be priced comparably to the American-made seasonal loads but will give markedly better performance. Again, the *only* way to know the efficiency of *any* gun/load/choke combination is to spend some time on the pattern board.

NONTOXIC SHOT

Since the 1980s, lead shot has been banned from use in the United States for all waterfowl hunting. This has expanded to upland hunting in waterfowl hunting areas and also in areas where waterfowl feed or breed. The current trend is to expand the areas where nontoxic shot is required for all hunting. I think the day is coming when the use of lead shot for any hunting will be banned.

The first nontoxic shot was steel. Steel was harder than lead but had less weight, so 1 ounce of steel pellets contained the same number of pellets as $1\frac{1}{4}$ ounces of lead. Since steel was much lighter, it lost velocity faster. This restricted the range and kinetic energy of the shotshells. Lead pellets could kill at greater ranges than the same-sized steel pellet. Steel pellets are also considerably harder than lead, and some damage was done to shotgun barrels by some of the earlier loads.

I stated in another chapter that I was involved with the Colorado Division of Wildlife in an education project prior to the lead-shot ban. Thus, I have been involved with nontoxic shot since before it became mandatory. Yes, some of those early loads were pretty bad. The ballistics were erratic, they could and often did damage a gun barrel, and the down-range performance was questionable. Unfortunately, too many shooters had bad experiences with these early steel shells and continue to badmouth steel's performance today.

Although many would like to see me drawn-and-quartered for saying so, I believe the nontoxic requirement for waterfowl was one of the best things to ever happen to the shotgun industry. It mandated that companies research and develop the nontoxic loads that led to improvements in cases, powders, primers, and wads. This development rolled over into lead loads and has provided a level of performance never seen before. Many people will disagree, but the performance of the various nontoxic loads of today are superior to many of the lead loads of the past and even to some of the lead loads manufactured today.

One factor that has not changed in the last twenty-five years is the high price of nontoxic loads in relation to lead loads. This is a major complaint among shooters. There have even been comments that this is a ploy to end hunting by making it too expensive for the average person. This is rubbish. Nontoxic shells cost more for a number of reasons. Today, steel loads can be found at costs similar to premium duck loads in the past. Other nontoxics are bismuth, iron-matrix, and Hevi-Shot. Each of these costs more, with some shells approaching $1 per shell.

It is simple economics. The compounds used to manufacture nontoxic pellets are more expensive than lead. The machinery used is new machinery. The

Older Guns and Modern Ammunition

In the days of paper cases, the metal head on the outside of the case was used to strengthen the case and prevent burn-through on the paper shells from the burning powder gasses inside. Heavier loads contained more powder so the brass was extended up the side of the case. These were high brass cases. Target and field loads did not need this extra strengthening, so the brass only extended a short way up the side of the shell. These were low brass cases.

An erroneous but common phrase also called these high base and low base cases. This is a misnomer because the base refers to the basewad inside the case that was opposite of the brass on the outside. High brass cases had a lower basewad to provide the extra room in the case for additional powder and shot. Low brass cases had a higher basewad inside the case because there wasn't the need for the extra space with the lighter loads.

Blackpowder and the early smokeless powders were loaded in bulk amounts. This is where the old dram rating we talked about earlier came into being. A 3-dram load had three drams or 82.2 grains of powder by weight. The early smokeless shotgun shell powders were designed to be used in bulk loadings similar to the bulk required by blackpowder. These loads seldom generated more than 6,000 pounds per square inch (psi) of pressure and most were in the 4,000 to 5,000 psi range. This is no longer true!

increased hardness of the pellets requires wads and cases that are stronger and stiffer than those used for lead loads. Special machines are also required to mold, make, and load these new cases and wads. The gun and ammunition companies have spent millions of dollars on the research and development of nontoxic shot and on the costs to get it into production.

These loads had to be safe, efficient, and effective. They also had to be reasonably priced but still enable the company to recoup the research and production costs and make a profit. Several people employed by the ammunition companies have told me that nontoxic shot was in production for fifteen years before all of the costs of the development and manufacturing were paid off and a profit was actually made. One friend of mine in the gun industry told me that over 40,000 rounds were expended in just one shotgun line to determine the choke restrictions that worked best with both lead and nontoxic shot.

Older Guns and Modern Ammunition *continued*

Modern shotgun powders are varied and designed to be used within specific parameters (recipes) to be loaded within certain limits. The Sporting Arms and Ammunition Manufacturers' Institute (SAAMI) sets the pressure limits for all modern shotshells. These pressure limits are designed for modern shotguns in good condition. Most modern shotshells operate within a pressure range of approximately 7,000 to 13,000 psi. All modern shotguns and those produced after about 1920 will safely handle all modern loads. If there is a doubt, the gun should be checked out by a competent gunsmith to be certain it is safe with modern loads.

Prior to 1920, many shotguns were designed to be used with blackpowder or the early bulk smokeless powders. These guns were safe with loads that didn't exceed 6,000 psi. These guns should never be fired with modern ammunition. The results can be catastrophic to the gun and the shooter, causing damage, injury, or even death!

Many of these fine old guns are beautiful examples of the art of gunmaking. Many of them have Damascus or twist-steel barrels in which soft steel or iron was twisted around an iron mandrel and then welded to make the barrel. Modern barrels are formed from a solid block of steel that is machined and bored to the proper size.

Damascus and twist-steel barrels should only be used with blackpowder cartridges and only then after a check of the barrels has been made by a competent gunsmith and certified as safe to shoot. Some

Since those early steel shells, there have also been changes and developments in the pellets. Other compounds have been used and these have proven to be better performers than steel. While more efficient than steel, they are also more expensive. Some of the alternative nontoxic shot currently available as I write are Bismuth, Tungsten-Iron, Tungsten-Matrix, and Tungsten-Nickel-Alloy. Tungsten-Nickel-Alloy is marketed under the trade name of Hevi-Shot. It is denser than lead, which actually makes it heavier than lead and also ballistically superior to lead. I have used all of the types of nontoxic shotshells currently and previously produced on both waterfowl and upland game and have found Hevi-Shot to perform the best out of all of the guns and loads used.

Because of the toxicity of lead to the environment and to humans, I foresee the day when lead shot will be outlawed for all upland hunting also. This aftermarket companies that specialize in shotgun modifications offer a steel sleeve that can be fitted to the gun to allow it to shoot modern ammunition. These usually reduce the gauge of the gun. We will discuss these more in the chapter on aftermarket accessories.

At least once a month I will receive an inquiry from a reader who wants to shoot his grandfather's or great uncle's old shotgun. He has been told it is safe to shoot as long as low brass loads are used. His local gun shop, his hunting buddies, or the kid at the gun counter in the local megamart has told him this. The answer from me, however, is a resounding NO! Even modern low-brass loads will have pressures in the 10,000-psi range and this is way too much pressure for a gun of this type. Also, in today's shotshell market, the height of the brass on the outside does not reflect the power of the shell as it once did. I have seen target shells that had high brass and high-pressure/high-velocity loads that had low brass.

I have a lovely old Parker exposed-hammer side-by-side that belonged to my great-grandfather. It is a beautiful old gun but as loose as a politician's campaign promises. It has Damascus barrels. I love this old gun, but it hangs on the mantle over the fireplace. It is unsafe to shoot with any loads, even blackpowder. Restoring it to a safe condition would reduce its sentimental value. This may be the best thing to do with that old gun. Enjoy the sentimental value and shoot your modern guns.

is already true in some foreign countries and some areas of the United States. The ammunition companies are also aware of this and are working to produce better and lower cost alternatives to lead. New alloys are being developed all of the time. It takes time to get these new alloys out to the shooter because they have to undergo testing by the U.S. Fish and Wildlife Service and also the Environmental Protection Agency.

I believe the days of inexpensive lead shotshells are numbered and that the cost of ammunition may become a major factor in the future of hunting. I can remember when gasoline was 30 cents a gallon instead of $3. Quality shotgun shells can still be bought for under $5 a box, so these have not kept up with the rising costs of other goods.

There is a natural nontoxic solution to lead shot. Found in nature and throughout the world, this alloy is heavier than lead, easily formed into pellets, and will give better performance than lead. So why don't the ammunition companies use this? Cost is the reason. This natural alloy is gold. How about shotshells that cost $500 each? That's only $12,500 for a box of shells! The next time you complain about the cost of a box of shotshells, consider the alternative.

9 Matching the Shell to the Game

When looking at the bags and bags of various shot sizes on and around my loading bench, I often ponder if there truly is a magic pellet or a real all-around pellet size. I previously mentioned one of my hunting mentors, Mr. Kilgore, who used a Browning A-5 Sweet 16 with a 26-inch Improved Cylinder barrel and Winchester Super-X high-brass shells in No. 7½ shot for all of his hunting. I hunted with Mr. Kilgore in an area of the Midwest where we alternated with brushy fencerows, small woodlots, and small ponds for ducks and geese. Mr. Kilgore was an excellent shot, and I seldom saw him take a

Picking the right loads for your quarry is an often-overlooked key to success in the field.
WINCHESTER

shot over 30 yards. This was also years before the ban on the use of lead shot for waterfowl. His gun, choke, and shot-size choices were perfect for the terrain, cover, and distances he encountered. Much of what he taught me was the opposite of the trends of those times, which often ran toward tighter chokes, larger shot sizes, and heavier loads. Over the years, I have had opportunities to hunt birds and locations that Mr. Kilgore never did. I found there was a lot of wisdom in the choices of heavier loads, larger shot sizes, and tighter chokes.

I also learned that Mr. Kilgore would not be undergunned in probably 90 percent of the hunting situations in which I found myself.

The No. 7½ pellet that was his favorite can be used on any clay-target field and will bust clays with gusto from low house 1 on the skeet field to the toughest crossing shot on a battue target on a sporting clays course. It will also perform very well on just about any feathered or furred game that can be taken with a shotgun. I have taken all types of birds with loads of No. 7½ over the years, and if I had to live with one pellet size, it would probably be 7½. Fortunately, we don't have to live with just one shot size and can use sizes that are more appropriate for the game, cover, terrain, and various hunting techniques. Because there are so many types of ammunition available to today's shooter, for the sake of simplicity, we will lump them into three categories: target, game loads, and high-velocity loads.

Target loads are the excellent loads made by most manufacturers for the demands of the various clay-target games. These are top-of-the-line shells with hard shot, consistent powder charges, good wadding, and good crimps. With the high volume of these loads made by different companies, they are often the best buy out there. A major outdoor chain has a store about a mile from my house. There you can buy a Heavy Game Load from one manufacturer at a price of $3.29 a box or $32.90 a case. The well-known, top-of-the-line target ammo from another maker is available for $3.99 a box or $38.00 a case. This is a much better buy even though the price is slightly higher.

Game loads are the lower-velocity loads made by almost every shell manufacturer. These will be marketed under a specific name. These are *not* the low-end promotional (and low-performance) loads found on the shelves prior to and during the seasons.

High-velocity loads are the loads made with shot at a higher velocity. These may be premium loads with plated shot or just a specifically named load with standard lead shot.

Rabbits

Gauges:	12, 16, 20, 28, 410
Shot Sizes:	4, 5, 6, 7½
Loads:	Game or target
Chokes:	Skeet, Improved Cylinder, Modified, Full

If still-hunting cottontails in heavy brush and around brushpiles, any shotgun choked Improved Cylinder with a game load of No. 6 shot will work fine. When hunting with beagles, I have always preferred a 20 gauge loaded with light 1-ounce loads of either No. 6 or 7 1/2. Since shots may be varied, an Improved Cylinder is fine for close shots, but I would prefer a Modified choke for the longer shots.

When hunting snowshoe hares, I have always used a 20-gauge over-and-under choked Improved Cylinder and Modified. I prefer 1-ounce loads in No. 6 shot in either game or high-velocity loadings. Since a common way to hunt these is on snowshoes, a lightweight, easy-handling gun is convenient and practical. Any 12, 16, 20, or 28 can be used. The 410 lacks adequate pattern density for these larger hares.

Jackrabbits are a great species to hunt. They are considered varmints in most areas and can be hunted year-round. They are a very challenging target and surprisingly difficult to kill cleanly. I have seen more than one accomplished game shot shoot great clouds of dust behind a rapidly accelerating jack. Although I have shot many jacks with No. 6 shot, I have found loads of No. 5 or even No. 4 shot will provide better penetration and fewer wounded rabbits. A full choke will provide sufficient pattern density for the longer shots.

Quail	
Gauges:	12, 16, 20, 28, 410
Shot Sizes:	6, 7 1/2, 8
Loads:	Game or target
Chokes:	Cylinder, Improved Cylinder, Light Modified, Modified

An older Browning A-5, an Ithaca 16, and a successful quail hunt.

For bobwhite quail, any gauge shotgun can be used. There are times a 12 gauge is overkill, but there are also times when a 12 gauge is just right. I have hunted quail on warm, humid days when the scent was thick for the dogs, the birds sat tight, and shots were all at 20 yards or less. I have also hunted them at the end of a four-month-long season in the seventh year of a drought. The air was dry, there was very little scent for the dogs, and the quail ran like marathon runners. Thirty-yard shots on covey flushes were the norm and 40 and 45-yard shots were not uncommon. In the first instance, a 12 gauge would be overkill. In the second, a 12 gauge with heavy loads was just right.

With the wide variety of cover, hunting conditions, and terrain in which bobwhites are found, it is very hard to recommend a load and choke combination that works well in all of them. The hunter in thick cover in the Southeast where even on covey rises seldom has shots over 20 yards would have the perfect combination with light loads of No. 8s and a Cylinder or Skeet choke. A hunter on the great plains of the Midwest may do better with an Improved Cylinder or even a Modified choke and moderate to heavy loads of $7\frac{1}{2}$s. I have been in situations where the best combination was a Skeet or IC choke in one barrel with a light load of No. 8s and the other barrel choked Improved Modified or even Full with a heavy load of $7\frac{1}{2}$s. This was in hilly terrain where the birds would hold tight. A quick short-range shot on the initial covey rise was common, while the second shot took place after they cleared the immediate brush and were headed either up or down hill. This is often very common when hunting some of the western quail species, and I know several hunters in Arizona and Nevada who use this combination to consistently take Gambels, Mountain, and Valley quail.

Two of my best hunting companions, Jeff McVay and Dee Dee, after an opening day quail hunt.

For scaled quail, No. 7½ is the lightest pellet that should be used and a lot of scaled quail hunters use No. 6 shot. For the hunter willing to do some preseason Internet scouting, several companies offer loadings in 12, 16, and 20 gauge of the No. 7 pellet. A very experienced scaled quail hunter friend of mine swears that the No. 7 is the perfect size for these running, far-flushing speedsters. He likes heavy loads of 1⅛ to 1¼ ounces out of a 12 gauge with a Light Modified or Skeet II choke. Since he consistently limits out on these birds in several states, I believe in his choices.

Grouse

Gauges:	12, 16, 20, 28, 410
Loads:	Game, target, or high velocity
Shot Sizes:	4, 5, 6, 7½, 8
Chokes:	Cylinder, Improved Cylinder, Light Modified, Modified

---

Ruffed grouse are the classic gamebird to many upland hunters. They have an almost cult-like following. The classic gun for grouse hunters is a lightweight side-by-side double barrel choked no tighter than Improved Cylinder and Modified. I have seen hunters in a grouse camp almost come to blows over the choice of gauge and shot sizes. Again, the terrain and cover will influence the choice of gun, choke, and load. A ruffed grouse is not that difficult to kill but can be very difficult to hit. When the leaves are still on the trees, many grouse hunters prefer heavier loads that put more shot in the air than when the leaves have fallen and there are more shots where you can actually see the bird. Back when I did a lot of grouse hunting in several states, my choice was a 20 gauge choked Improved Cylinder and Modified. Copper-plated 1-ounce loads in either No. 8 or 7½ were my favorite. Several of my grouse hunting friends have had great success with Fiocchi's Golden Pheasant loads in both 20 and 28 gauge. These excellent shells use nickel-plated lead shot and are available in No. 6, No. 7½, or No. 8.

For the blue and spruce grouse of the western mountains, loads of No. 6 or No. 7½ out of an Improved Cylinder or Modified choke are almost ideal. A big blue or spruce grouse will weigh 2 to 3 pounds, but in my experience, they are not a difficult bird to take with relatively light loads. My old blue grouse hunting buddy from Colorado often said he never needed more than 1-ounce loads to take blues. He used a 1-ounce load of No. 7½ or No. 6 whether he was shooting a 12, 16, or 20 gauge, and I never saw him lose a bird in five years of hunting with him.

Sharp-tailed grouse and prairie chickens are taken in open terrain and shots are usually long. When using a double-barreled gun, the combination of Modified and Full is hard to beat, and when using a single-barreled gun, a Modified or even an Improved Modified choke is a good choice. Although I am not much of a fan of No. 6 shot, I will admit it is probably the best size to use on these birds. Heavy, high-velocity loads are not needed. I have had very good luck with either pigeon loads of $1\frac{1}{4}$ ounces of No. 6s at 1,220 feet per second in a 12 gauge or $1\frac{1}{8}$-ounce loads at 1,200 feet per second in either the 12 or 16 gauge. If using a 20 gauge, I would recommend heavy 1-ounce loads of No. 6 shot.

Sage grouse are our biggest upland gamebird. It is not unusual to have one weighing 5 pounds and some birds go as heavy as 7 or 8 pounds. The wide-open terrain they like to inhabit often makes for long shots. Although my personal sage grouse hunting experience is limited, I have had excellent results with a 12 gauge with an Improved Modified choke and heavy loads of No. 5 shot. Several Wyoming and Montana hunters of my acquaintance prefer Full chokes and heavy loads of No. 4 shot for these gigantic birds.

Woodcocks	
Gauges:	16, 20, 28
Shot Sizes:	$7\frac{1}{2}$, 8, $8\frac{1}{2}$, 9
Loads:	Game or target
Chokes:	Cylinder, Skeet, Improved Cylinder

Although where I live now provides me the opportunity to hunt birds for almost six months out of the year, I live over a thousand miles from decent woodcock habitat. Woodcocks hold a special, very fond place in my heart and there is no other gamebird I enjoy on the table as much as I do woodcock sautéed in butter and wine sauce with portabella mushrooms.

Yes, woodcocks can be shot with a 12 gauge, but at the distances that these delightful birds are usually taken, a 12 gauge, even with light loads, is overkill. In good woodcock cover, birds are taken at distances measured in feet, not yards. I had one favorite cover years ago that never offered a shot over 10 yards. By the time a bird had gone 10 yards, it was above the willows or on the other side of the brambles where it couldn't be seen. I was in a local gun shop one time and picked up a little side-by-side 20 gauge on which the previous owner had cut the barrels back to 22 inches. This was the perfect gun for my favorite woodcock covers, and I used it for several years before leaving it with a hunting buddy when I moved from the Midwest. He passed on several years ago, and I never got this little jewel back. Winchester AA skeet loads with $7/8$ ounce of either No. 8 or No. 9 shot made this a great combination, and I ate my favorite meal of woodcock breasts a number of times.

The 20 gauge is a great gun for woodcocks, but the 28 gauge is ideal. On my last foray into woodcock covers, I used a delightful little 28-gauge over-and-under that weighed in at $5^1/2$ pounds. With the Cylinder and Skeet chokes screwed in the barrel and $3/4$-ounce loads of Remington STS in size $8^1/2$ shot, I collected five of the six woodcocks at which I took shots.

Partridges

Gauges:	12, 16, 20, 28, 410
Shot Sizes:	5, 6, $7^1/2$, 8
Loads:	Target or high velocity
Chokes:	Cylinder, Skeet, Improved Cylinder, Light Modified, Modified, Improved Modified, Full

The chukar partridge is an interesting bird. Originally imported from Asia, it have become a huntable species in a number of western states. They also are very adaptable to captivity and provide enjoyment on countless shooting preserves throughout the United States. Captive birds are well known for their propensity for tight-sitting, close flushes, which is just the opposite of their wild brethren. I have had the opportunity to shoot hundreds of chukars as part of dog training sessions and trials, and I seldom needed more than a 20 gauge with an Improved Cylinder choke and a light load of No. $7^1/2$ shot. My favorite chukar gun for this type of shooting is a 28 gauge with $3/4$-ounce loads of No. $7^1/2$s. If shooting a side-by-side or over-and-under, it will be choked Skeet and Improved Cylinder. If I am shooting a single-barreled gun, then Improved Cylinder is my choke of choice.

Wild chukar hunting is something else. These birds live in some of the most beautiful, stark, and wild areas of the west. The steeper the canyon walls and the sharper the drop-offs, the better the chukars like it. I know that when chukar hunting I have actually climbed down hills, but by the end of a typical day in chukar country, you will swear you spent the entire day hiking only uphill.

Chukars like nothing better than to run ahead of you and your dog up the steepest canyon wall they can find. Then, when you are on a slope so steep that you are parallel to the ground with your face about 4 inches off the rocks, they flush right back over you, heading back downhill. As they buzz by you, you try to keep your balance and take a shot at the same time. The birds land several hundred yards below you and you can see them walking around. The only problem is it will take you an hour and over a minimum of a half mile detouring around and over canyon walls, rocks, and impassable grades to get where the birds landed. As you finally reach the flat area where they landed, you hear the distinctive call of the chukar . . . above you! Then you start the entire process all over again.

There are many times when I have felt that I own the perfect chukar gun. My little 17-caliber HMR with a 3 x 9 variable scope should be just right for wiping that smirk off a chukar's face out to 100 yards. Alas, this is frowned upon by the wildlife officers, so I have to make do with a shotgun. A light-weight 20-gauge side-by-side or over-and-under is an ideal chukar gun. Believe me, you will carry it a lot more than you will shoot it! One-ounce loads of No. 7½ or No. 6 shot are perfect. I have used an Improved Cylinder and Modified fixed chokes with success. A chukar hunting friend from Nevada has a 12-gauge side-by-side that weighs in at a little over 6 pounds. It is choked Skeet 1 and almost an Improved Modified. He favors Remington International Trap ammunition with ⅞ ounces of nickel-plated No. 7½s at almost 1,400 fps. He hunts chukars several days a week during the season, and this combination fits his personal hunting style perfectly. Dedicated chukar hunters are a different breed, and if hunting these wily and clever birds for the first time, I would take the time to find out what gun, choke, and load the local fanatics favor before venturing out.

Nickel-plated shot will increase the performance of any load.

Hungarian or gray partridges are a special little bird to me. An import from the vast area of Eastern Europe that includes the Russian steppes, they have thrived in the upper Midwest. The amazing thing to me about these delightful birds is that they are found in cover you would swear could not conceal an overweight field mouse. Larger than a quail, they flush in coveys and singles similar to quail, and even though they favor wide-open terrain, they are fast and tricky enough fliers that shots are not easy. In much of the terrain they favor, the prairie wind is a constant factor, and when a covey comes up and catches the wind, they are gone! My gun of choice when hunting them has been an over-and-under choked with my open/tight choke combination. An

Improved Cylinder and an Improved Modified or even Full choke has worked very well. Any 12-, 16-, or 20-gauge shotgun with No. 7$^1/_2$ loads in the open barrel and a load of high-velocity No. 6s or even No. 5s in the tight barrel works very well. With a single-barreled gun, it is hard to beat a Light Modified or Skeet II choke with a light load of 7$^1/_2$s backed by high-velocity loads of No. 6 or No. 5 in the magazine. Sharptail grouse overlap in many areas with the Hungarians. The sharptails are slightly larger but offer similar shots. The choice of guns and loads for Huns will work fine on sharptails.

I must confess that I have never had the opportunity to hunt ptarmigans in their native habitat. This will be corrected by the time this book is published because I have two different invitations to Alaska for ptarmigan hunting and fishing within the next year. On the advice of several Alaskan friends and others who have had a chance to hunt this unique bird, I will be toting two guns on my trip. Both will be over-and-unders with choke tubes. One will be in 20 gauge and the other in 28 gauge. I will take a supply of Fiocchi Golden Pheasant loads in No. 6 and 7$^1/_2$ shot for each gun. My vet and hunting buddy had a chance to hunt these birds for the first time this past year. He took a little 410 side-by-side and 3-inch shells loaded with No. 7$^1/_2$ shot. He did not have any problems with this combination. He told me he wished he could have taken his German Shorthair along with him because he would have loved to see how Lola handled these birds.

Doves	
Gauges:	12, 16, 20, 28, 410
Shot Sizes:	7$^1/_2$, 8, and 8$^1/_2$
Loads:	Game or target
Chokes:	Cylinder, Skeet, Improved Cylinder, Light Modified, Modified

Doves are a true challenge. I love hunting these little gray speedsters, even though they can frustrate the most experienced shotgunner and make him look like he is shooting blanks. I was in my thirties before I got to shoot my first dove. I had heard how difficult they were to hit, so when I was invited on my first dove shoot, I took my faithful little 20-gauge over-and-under and four boxes of shells. I was hunting on the edge of a sunflower field and the birds were coming in fast and furious. Three boxes of shells later, I had taken exactly four birds! Fortunately, a friend with years of dove-hunting experience took pity on me and started giving me tips as to when to shoot and how fast to swing and lead the gray blurs streaking by my stand. I did manage to take the last six birds of my limit with the last box of shells. I wish I could say I have never repeated that day, but doves manage to give me several lessons in humility every year.

Since that day over twenty years ago, I have had the opportunity to shoot doves in numerous locations and with many different guns and loads. Although my personal preference is a 28 gauge, I think the 20 gauge is almost the ideal dove gun. A 20-gauge semi-auto will provide the opportunity to burn up more shells than you care to carry, but it will adequately take any dove within range. Last year on the opening day of the Texas dove season, I was right in the middle of testing a Ruger Gold Label 12-gauge side-by-side for a magazine assignment. We were on a flyway between a feeding area, a roosting area, and a waterhole, so birds were flying in all directions. I used the Skeet and Improved Cylinder chokes in the little Ruger with light 1-ounce loads of No. 8 shot at 1,200 fps. By waiting the birds out, and not shooting at every bird that went by, I took most of my shots at less than 30 yards. I still had eighteen shells left in my second box of shells when the fifteenth and final bird hit the ground. Of course there are other days when the amount of lead I put in the air outweighs the dove in the bag by a considerable amount.

The choices of gun, choke, and load for dove depends, as with many game birds, on the way they are being hunted. If you are hunting doves on a flyway where most of your shots are passing shots at birds rapidly moving from Point A to Point B, you will usually require a tighter choke and heavier load. If you are taking birds as they come into feed, water, or roost, you will often be able to use light loads and a very open choke. A good friend of mine had always hunted passing birds, and his favorite dove gun was a 12 gauge with a Modified choke. He hunted with me on one of my favorite waterholes one day where shots were seldom over 15 yards. He is an excellent shot and hit doves consistently, but many of the birds he hit that day were practically destroyed by his tight choke and heavy load. The next time he hunted that waterhole, he was using a 410 and had an absolute ball with the little gun.

In my area of Texas, our dove season runs through the months of September and October. In other areas of Texas, I can hunt doves until January 15. The first week of our dove season may see temperatures at or above the 100-degree mark. T-shirts and lightweight clothing is the rule, and you don't want to be pounded with heavy loads in even a 20 gauge. One nice thing about dove hunting is that you get to sit and let the birds come to you. On the few occasions that I do use a 12 gauge, I will usually use either my competition over-and-under weighing in at 9 pounds or my competition semi-auto at 8 pounds. I shoot mostly 1-ounce loads in competition, and these moving at about 1,200 fps are perfect dove medicine. My favorite skeet practice load is $7/8$ ounces of No. 9s at 1,200 fps. When I am loading some of these close to dove season, I will load a case or two with No. $7^1/_2$s or No. 8s. Another fun thing to do in the dove fields is to use sub-gauge tubes or reducers in an over-and-under or side-by-side. I haven't gotten brave enough to use the 410 tubes in my over-and-under, but I enjoy using the 28-gauge tubes on a dove stand.

By the end of October, we may still be in shirtsleeves or have temperatures around the freezing mark. The migratory birds are warier and shots are often at longer ranges as the birds fly higher. One of the best dove shoots I have ever had was as a "blue northern" was blowing in and the wind chill was about 15 degrees. The birds were big northern birds, and they were moving with the wind behind them. That day, I used my 12-gauge semi-auto with a Light Modified (Skeet II) choke and heavy $1^1/_8$-ounce loads moving at 1,400 fps.

I handload most of my dove loads with the same hard shot and components that I use in my competition loads. I avoid the seasonal loads like I would a West Texas Coontail (Western Diamondback Rattlesnake). When I do shoot factory loads, I prefer the target loads as loaded by any of a number of different manufacturers. These will perform much better than the cheaper loads, and I save my cases for reloading. I have found that using quality loads enable you to use a lighter degree of choke, which increases your patterns and your ability to hit these tricky targets.

Although some hunters prefer No. 9 shot for dove, I have found that unless all your shots are at less than 20 yards, No. 9s are not that efficient on dove. Although only slightly larger, I have had much better luck with No. $8^1/_2$ shot. I use No. 8s also but would not be unhappy if I was limited to only size $7^1/_2$ pellets for doves.

Pheasants

Gauges:	12, 16, 20
Shot Sizes:	4, 5, 6, 7, $7^1/_2$
Loads:	Target or high velocity
Chokes:	Cylinder to Full, including everything in between

I have no idea how may pheasants I have taken in my lifetime. I have hunted them for over forty-five years in thirteen different states in all kinds of cover, terrain, and weather conditions. As I am writing this, it is in the middle of the Texas pheasant season, and I have already hunted in Iowa and Kansas and have trips planned to Nebraska and back to Kansas. I have hunted in the classic block-and-drive-type hunt in large groups, but my preference these days is with just my dogs and one or two companions. I seldom hunt opening weekends any more, but the last few weeks of a season will often find me out every day. I have shot pheasants with everything from a 10-gauge muzzle-loading shotgun to a single-shot 410. I have shot planted birds for dog trials and at hunting preserves and wild birds in a blizzard on the last day of January.

I consider any wild pheasant a trophy bird. I absolutely hate to wound and lose a bird, so I use the guns, loads, and chokes that I have found to be the most efficient for this magnificent bird. I will also tell you upfront that some of my observations will run contrary to much of the information you will read elsewhere. I ask you to remember as you read this that my background in law enforcement slants me *very* heavily toward fact and not opinion.

My preference for pheasant loads contains four words: high-velocity plated shot. Copper-plated is good, but nickel-plated is even better. Plated pellets moving at sufficient velocity provide the penetration and power needed to penetrate the thick skin and feathers into the vitals and to break the heavy wing and leg bones and prevent the bird from escaping. My best hunting buddy Jeff McVay puts the toughness and tenacity of a rooster pheasant quite succinctly. Jeff says that if from the day you were born something was trying to make you dinner every day of your life, you would be tough, smart, elusive, and tenacious also.

Even the pen-raised bird shot on shooting preserves and in some states as part of stocking programs has the same genes and bone and muscle structure. I don't care if you are shooting thirty planted birds a day on a shooting preserve or hunting in 2 feet of snow at the tail end of a 3-month season. Any shot at a pheasant will require an adequate gun, load, and choke. There may be differences in what is used under these varying circumstances, but the ability to put the bird on the ground either dead or severely wounded so that it cannot escape is the essence of sportsmanship.

The most common shot size recommended for pheasants is No. 6. I haven't voluntarily used No. 6 shot for hunting pheasants on preserves or in the wild for years. In the few times I was forced to use No. 6 because there was nothing else available, I have utilized plated shot. Even then, I have had failures in penetration or lack of sufficient pattern density to take the bird with the effectiveness I prefer.

Yes, I know. Millions of pheasants are shot every year with loads of No. 6 shot. Many more are hit and wounded to either die a lingering death or have areas of infection from No. 6s. Over the years, and as recently as last week, I have had my dogs either run down a cripple I have not shot or retrieve a wounded bird that couldn't run. I have also cleaned many a late-season bird and found an infected area around a flesh wound caused by a shotgun pellet. I have never found a pellet larger than No. 6 in any of these birds, and the vast majority had lead No. 6 pellets in their bodies. Part of the reason for this is the poor shooting and inexperience of many pheasant hunters. Even good shots and experienced hunters, though, will often have a bird hit hard with No. 6 shot fly off.

Another big reason is that in many different guns, loads, gauges, and chokes I have tested over the years, No. 6 shot is one of the most inconsistent performers. I have had numerous tests where a gun performed very well with everything I put through it *except* No. 6s. I have a set of 26-inch barrels for one of my 12-gauge over-and-unders that has all of the bells and whistles. The barrels are ported and backbored, the forcing cones have been lengthened, and I have a complete set of choke tubes custom-made to the barrels. George Trulock of Trulock Chokes made these choke tubes for me, and beginning with a pure cylinder bore, they are in .05-inch increments all the way up to .30 for a super full choke. This set of barrels was modified as part of a series I did several years back on modifications to gun barrels. All of these modifications increased the efficiency of the barrels with loads of all but one shot size. No. 6 continued to be a mediocre performer in these barrels, as it has in many other guns I have tested.

My preference in shot size for wild pheasants is hands-down No. 5. I have been using No. 5 for almost twenty years now, and it has performed magnificently on pheasants in all types of conditions, chokes, guns, and gauges. A few years back, it was hard to find No. 5 shot in factory ammo. Now it is one of the biggest sellers in premium loads during pheasant seasons. For late season birds or in windy conditions, I will often move up in size and use No. 4 shot.

Recently I was at the large Cabela's store in Kansas City, Kansas, the week before the Kansas season opener. Cabela's had stacks and stacks of premium plated loads for sale on special displays. What amazed me was how many of these were 3-inch-magnum loads in 12 gauge. In all the years I have hunted pheasants, I have *never* had a shot at a rooster that required a 3-inch lead load to take the bird. I have used 3-inch shells on pheasant hunts when hunting in nontoxic areas and the only local steel shells in No. 3 shot (which equates to No. 5 lead) were 3-inch shells. It never ceases to amaze me that hunters think they need a 3-inch shell for roosters. I personally believe that if you think you need a 3-inch load to hunt pheasants what you need to do is get your gun out of the closet in the off-season and practice shooting. That will help you take more pheasants than the heaviest 3-inch shell.

Over the years, I have used shells of all velocities and weights of shot. I mentioned earlier the advances that the lead-shot ban brought about in shotshell powders and loads. Some of the powders developed for nontoxic loads pushed lead loads to unheard-of velocities. One of these is the Longshot powder developed by the Hodgdon Powder Company. I had a chance to begin experimenting with Longshot before it became available on the commercial market. The higher-velocity loads, when combined with plated shot, gave new meaning to the old street saying, "speed kills." When pushed into the 1,500 fps range, plated No. 5 pellets were absolutely amazing in their penetration and power on pheasants.

Yes, I know that the faster a round lead sphere is pushed through the air the faster it will slow down. I've read the articles and looked at all the tables that say that at 40 yards there is little or no difference between a lead pellet started at 1,200 fps versus one started at 1,500 fps. All I can tell you is that at the ranges I have taken pheasants since I started using higher-velocity loads, it makes one helluva difference. I took several boxes of Fiocchi's GPX Golden Pheasant loads to Iowa one year. These push $1^3/8$ ounces of nickel-plated No. 5s at 1,485 feet per second. Now, I have had good luck with the standard Golden Pheasant load of $1^3/8$ ounces at 1,250 feet per second, but the GPX loads were so noticeably more potent that Ty Green, my Iowa hunting buddy, started calling them swatter loads because he had never seen a load that swatted pheasants out of the sky like these did. Winchester, Federal, Fiocchi, and

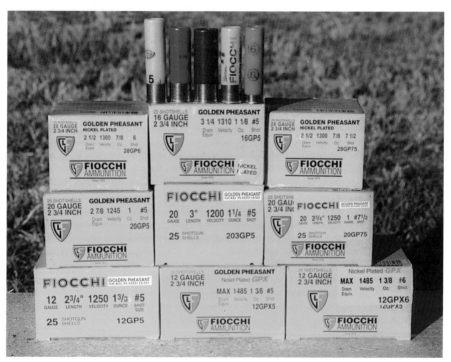

Fiocchi's nickel-plated Golden Pheasant loads work very well in a number of applications.

Remington, among others, all make high-velocity loads in the 12 and 20 gauge with plated shot. Fiocchi also offers them in 16 and 28 gauge. These will also help the average hunter with his shooting because the higher velocity requires less lead and will hit those birds in the front half, where the pellets do the most good, instead of in the tailfeathers.

Besides practice and more efficient shells, I think the average pheasant hunter will increase the number of birds he takes by lightening up a degree or two on their choke choice. It is rare that I have anything tighter than a Modified choke tube in my pheasant guns, and most of the time I am shooting considerably looser (the chokes, not me, as my shooting is always loose).

On a recent pheasant trip to Iowa and Kansas, I spent a day resting and doing some research in Kansas City. Part of my research was spending the afternoon at the U.S. headquarters for CZ-USA Firearms. While there, I picked up one of their Redhead over-and-unders in 12 gauge to use for this book and a magazine article. I had given away all of my 12-gauge ammo up in Iowa, and the only loads of plated shot I could find were copper-plated No. 4 shot. These were the excellent Remington Nitro-Pheasant loads that push $1\frac{1}{4}$ ounces of shot at 1,400 fps. This load took twenty-one roosters with twenty-three shots during the Kansas portion of my hunt. I had the Cylinder and Improved Cylinder choke tubes screwed in the barrels of the Redhead, and the Improved Cylinder barrel was only fired four times and two of those were on doubles. The combination of a high-speed plated-shot load and an open choke was deadly and not a single bird was wounded or lost.

These are my choices for wild birds. When hunting preserve birds or released birds, I have seldom found the need for heavy loads. I still prefer open chokes, but will usually use a quality target load of $1\frac{1}{8}$ ounces of No. $7\frac{1}{2}$ shot. This is also a good load for the chamber of a single barrel or the open barrel of a double in an area where quail and pheasant overlap. An even better choice is a quality pigeon load with $1\frac{1}{4}$ ounces of very hard or plated shot at 1,220 fps. In a 20 gauge, the combination of 1-ounce plated $7\frac{1}{2}$s backed by a load with 1-ounce plated No. 5s is hard to beat.

It should be obvious to you by now that I have a passion for pheasant hunting, and you have probably also figured out that I have a passion for the 28 gauge. You may have wondered why I didn't list the 28 gauge in the recommended gauges for pheasants. That is because the only time I will use a 28 gauge on wild birds is when the conditions are perfect, with good scenting conditions and very little wind. I have had too many experiences with the 28 just not being big enough for wild birds. For preserve or trial birds, it is one of my favorite choices. I prefer plated No. $7\frac{1}{2}$ shot and Skeet 1 and Skeet II chokes, or Improved Cylinder if using a single-barreled gun.

Now I know there are those out there that will disagree with some or all of my choices. That is fine. If what you are using works consistently for you and your style of hunting, then go for it! I have adapted to changing conditions and covers during a hunt or when hunting a new area or species. I have also found that many times what works for one style or bird will work very well when hunting a different species hundreds of miles away.

10 The Shotgun Barrel

The essence of any firearm is the barrel. This piece of steel is what the gun is all about. Modern shotgun barrels are the best ever made. Constructed with high-grade steel, they are designed to withstand pressures unheard of even a decade or two ago.

The modern shotgun barrel is machined from a solid piece of steel. In many cases, the receiver slots, barrel lugs, and other parts are machined with and are part of the barrel. After the basic barrel is formed, it is reamed to the proper diameter, tapped for choke tubes if needed, or the fixed choke is machined in the barrel. Bluing and polishing follow before the barrel is fitted to the receiver or action.

In the days of blackpowder, a longer barrel was needed to allow the powder to completely ignite. Heavier charges required a longer barrel. This increased the velocity of the load. These guns were said to shoot harder. This myth still exists to this day. The powders in a modern shotgun have fully ignited and reached peak operating pressures within the first 14 inches of barrel. A longer barrel will not increase the velocity and in some case will actually decrease it. The length of a shotgun barrel is a matter of personal preference and current trends. Even then, there is little more than a foot of difference in the most common lengths used.

The 1933 Federal Firearms Act that outlawed "sawed-off" shotguns set the minimal barrel length for a smoothbore weapon (shotgun) at 18 inches. The longest modern shotgun barrels of which I am aware are some of the single-shot "Long Toms" made by various manufacturers. These are sometimes found with 40- to 42-inch barrels.

The most common barrel lengths found on modern shotguns for upland hunting are between 24 and 32 inches in length. Probably the most common barrel length on either double barrels or repeaters is 28 inches. The current trend in competition over-and-unders for trap, sporting clays, and even skeet is toward long (32- and 34-inch) barrels. These are excellent for smooth follow through on a difficult clay target course, but are seldom needed in the upland fields. The additional length and weight may actually be a detriment to the average hunter. Inside the metal tube of the barrel are three things that influence the performance of the gun. These are the chamber, the forcing cones, and the choke.

CHAMBER

We have discussed chamber lengths in several different chapters. Modern shotguns made after World War II have been standardized with chamber lengths of $2^3/4$-inch, 3-inch, and $3^1/2$-inch chambers in the 12 gauge. The 10 gauge has chamber lengths of 2-$7/8$ and $3^1/2$ inches. The 16- and 28-gauge guns have a chamber length of $2^3/4$ inches. Twenty-gauge guns have chamber lengths of $2^3/4$ and 3 inches, and 410s have a chamber length of $2^1/2$ and 3 inches. It is important to note that these lengths are for a fired shell. A loaded $2^3/4$-inch shell actually measures about $2^1/4$ inches in length. A loaded 3-inch shell measures $2^1/2$ inches in length, which means a loaded 3-inch shell will fit in a $2^3/4$-inch chamber. Firing it will raise pressures to a dangerous level and could cause damage to the gun or injury to the shooter.

Shotgun Barrel

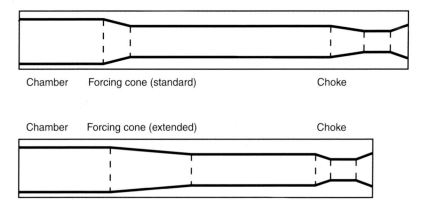

Of course, it is safe and very common to fire $2^3/4$-inch shells in a 3- or even $3^1/2$-inch chamber. There is still another old wives' tale out there that says firing a $2^3/4$-inch shell in a 3- or $3^1/2$-inch chamber will cause velocity loss and disrupt the pattern. I did some extensive testing of three Browning Gold semi-auto shotguns a few years back. One had a $2^3/4$-inch chamber, one had a 3-inch chamber, and one had a $3^1/2$-inch chamber. Using identical Winchester shells, I had less deviation in the velocities between the three chamber lengths than I had in the individual shells fired. I also obtained beautiful, well-defined patterns from all three chambers. The same choke tubes were used in all three guns. As a matter of fact, I had the most perfect IC pattern I ever shot out of the 3-inch chambered Browning.

FORCING CONE

In front of the chamber is the forcing cone. This is one of the most misunderstood but critical portions of the barrel. The purpose of the forcing cone is to reduce the diameter of the shot column from the diameter of the chamber to the diameter of the bore. This enables the wad to seal in the bore and prevents gas from blowing by the wad and disrupting the pattern. Traditionally, forcing cones were made short with very steep angles to prevent the fiber and paper wads of the past from being deformed or turned in the barrel to allow gas to escape past them. The modern one-piece plastic wad allows for an expansion of the plastic to prevent this.

Unfortunately, most forcing cones are still made very short with extreme angles. This literally forces the wad down to the diameter of the barrel and forces the shot charge down to the diameter of the barrel. In this short distance, the extreme angles add to the pressures in the barrel and may still cause some disruption of the shot charge, ultimately affecting the efficiency of the pattern. After passing through the forcing cone, the wad again expands to fill the barrel until it reaches the choke.

CHOKE

At the choke, there are restrictions in the barrel that force the wad down and slow it somewhat. After the wad passes through the choke, the wad and shot charge exit the barrel. The heavier shot charge separates from the lighter weight wad, and the shot charge continues on to strike the target. Picking up any fired wad at the range will show you the forces in effect here because there will be indentations made in the plastic of the wad by the pellets as they are forced through the forcing cone and the choke.

The purpose of the choke, of course, is to control the spread of the shot. This shot spread is the pattern we have talked so much about. Ideally, a pattern should be equally distributed with no gaps or areas where it is weak and no areas where the shot is clumped together in small clumps.

The most common type of choke in use today is the detachable choke tube. This concept was first developed in the Cutts Compensators, which had screw-in tubes to change the choke. Later, Winchester offered a version of a venti-

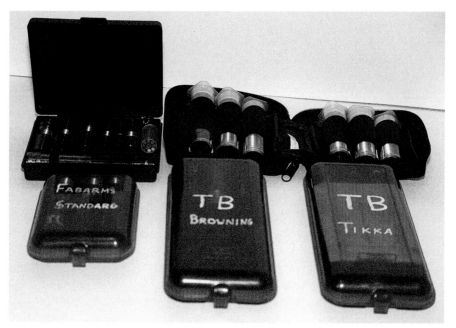

Various types of choke tubes and carriers.

lated, screw-in choke tube in their Model 59 autoloaders. Winchester brought out the first fully interchangeable choke-tube system that I am aware of in the 1970s. This was in their Winchester Model 1200 pumps and 1400 semi-autos. Many gunsmiths began offering the conversion of tapping existing barrels for this new choke system. Soon an entire sub-industry was born, and there are very few companies that offer a shotgun today without interchangeable choke tubes. There is also a large market of companies making aftermarket tubes in many different styles for most common brands of shotguns.

The choke is not the ultimate answer to the performance of the gun. I have said it before and will say it again: the *only* way to know the performance of your gun with a given choke or load is on the pattern board. It is not uncommon on a sporting clay course to see shooters with a full line of chokes for their guns. Most common are 0.05-inch increments, but I have seen choke sets that had 0.02-inch increments. These shooters will often be changing chokes between stations. It never ceases to amaze me how few of these shooters know what type of performance to expect from a given choke and load. They know what the theoretical numbers are for that choke, but they have no idea how that choke is performing out of their gun with the load they are using.

I have had a choke that was marked and measured very tight that gave very loose and spotty patterns, and a choke that was relatively light that gave very dense and tight patterns. I have a complete set of choke tubes in 0.05-inch increments for one of my over-and-unders. I also have a set of 26-inch and 30-inch barrels for this gun. I use the 30-inch barrels for competition and some hunting and the 26-inch barrels for much of my upland hunting. I have spent the time to pattern this gun with the various chokes and my favorite loads. For several of my favorite pheasant loads with nickel-plated No. 5 shot, I will often shoot a choke that is marked lighter than the performance I am getting with that particular load. For example, if I want to have chokes that are giving me Improved Cylinder and Improved Modified performance with a favorite load, the actual chokes in the barrel will be marked Skeet I and Light Modified. If I want that same performance with a light handload of No. 7 pellets for late season quail, I will be using the Improved Cylinder and Improved Modified tubes. With the nickel-plated No. 5s, my Improved Cylinder tube gives percentages that run around 55 percent, which is Light Modified performance, and my Improved Modified tube gives a percentage of around 82 percent, which is extra full.

MODIFICATIONS

Now I will admit that this gun has some other modifications to the barrel that affect performance. The standard 0.729-inch barrel diameter on this gun has been expanded to 0.735 inches. This is called overboring or backboring. This reduces pressure and allows the shot cup to expand fully to fill the bore. The forcing cones on this gun have also been modified. They have been changed from the standard $3/4$-inch long cones with a 45-degree taper to cones that are $2^1/2$ inches long with a gradual 25-degree taper. This prevents the sudden forcing down of the shot charge to fit the diameter of the barrel. With the longer cones, lesser angle, and the larger bore, the shot cup and the pellets within are subjected to less stress during the firing process. This causes less deformation of the pellets within the shot cup, and as they exit the barrel, more of the pellets are still round and fly truer. Because there are fewer deformed pellets to fly out of the pattern, the pattern is tighter and denser.

Another modification is porting of the barrel to reduce muzzle rise and felt recoil. In this modification, holes are cut in the end of the barrel to use the exiting gases from the fired shell to push down the barrel and reduce barrel rise. This lack of barrel rise also decreases the amount of felt recoil since the barrel is not rising as high and the gun is not being pushed as far back into the shoulder or the cheek. I have several guns that are ported. They either came that way from the factory or I had the modification done. Many people will disagree with me, but after shooting thousands of rounds from a fixed, stationary position for pattern and velocity tests, I believe that porting does reduce the felt recoil. Just last week I was testing some loads out of two different 12-gauge pump guns. I was using the same load, and these two guns, although of differ-

Porting on an over and under as done by Magna-Port.

ent makes, weigh within one ounce of each other. One comes standard with a ported barrel; the other does not. I was testing some new very-high velocity steel loads for a manufacturer. These loads chronograph at over 1,500 feet per second. I was alternating between guns at the chronograph and the pattern boards. I could definitely tell a difference in the felt recoil between the two guns. The one with a ported barrel had less perceived (felt) recoil and muzzle rise than the other one, which made it more comfortable to shoot.

A word of caution about porting: although it appears to be nothing more than holes drilled in the end of the barrel, porting must be done properly. I know of several people that had local "gunsmiths" port the barrels on their guns. Especially on semi-auto shotguns, this has caused the gun to malfunction with some loads. One friend of mine had a Remington 1100 that would function perfectly with any load. He found a "gunsmith" who would port his barrel for $25. This "gunsmith" clamped a template over the barrel and went to work with his portable hand drill and ⅛-inch drill bit. After this ironmonger got through drilling, he took a polishing tool and "cleaned up" the inside of the barrel.

When my friend tried shooting this gun with 1-ounce loads, it would no longer function. To function reliably, he needed to use heavy (1,200 fps) loads with 1⅛ ounces of shot. He had the gun ported to reduce the felt recoil, but with the heavier loads now needed to make it function, he was getting more recoil than he had with his 1-ounce loads prior to the porting job. When we put a micrometer to the inside of the barrel, we found that the clean-up job had caused the interior of the barrel to go out of round. At several places, the barrel had indentations running 0.03 to 0.11 inches. My friend saved $50 by not having a well-known firm do the work. Of course, in the long run, by the time he replaced the barrel, had the work done by a national firm, and got the gun back to what he wanted, he was out several hundred dollars, a lot of time,

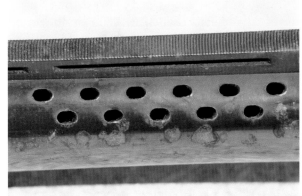

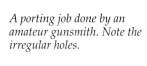

A porting job done by an amateur gunsmith. Note the irregular holes.

and experienced much frustration and grief. There are several companies that specialize in either shotgun modifications or porting that I would recommend highly for this type of work. Two that I have used and have been very pleased with both the work done and their customer service are Magnaport and Angle-Port.

These modifications used to be done only as aftermarket custom work. Now, there are several companies that offer these modifications as standard on various models. My competition semi-auto is a 12-gauge Browning Hunter Sporting Clays model and it came from the factory with a backbored barrel, porting, and lengthened forcing cones. One of my future research projects is to take a standard model gun from the factory. I will get several cases of factory ammunition from the same lot number to test through the various factory chokes and for velocity. I will then have one modification at a time done on the gun to see the difference in the performance. First will be lengthening of the forcing cones. Next will be backboring of the barrel followed by the porting of the barrel. Finally, I will have a set of choke tubes custom made for the bore diameter of the new barrel. Since this will involve over a year of work and be very expensive, it is still on the to-do list.

With the testing I have done to date, I will say that lengthening the forcing cones has had the most consistent and practical use. Every gun to which I have had this modification done has increased pattern efficiency, density, and performance. As time and budget permit, I am slowly working my way through the gun safe and eventually will have this modification done on all of my shotguns.

As these modifications become more and more common, I hope more manufacturers will add them to the standard models. This has happened in the past. The ventilated rib, which was used by trap and skeet shooters to give them a more uniform sighting plane and to reduce mirage from barrel heat, is

found on most shotguns today after getting its start as an aftermarket acces-
sory. I can remember when a ventilated rib was first offered at an additional
charge on such guns as the Remington Model 1100 and 870. Now these and
most other guns come with a ventilated rib standard, and off the top of my
head, I cannot think of a single pump, semi-auto, or over-and-under currently
marketed that does not have one.

SIGHTS

Since a shotgun is pointed rather than aimed like a rifle, the traditional shotgun sight has been merely a metal bead at the end of the barrel. This gives an
indication of the point of the barrel in relation to the target. To prevent canting of the gun and misalignment, target shooters began using a center bead of
one half the diameter of the front bead. When the gun was properly fitted, the
front bead appeared to sit on top of the center bead to give a figure eight alignment. This would tell the shooter the gun was properly aligned, and center
beads became very common after pre-mounted guns were allowed in both
trap and skeet.

There is a lot of controversy about whether the front sight or center
bead/front sight alignment is actually seen by the shooter in relation to the
target. I have a 20-gauge over-and-under that I often use as a training gun for
new shooters. It has no front or center bead. This prevents a new shooter from
getting focused on the sight and forces them to keep their eyes on the target.

A recent development is the use of a colored fiber-optic bead as a front
sight. These come available in various colors and dimensions and are designed
to be used against different backgrounds. I have these on several of my guns
and use them on a regular basis. I don't use them for aiming, but they are
"seen" by my eyes in relation to the target. Although I don't consciously focus

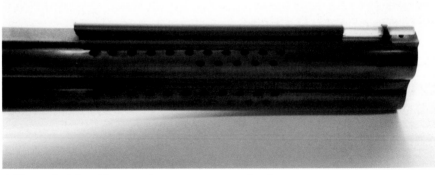

A fiber-optic sight with a tunnel prevents cross-eye shooting.

on the front sight, when I miss a target, I will know whether I was above, below, or behind the target by what I saw with the sight in relation to the target. This is especially useful in preventing the lifting of the head off the stock, which will almost always result in a miss. The eye is naturally drawn to motion and there is a tendency to lift the head to get an unimpeded view of a flying clay target or rising bird. Lots of rounds fired in practice with this type of sighting arrangement will teach your brain what is needed to hit the target and cause you to subconsciously shift to the proper eye/head/cheek position even in the excitement of the cackling flush of a rooster.

There are variations of these sights. Some have tunnels that focus the eye on the sight to help a shooter who has a problem with cross-eye dominance. We will discuss this phenomenon more in another chapter, but it is something that can severely affect a shooter. I am right-handed but have a very dominant left eye that prevents me from shooting with both eyes open, which is the proper way to shoot a shotgun. I developed a method of coping with this long before these sights ever became available. I have worked with a number of new shooters who have the same problem, however, and these devices enable them to effectively shoot with both eyes open.

As we have seen, the barrel on a shotgun is more than just a simple steel tube. It is a complex piece of machinery that must be properly used to give the best performance in the field. Are all of these modifications necessary? No, but one of them may be the one you need to not only increase the performance of your gun but also your enjoyment of it.

11 Making it Your Gun

The first week of our current pheasant season coincided with a blast of Arctic air. The first day I was able to go also was a new record-low temperature for that date. When I headed out that morning, the temperature was a brisk 7 degrees above zero and the wind chill made it feel like 17 below. Needless to say, I had a few more layers of clothing on than I normally wear. Now, I knew that these extra layers of clothing would affect the length of pull and the fit on the favorite 16 gauge I was using. Of course, I didn't think about this until I had missed two roosters in a row. When I got back to the truck and before moving on to the next field, I took a screwdriver and removed the recoil pad from the stock. This shortened the length of the stock by an inch and made it the same effective length needed when not wearing heavy clothing. The next two shots I fired put two roosters into my game bag instead of empty shells.

How well or how poorly your gun fits you will affect how the gun performs for you. Too many shooters "make do" with a standard gun when just a slight modification or two will fit the gun very well to their individual physique and shooting style and increase their shooting skill.

A shotgun stock usually has two parts: the buttstock and forend. How well these pieces of wood or synthetic material fit your shoulder, face, and hands determines how well you will be able to shoot with that gun.

BUTTSTOCK

The buttstock is the connection between the shooter and the gun. It is where the shoulder comes into contact with the heel and toe of the stock. It's where

A quality shotgun like this Franchi Alcione Titanium might look great, but make sure it fits you before you make the investment. BENELLI U.S.A.

the cheek comes into contact at the comb of the stock and where the hands grip and control the trigger. Custom fitting a stock to a particular person's physique and shooting style is a complicated and usually expensive project. A true custom-made stock will have over thirty measurements that are specific for the person who ordered the stock.

Fortunately, gunstocks are not like dentures, and we can usually get one that fits comfortably and enhances our shooting without a lot of changes. Also, the different gunmakers do a good job of making their stocks fit the average shooter, so that for most shooters very few adjustments are needed. I did the entire measurement system with a try gun and a custom fitter at a national clay target event a few years ago. The final measurements showed I needed to make a total of two relatively minor adjustments to most stocks to get them to fit me almost perfectly.

A friend of mine spent some time in London and was fitted for a stock by one of London's most prestigious makers. Interestingly, they would not tell him what the measurements were unless he ordered a gun. After a wait of several years, he received his very expensive custom-made gun. After he had used the gun a few times, he told me that the stock seemed incredibly familiar to him. He at first decided this was because it was fitted so well that it felt familiar the first time. One week he left the new custom gun at home and took his old Beretta over-and-under to the range. Suddenly, a light bulb went off in his head. When he got home, he took the measurements for his custom stock and compared them to his old Beretta. The only alteration he had made on the Beretta stock was to add a spacer and recoil pad to his length of pull. All of the measurements were *exactly* the same. He later sold the custom-made gun and refers to this whole experience as his "three-year, $20,000 lesson in stock fitting."

Critical Areas of Fitting on a Stock

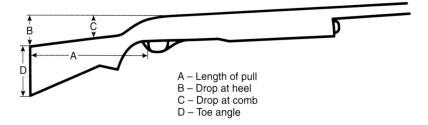

A – Length of pull
B – Drop at heel
C – Drop at comb
D – Toe angle

Fortunately, most of us don't have to go to this extreme to get a gun to fit us properly. The areas of concern for most shooters are as follows:

1. Length of pull
2. Drop at comb
3. Drop at heel
4. Toe angle or pitch

LENGTH OF PULL

I have often described my build as a "fireplug with legs." I am very broad in the chest but have short arms and almost no neck. I can take a size 44 suit coat off the rack and it will fit me perfectly across the chest and shoulders. The arms are usually somewhere down around my fingertips, though. I have a similar problem with shotgun stocks. I did some research while writing this book and measured over 160 shotgun stocks from fifteen different manufacturers. Just in the length of pull, the lengths ran between $13\frac{7}{8}$ inches to $14\frac{5}{8}$ inches. I found variations of over a half an inch on guns of the same model. On one model, of the five guns I checked, they were all of different lengths between 14 and $14\frac{1}{2}$ inches. I wish I could say that this was a rare incident, but I found very few guns where the stock was exactly the same length from gun to gun. Sometimes it was as small as $\frac{1}{32}$ of an inch; other times it was as large as $\frac{5}{8}$ of an inch.

What this means is that a factory stock may fit you, but another gun by the same maker may not. A proper length of pull should fit you and your shooting style. If all you do is shoot a pre-mounted gun in clay-target competitions, you will usually have a longer length of pull than if you shot low gun. If you have one gun set up for doves when the temperature is likely to be at or around 100 degrees, that gun will have a longer length of pull than your goose gun that you use in below-freezing weather from a sitting position.

Testing a gun on the range under the watchful eye of a knowledgeable instructor is a great way to determine whether the fit is right for you. BERETTA U.S.A.

So what is the perfect length of pull for you? When you have shouldered the gun, it should be in full contact with your shoulder and cheek. Your eye should be positioned so you have a sight picture of part of the rib and the front sight or the figure eight of the center bead and front bead. There should be sufficient distance between your thumb and cheek so the recoil doesn't give you a bloody nose. If the gun is going to be used for hunting or low-gun clay shooting, the stock should be short enough to not hang up on clothing while being mounted. This should apply to the clothing you will be wearing while using the gun, not just the shirt you have on when trying the gun at the store or the gunsmith's. Besides a lack of practice, I believe the difference in pull length is one of the main reasons why many shooters miss birds in the field. They may be wearing clothing that lengthens the stock by as much as an inch, which adversely affects the gun's point of aim, balance, and maneuverability. There is an easy way to check this. While wearing just a shirt, take your shotgun and hold it as you would in the field. Now focus on a point on the wall about 10 feet away. Keep your eyes focused on this point and bring the gun up to your shoulder in your normal mount. Does the gun point at the point on the wall? If so, then the gun is close to the proper length for you. Does the gun point above the focus point? Then the stock may be a little short for you. If it points below the focus point, the stock may be too long for you. Now take several handkerchiefs or fold a T-shirt to the approximate thickness of your cold-weather hunting gear and try the same experiment. Usually you will find that the gun is much too long for you. If that is the case, the simplest solution is to have guns of different lengths so that you can change guns to fit your clothing in much the same way many women change their shoes. This, obviously, is not a very practical solution for most of us. I have seen, however, a set of eight perfectly matched doubles made by an English firm for a Lord of the Realm that had different lengths of pull and stock heights to accommodate His Lordship's choice of shooting attire for that day. No wonder my Scotch, Irish, and Welsh ancestors rebelled so often!

There are several other simple solutions to these length-of-pull differences. The first is to have a set of spacers installed that can be removed or replaced as needed to change the length of pull. I have this set-up on several guns and it works very well. Another solution is to have recoil pads of different thickness fitted to the stock. A friend of mine has this set-up on a Benelli Black Eagle. He has a 1-inch pad on the gun for clay-bird practice during the summer and dove season. For early-season hunting, he uses a half-inch pad. For late-season hunting in cold weather, he takes the recoil pad completely off. Thus, the gun is at the proper length of pull for him whether he is wearing a T-shirt, a heavy shirt and hunting vest, or several layers of clothes and an insulated jacket. A third solution is to have the gun length set for your shorter length of pull. Then a slip-on pad will give you the proper length for shirt-sleeve shooting.

All this changing of recoil pads and spacers can cause the screw holes to enlarge and require larger screws. A solution to this is a nut-and-bolt system. These have a female part screwed into the stock and then a male bolt with an Allen head that screws down into the female nut. This system is available from several different suppliers, or at your local hardware store. I have used this system, and it is much easier and more convenient than just the standard recoil pad screws.

DROP AT COMB

The comb of the stock is where your cheek comes into contact with the gunstock. With a shotgun, your eye is the rear sight and the relationship of your eye to the barrel affects the point of impact at various ranges. Most modern stocks have a relatively straight stock with approximately 1- to 1$^{1}/_{2}$-inch drop at the comb. Some target stocks will have less, especially trap stocks designed to shoot a rising bird. Visit any clay-target competition and you will find a number of shooters using stocks that allow them to adjust the height of the comb. This is a very common alteration on a target gun and is well worth the money and time invested for clay-target games. Since most of these are shot with a pre-mounted gun, this alteration allows the shooter to get exactly the sight picture they want for the target being presented. Very few hunters use this modification, though it could be of value to them. Fortunately, you don't have to go to the expense of cutting the stock and installing adjusters to raise

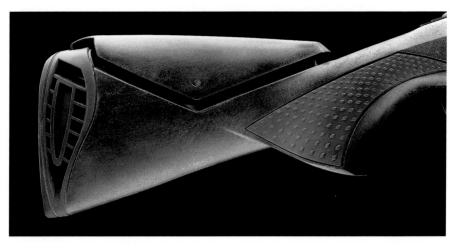

An adjustable stock, such as shown on this Browning Cynergy, is one option for ensuring shotgun fit. BROWNING ARMS

the comb on your favorite hunting shotgun. Several companies make ure-thane or rubber pads in several thicknesses that are attached to the stock with either Velcro or tape. A very inexpensive solution, and one that has been used by target shooters for years, is to buy moleskin pads at your local drug store. These can be added to each other until the required thickness is achieved. These can also be used to add thickness to the comb itself. Many old guns and some European guns have relatively thin combs. These increase the felt recoil on even a proper-fitting stock. They can also be used to cover the seam on some synthetic stocks. I have previously told of my painful experience with this seemingly insignificant little seam. Now if I am testing a gun with this style stock, I make sure I have some type of covering over the seam to prevent discomfort and possible injury.

The thickness of the comb can also vary. Since I have a round (read fat) face, I prefer a gun with a thicker comb. A sharp, thin comb greatly increases felt recoil for me. Shooters with a thinner face may like a thinner comb. Again, this can be changed with the addition of a pad.

DROP AT HEEL

The heel of the stock is where the gun fits into the shoulder. Most modern stocks are relatively straight and the drop at the heel is between $1^3/_4$ and $2^1/_2$ inches. Again, older stocks and some European stocks designed for a "head-up" shooting style will have significantly more drop at heel. I have seen some of these stocks with as much as $3^1/_2$ to 4 inches of drop. With a proper amount of drop at the heel, the gun should fit comfortably and completely into the shoulder pocket, which is between the shoulder bone and the collarbone. To

A perfectly fit shotgun is essential to consistently breaking clays on the range—and bringing down birds in the field. BROWNING ARMS

prevent injury and for comfort, the pad or buttplate should fill this space and not come into contact with either bone.

Another feature found at the heel of the gun is cast. Cast is where the stock is slightly off-center to accommodate the shooter and prevent canting of the gun. For a right-handed shooter, this is called "cast off." For a left-handed shooter, it is "cast on." If there is no cast, it is called neutral or zero cast. Most modern stocks are built with neutral or zero cast. This is a relatively minor adjustment that can be made by a competent stock fitter and one that can greatly improve your shooting. Canting of the gun can change the point of impact and cause a shooter to cramp up during the swing. A properly cast gun will prevent canting and enable the shooter to have a constant point of impact.

TOE ANGLE OR PITCH

This is an often overlooked but very crucial dimension. The toe angles can be positive, neutral, or negative. To check the toe angle of your gun, set the gun with the action flat against a wall. The butt should be flat on the floor. If the end of the barrel is also flat against the wall, then the gun has a neutral toe angle. If the end of the barrel is away from the wall, the gun has a negative toe angle. If the action will not fit against the wall because the barrel is touching the wall, the gun has a positive toe angle. Now this might not seem that important, but what you need to realize is that this critical area affects how well your gun fits into the pocket of your shoulder. This not only affects how well the gun fits and conforms to your body, but it can also have a drastic effect on recoil and making the gun comfortable to shoot.

Most guns as they come from the factory have a negative toe angle. This is because the bottom of the stock or recoil pad (the toe) has a sharp angle that conforms to the line of the stock. If this angle is reduced, then the toe of the stock will fit into the shoulder pocket better and make the gun more comfortable and less punishing.

Ideally, the entire butt end of the gun's stock should fit in the pocket between the clavicle and the rotator cuff of the shoulder. If you reach up with your off hand, you will find there is a natural pocket between these two bones, with the top of the clavicle forming the top of the shoulder. Now try a little experiment. Go to your bookshelf and find a hardback book that is about the same width as the buttstock of your gun. If you have an extensive book collection, you may be able to find one that is about as long as it is from the top to the bottom of the buttstock. If you do, use that. If not, any hardback book that is as wide as the buttstock will do. Hold the book by the front opening with the binding pointing towards your shoulder. Now place the center of the book in the pocket on your shoulder and press it in. You may want to extend and flex your arm as though you were holding the gunstock. Do you notice that the top of the book is at a steep upward angle away from the shoulder? This is what happens when the toe of the buttstock is flat and is an extension of the line of the stock. Now rotate the book 90 degrees and hold it by the bottom with the binding pointing down. Place it back in the pocket of your shoulder. You will find that the book is level and is in a comfortable position for you to put your cheek on it. This is the difference between a negative and a neutral toe angle. That is why on many guns used by competition clay-target shooters you will see adjustable recoil pads at angles that seem strange to the gun. These shooters know the importance of having the gun firmly locked into the shoulder pocket, and they adjust their pads to the angle that fits them. Rifle shooters have known this for a long time, and you will seldom find a rifle with the exaggerated toe angle found on many shotgun stocks. As a matter of fact, the more recoil a rifle will produce usually the more tailored this area is.

Adjustments to this area of a gun can make a drastic difference in how it performs for you. It will not only increase your performance but will also enhance the comfort of the gun by reducing felt recoil. Most of my personal guns have this modification done to give them a neutral angle. This can be accomplished in one of several ways. A spacer with either a positive pitch or angle where it is thicker at the top can be added. A negative-pitch spacer is thicker at the bottom and this can be added also. The recoil pad can be ground down to be thicker at either the top or the bottom. Just grinding the toe of the recoil pad off so that it is flat along the bottom rather than extending the line of the stock can make a big difference.

Kick Eez has come out with a new recoil pad to fit the pocket of the shoulder called their Rocker pad. At first, this pad feels very different when compared to older-style pads. By the end of your first round of clays, though, you will be calculating the cost of equipping all of your guns with this type of pad.

FORENDS

Technically, the forend is just where the gun is gripped with the off hand. Forends on either doubles or repeaters come in a number of different styles. They may be a "splinter" forend on a double barrel that is just large enough to contain the metal parts, or they may be the large "beavertail" style found on some doubles and many repeaters. There are many different styles, thicknesses, and configurations of forends. Some are aesthetically pleasing and comfortable while others have all the eye appeal and handling characteristics of a cement-covered 2x4.

I have a relatively small hand, and I find that a smaller forend is more comfortable to me. This does not mean I like splinter forends. I have to constantly adjust my left hand so that my thumb and fingers don't obstruct the sight picture when grasping the barrels on a side-by-side with a splinter forend. This is a pain! On a double, I prefer a semi-beavertail forend. Surprisingly, the most comfortable factory forend I have found on any side-by-side double barrel is

on the Spartan line of guns imported by Remington. These are thin but extend to the outside of the barrel. This forend is very comfortable and provides a good grip and consequently good control of the gun without placing the off hand at an unusual angle.

A very popular forend found on over-and-under guns is the Schnabel-styled forend. This is a relatively thin forend with a pronounced lip at the end. A very comfortable style, shooters with various gripping styles will easily adapt to it. Other over-and-unders will come with a standard forend that is rounded on the bottom and at the front end. This style will usually be

When the fit is perfect, the mount and swing soon become effortless. WINCHESTER

somewhat thicker but will still provide a comfortable grip for a number of gripping styles.

Beavertail forends are often found on specific target guns and some hunting guns. With a full grip in the palm of the hand and the fingers wrapping into the grooves on the wood, these are designed to give the off hand a solid hold on the gun. With my small hand, these styles are very uncomfortable, and I have less control with them than I do with a standard style. One shooting companion of mine has very large hands with very long fingers. The forends that are comfortable to him feel like a chunk of a 4x4 wood in my hand.

Many repeaters, pumps, and semi-autos will have large forends. On a semi-auto, this is required for the gas or spring mechanisms that are part of the operating mechanisms. One common type found on pump guns is the "ring-tail," which is a small piece of wood with vertical grooves for gripping. Many other pump guns will have a large beavertail forend. Like so many other features on a gun, the forend is a personal preference. Fortunately, many manufacturers offer different styles, and even if the model you prefer doesn't offer the forend you want, they can be changed out with a minimal amount of work and at a relatively low cost. These may be ordered from the factory or from an aftermarket parts supplier.

Combining these changes on the buttstock and forend, along with the barrel modifications discussed in chapter 10, will enable you to have a true custom shotgun that fits your style, method, and type of shooting.

12 Protecting Your Investment

I have seen shotguns over a hundred years old that could pass for brand new. I have also seen guns less than five years old that have been reduced to battered, rusty hunks. It is not how much use a gun receives that determines how long it lasts. How well it is cared for, transported, and stored will often have a greater effect than the amount of use. I have seen guns that the owners used on a regular basis for thirty years. They showed some areas of use, but the bluing was still bright and the wood was in good condition. I have also seen guns that the owners thought they were storing properly covered with rust, and the wood had cracked and dried or become spotted from moisture after less than two years. Proper maintenance, storage, and transportation of your guns will provide you with years of enjoyment and enable you to pass the gun on to future generations.

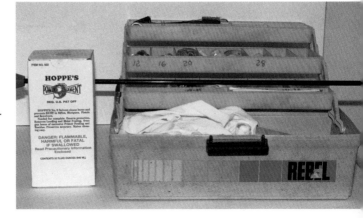

The author's gun cleaning kit has more than the basics.

MAINTENANCE

Fortunately, the guns and modern ammunition of today contain none of the elements that could damage or destroy a gun just a generation ago. Modern wood and metal finishes are almost impervious to moisture. Today's ammunition no longer contains corrosive powders and primers that were magnets for moisture and consequent rusting problems.

Moisture is still the enemy, however, and proper gun care must be done to remove it, prevent it, and protect from it. Unfortunately, too many gun owners think spraying the entire gun down with a moisture-displacing lubricant is the way to do so. This is not true. The individual parts of the gun need individual attention and separate types of maintenance, cleaning solutions, and lubrication to function properly and stay in like-new condition. We are very fortunate that there are a wide variety of products available for today's shooters to clean and maintain their cherished firearms. All of these products are very good, and it is just a matter of personal preference as to which one is used.

Ideally, at the end of every day of hunting or shooting, the gun should be cleaned and lubricated properly for storage. When I was first introduced to hunting and shooting by my father, this was an inviolate rule that I always enjoyed because it gave me more time with my dad and with the guns. I must confess that as I have gotten older I have become lax about this and instead of doing every gun every time, I will schedule specific days for gun cleaning and maintenance. Often, I put it off to the point that when I finally get around to it, it turns into several days or even a week of gun cleaning.

I am fortunate to live in an arid climate with very low humidity, and seldom do I have to deal with moisture on my guns from a day of hunting. There are, of course, exceptions to this, and when my guns are exposed to external moisture, they do get cleaned and wiped down at the end of the day. It doesn't take much moisture or a great amount of time to damage a gun. A friend and I were quail hunting one morning last year. It was a rare day for West Texas, with a cool, damp, and foggy morning. My friend uses a hard case with a fleece lining to store his gun. He takes the top half of the case off and uses the bottom half as a scabbard while in the truck. During the course of the morning, he probably took his

This barrel rusted after being stored in a lined case.

gun out and placed it back in the
scabbard a half dozen times. The
scabbard was in a muzzle-down
position in the truck. Moisture that
had accumulated on the gun got
onto the fleece lining, and gravity
and capillary action took this moisture to the bottom of the scabbard.
At the end of the day, he wiped
down the external parts of the gun
and placed it back in the scabbard.
The next week when he pulled his
gun out of the scabbard, the last 2 to
3 inches of the barrel had a substan-
tial amount of rust on it. This rust
was also on the inside of the barrel

*A rusted-in choke tube requires lots of hard,
careful work to remove.*

and had frozen the choke tube in place. It took several days of soaking and
work with very fine steel wool, but I was able to remove the choke tube and
the rust. Some touch-up bluing has the metal covered again, but close inspec-
tion will show where this rust was.

Another enemy of your gun is lubrication. Not under-lubrication, but
over-lubrication. If your car is designed to run with five quarts of oil, you
know it will not run any better and will actually be damaged if you use ten
quarts of oil in it. The same is true with your gun. Over the years, I have had
a lot of experience with malfunctioning weapons, both as a civilian and as a
law enforcement firearm instructor and armorer. For every one gun that I have
seen malfunctioning because of a broken part, I saw five or more that were
malfunctioning because they were over-lubricated. Over-lubrication can also
damage the gun when the oils and lubricants attract dirt particles. These act
as an abrasive compound on moving parts and may increase the rate of wear
and cause malfunctions. I used to teach students in law enforcement classes
to use an eyedropper instead of a spray can to lubricate their duty weapons.
This same philosophy applies to hunting and sporting weapons.

Over the years I have developed a system for cleaning and storing guns.
This system has four levels. Now, I am not going to go through these levels on
a step-by-step basis. I am simply going to touch on the points of interest at
each level and discuss when each level is required.

LEVEL ONE

This is the quick maintenance performed at the end of a long day of hunting.
One of the worst possible sources for moisture is the human hand. I have one

friend who has such strong salts and oils in his natural moisture that one of his fingerprints left on a gun will be visible in rust within 24 hours. When he has been handling a gun on the skeet range or a hot afternoon dove hunt, his guns require a more extensive wipe-down than others do.

Fortunately, most of us aren't this toxic, so a quick wipe-down with an appropriate cloth at the end of the day will suffice. For years, I kept a lubricant-saturated cloth in a plastic baggie in my gun case. I still use this, but there are some commercial products that are easier to store, use, and dispose of. Various makers make gun wipe-down cloths saturated in a cleaning/preventative solution. Some are in multi-pack holders, where one or more can be pulled out and used as needed. Others are in one-time individual packages that can be used and then thrown away. I have used both, and just for the convenience, I prefer the one-time packages. I keep a few in my truck and in my gear bags. In the gear bags, I will also usually have a takedown cleaning rod and tips for various gauges. A quick pass of one of these cloths through the barrel will remove moisture and residue. After the outside of the gun has been wiped down, it is ready for another day.

There are some important points to remember about Level One. First, these after-hunt wipe-downs do not replace a thorough cleaning and are just a quick way to prevent possible damage from moisture. Second, if you are hunting in a cold climate, the gun should be brought inside and allowed

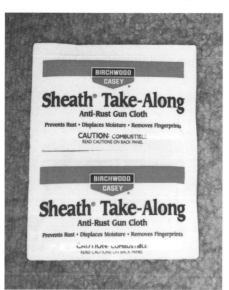

to come up to room temperature before any cleaning is done. The gun should be removed from the case and allowed to warm up. The metal on a cold gun will retain moisture, and leaving it in the case will cause moisture to be transferred from the gun to the lining of the case. It lurks here until the gun is put back in, and then it attacks the gun again. Ideally, the case should be allowed to air out as well.

These cloths have a shelf life of about a year. They will eventually dry out and be ineffective in transferring their protective lubricants to the gun. When this happens, you are just moving the moisture around on the gun rather than removing it.

Birchwood Casey's Sheath Take-Alongs work well for a quick wipe-down in the field.

LEVEL TWO

Level Two maintenance is the level at which too many guns are kept. This is when the barrel is removed and cleaned inside and out. The action should also be cleaned, but too often, instead of being cleaned, more lubricant is sprayed into the action and it is considered cleaned when in reality it has been made dirtier. There are many types of cleaners available today. I have used all of them and they all work quite well. My personal preference is still for Hoppe's No. 9. Although many people find the odor of Hoppe's unpleasant, I personally am very fond of it. Matter of fact, if I ever find a woman who tells me she loves that smell, I may propose right then and there! I will admit that some of the other products require less actual work than Hoppe's when removing lead and powder residues, but I still prefer to use Hoppe's.

At this level, the barrel is removed from the action. The choke tubes are removed from the barrel. The barrel is cleaned inside and out with a brush and swabs soaked in your favorite cleaner. The choke tubes should be cleaned separately, both inside and out. An important area to clean is the choke-tube threads, both on the tubes and inside the barrel. Debris or buildup in this area could cause damage to the gun from stripped threads or bulging of the tube and barrel.

This Otis compact cleaning kit can be carried in a gear bag or vest.

The action should be cleaned next. A quick and efficient way to accomplish this is to use an aerosol spray such as Gun Scrubber to clean out the action. This should be done with the action pointed down so the spray does not run down into the stock and affect the interior of the buttstock. After spraying out the action, it can be properly re-lubed with a high-quality gun oil or lubricant. There are many on the market. Again, this should be used *very sparingly.* For example, on the action-guide grooves found on the inside of the action on a pump or semi-auto, one drop of oil or lubricant should be applied in each groove. The action will properly distribute the lubricant when assembled and cycled.

Gas-operated semi-auto shotguns do require extra lubrication in one area. The gas mechanism on most of these guns fits over the magazine tube. Keeping the magazine tube covered with a good lubricant will ensure proper functioning of the weapon and help in clean-up. Any good lubricant can be used. I have used Break-Free for years, and it has performed very well. I was introduced to a great lubricant called FP-10 at a police armorer class a few years ago. It is of higher viscosity than anything else on the market, and one drop of it is the equivalent of several drops of any other lubricant I have used. This is one of the wonder lubricants that continue to lubricate even if you can't see it on the part. I have been very pleased with the performance of FP-10.

This is the amount of lubricant needed to keep a gas-operated semi-auto functioning. Other guns require even less.

Please note that if you have a long-recoil-designed semi-auto shotgun, you do *not* want to have any lubricant on the magazine tube. This will actually increase the felt recoil and may cause damage to the gun. The long-recoil design is made to function without any lubrication. Adding lubricant speeds up the compression of the spring and increases the recoil and the wear and tear on the parts.

After the action has been cleaned and lubed, the weapon should be reassembled. All of the exterior metal surfaces can then be wiped down with a cloth that has a small amount of lubricant. One of the wipes used in Level One can be used also.

LEVEL THREE

A Level Three cleaning is total disassembly of the gun. This is not as hard or as difficult as it may seem. There is an excellent series of books for disassembly of guns published by *Gun Digest.* Written by J. B. Wood and very well illustrated with photographs, they include step-by-step procedures for most modern guns. They are so well done I really think the series could be renamed *Gun Disassembly for Dummies*!

Many hunters and shooters do not realize there are actually areas on the gun that attract dirt and debris. When walking through the brush, weed seeds and particles will find their way into the gun's action. Unburned powder and plastic residues can also work their way into the action. When I have completely disassembled guns at the end of the bird seasons, I am constantly amazed by what I find hiding within the confines of the action. I have found feathers, weed seeds, pieces of bark, and small twigs. I have also found fired primers that were popped out of a case, and since I will sometimes try to squeeze one more reload out of some cases, I will often find shot that has come out of the shell. Although this will primarily occur on a repeater, an over-and-under or side-by-side can also acquire a surprising amount of debris in the area of the barrel lugs and receiver. Most of my guns will receive this level of cleaning at least once a year. If the gun has been exposed to severe weather or conditions, it will receive this level cleaning as needed. During the duck and goose seasons, it is not unusual for me to have to strip a gun down to this level after every outing.

Level Three requires total disassembly of the gun, including removal of the buttstock. Most guns are stored in a muzzle-up position in a rack or gun safe. This position allows solvents and oils to run down into the buttstock, where they can weaken or damage the wood. If you don't believe this can happen on your gun, take the buttstock off and put some paper towels or a clean cloth inside the buttstock, filling the cavity. Then let the buttstock sit with the grip down for a couple of days. You will be amazed at how much is absorbed by the paper towels or cloth. All of this is potentially damaging to the wood, as it weakens it and may cause it to split or break. The easiest way to prevent this is to store the gun in a muzzle-down position. With the configuration of gun racks and safes, this is often not practical. If possible, store the gun in a muzzle-down position for two days to one week after cleaning. Gravity will force most of the oils and solvents to run to the end of the barrel, where they can be wiped off. If this is not practical, then another more involved but more permanent solution is to seal the wood on the inside of the buttstock. This can be accomplished in a day or two with any of the excellent commercial sealers currently available. While this won't prevent the oils and solvents from getting into the buttstock, it will provide a level of protection to the wood. Also, inside the buttstock on many weapons are springs that are part of the action. These need to be removed and cleaned to prevent malfunctions. Although I currently do not own a Remington Model 1100, I keep a supply of these springs since several friends of mine have 1100s and replacement of this spring will correct many malfunctions with this gun. I have made considerable money over the years by buying malfunctioning 1100s. More times than not, a thorough cleaning and the replacement of this $8 spring will have the gun functioning flawlessly. I have then resold the 1100 for a considerable profit.

After the cleaning is completed at Level Three, the gun should be properly lubricated and reassembled. Again, the amounts of lubricant used should be much less than you would think. I use a total of ten drops of FP-10 on a gas-operated semi-auto shotgun. One drop is placed on each of the guide rails, one drop on the trigger spring, one drop on the safety, and six drops on the magazine tube. I spread the six drops on the magazine tube around with my fingers and reassemble the gun. After the exterior has been wiped down, the gun is ready for storage.

At this level, special attention should be paid to the buttstock and forend. Cleaning solvents should never be used to clean the wood. Even with modern finishes, these can still seep into and soften or damage the wood. Any good commercial wood cleaner can be used to clean the wood. An old toothbrush is useful for cleaning the checkering and other small places. Any good wood polish can be used to add a polish to the wood; just be sure to check the ingredients and read the label warnings. A friend of mine used a product on the polyurethane finish on his gun. Several months later, he noticed areas of discoloration on the wood. *Then* he read the warning label and discovered that this cleaner and polish should not be used on polyurethane finishes.

LEVEL FOUR

A Level Four cleaning is very similar to a Level Three, except there is an additional step of adding a protectant or preservative for long-term storage. Anyone who has served in the military has had the pleasure of dealing with a lovely substance named Cosmoline. This greasy, oily, wax-like substance did what it was supposed to do: cover every millimeter of a weapon's surface inside and out to prevent rust and moisture. It did the job very well, as anyone who was handed a Cosmoline-covered weapon can attest. Getting it off was another matter. Armorers had all kinds of tricks, like gasoline or special cleaning solvents. Recruits and boots were stuck with hot water, cloths, and lots of physical labor. Cosmoline is still available, and if a gun is going to be stored and not used for a long period of time, it is an excellent material to use.

Most of us don't want to go through the extensive cleaning Cosmoline requires when we want to use the gun again. Fortunately, any good storage lubricant or grease can be used on the gun to protect it during long-term storage. The gun should still be stored in a humidity-controlled environment since moisture is still the enemy.

An easy preservative is one I was introduced to by a hunting guide along the Texas gulf coast. His guns were exposed daily to salt air and water, and even in the off-season, the humidity runs so high it can rust a gun stored in a safe or even in an open rack. He uses a high-quality car wax on the metal parts of the gun, both inside and out. Designed to protect the finish on your car, these are almost impervious to moisture. I've seen him wash the mud off his gun with a garden hose, and the water just beaded on the metal. Prior to the season, he cleans the interior parts with kerosene or white gasoline and lubricates the gun as needed. He has one Model 1100 Remington that has had this treatment for over twenty years, and although it shows lots of wear, there is no rust to be found anywhere on it.

I have used this same wax on the outside metal of a weapon with a good preservative grease on the interior parts. When combined with a high-quality wood cleaner and preservative, it will keep your gun impervious to moisture for years. Hopefully, though, you will not be doing this to your hunting shotgun because you should be using it extensively for practice during the off-season.

TRANSPORTATION

How your gun is transported to the field or the range is a matter of personal preference, but it may be restricted by state or local laws. When I pheasant hunt in Iowa, for example, local law requires all guns being transported to be unloaded and cased or broken down.

Guns should be completely unloaded while being transported. While this should be an obvious safety rule for all of us, it is not always followed. A blue grouse–hunting friend in Colorado was accidentally killed because he violated this rule. He was hunting by himself, but the evidence showed he had placed his loaded gun on the floor of his Toyota Land Cruiser with the muzzle up. He was hunting with a year-old German shorthair that was not restrained in the cabin of the truck. Either the dog knocked the safety off or the gun was placed in the truck with the safety off. Either way, the results were the same. He had apparently seen some grouse from the road and parked the truck. As he was opening the door, he pulled the gun towards him by the barrel. The excited dog was jumping around on the front seat. The dog's paw managed to trip the trigger and the gun fired a load of No. 6s into Jim's neck and face, killing him instantly. When he didn't show up by sundown, his wife, who was one of our local EMS volunteers, called the sheriff's office and we started a search. I was a member of the local search-and-rescue team, and since I knew the areas where Jim grouse hunted, I was assigned leader of one of the teams. Unfortunately, it was my team that found him, and it takes a lot out of you when you

A soft case for transporting shotguns.

have to stand and watch as the crime scene is processed before wrapping and transporting the body of a friend. Jim was a very safety-conscious hunter, but this one series of mistakes with a loaded gun cost him his life.

Besides the safety issue, transporting a gun loose in a vehicle can cause damage to the gun. Not just the dents, dings, and scratches, but some serious damage. I know of several bent barrels, broken bolt handles, and even plugged barrels that have resulted from a gun being loose in a vehicle.

So what type of case should you use? A soft case will protect the finish of the gun and in some instances, especially with foam-filled soft cases, will protect the gun from more serious damage. I used these to transport guns in vehicles for a number of years and they worked very well. They are the least expensive way to protect your gun.

Next are the hard cases. These may be made of plastic or metal. Designed to protect the gun against the violence of airline baggage handlers, they have thickly padded foam interiors and good locks and hinges. The biggest drawback to these for a transportation case is their size. They are big and bulky. If you were going to use one of these as your transportation case in the field, I would suggest you use a single gun case or even a breakdown-style case. Get one that fits your gun well. Unfortunately, these are often made for the longest possible gun, and there will be lots of excess room inside when your shorter upland gun is placed in the case.

It may sound silly, but you should also make sure the case will fit in the vehicle you will be using in the area that you want to store the case. I drive a full-size GMC Yukon. The area between the rear wheel wells is 48 inches wide.

A hard plastic case for transporting shotguns.

I cannot put most hard cases in this area crossways since most of them are 50 to 54 inches long. A friend of mine has a small single-cab pickup. His hard gun cases will not fit behind the seat in the cab. When driving, the cases are in the open pickup bed. When he stops somewhere, he has to take the cases out of the bed and put them in the cab. Since they won't fit behind the seat, they are laid across the front seat and are very visible to anyone outside the vehicle. They offer good protection for his guns, but poor protection against possible theft.

Another type of hard case is the one designed as a scabbard for a single weapon. These may be made out of stiff saddle leather or molded plastic. Designed to protect the gun while on horseback or an ATV, they provide excellent protection for the gun. They are usually smaller and handier than the large multi-gun cases. Adjustable for size, they can be used for guns of different styles and action types. My veterinarian and hunting buddy Carl has several of these, and he has used them to transport guns all over the United States by car, horseback, and airplane. The cases show years of wear and tear, but they still protect the guns inside.

Now, I am well known for making poor investments. It is said that even a blind pig finds an acorn every now and then, and even I make a wise investment on occasion. One of the best investments I ever made was in a storage system for my truck that was specifically designed to transport guns and gear. There are a number of different systems available, but the one I chose is made by TruckVault. It is custom-made to my vehicle, and I can have four guns and all of the associated gear in it; and from the outside of the vehicle, nothing is visible. This is a valuable security issue and a safety issue also. My TruckVault is considered a safe under my homeowner's insurance policy.

I have stated before that I have driven what are now called SUVs for almost thirty years. I love this type of vehicle, but one thing that has always

The author's GMC Yukon with the TruckVault installed.

bothered me is the lack of storage space for all of the gear that an outdoors-
man carries on a regular basis. Tools, toolboxes, towing gear, ropes, etc. are
usually carried in a loose and haphazard manner in the rear cargo compart-
ment. This can be an important safety issue in an accident because each of
these items becomes a projectile. For a large part of my police career, I specialized in accident investigation. I worked several fatal accidents over the years
where one of these items became a deadly missile and struck the driver or a
passenger with sufficient force to kill. One case involved a relatively low-
speed intersection collision involving a Chevrolet Suburban and a pickup
truck. The Suburban struck the pickup broadside. Everyone in the Suburban
was seat-belted in and should have survived with very minor injuries. However, a 6-volt camping lantern that had been loose in the rear of the Suburban
struck the lady sitting in the front passenger seat. Even at less than 30 miles
per hour at impact, the lantern was moving with enough force to crush the
back of the lady's skull and kill her.

   With my TruckVault, I can keep all of the articles I normally carry stored
where they cannot become projectiles. I speak from experience here. I rolled
my Yukon in an accident in 2005, and although the exterior and the interior of
the TruckVault were damaged enough that the unit had to be replaced, the
two guns and all of the gear in the TruckVault was undamaged and remained
in the TruckVault.

Without a TruckVault or similar storage system, all of these items would be carried loose in the back end of the truck.

STORAGE

For years, there were two common ways to store guns. They were either stuck in a closet or displayed in the open on gun racks or in a wood-and-glass cabinet. These methods are still in use, but in the litigious society of today and with many laws requiring that weapons be secured, these methods are becoming less and less common. There are several ways to store your guns that are both safe and secure.

A lockable, hard gun case is a good, relatively inexpensive choice.

All of the items safely stored in the TruckVault.

The unloaded gun or guns can be placed in the case, the case locked and then stored in a location not visible to casual visitors. An additional level of security can be added by using individual trigger locks or cable locks on the individual weapons.

Probably the most common type of storage system today, especially for those of us who own what the news media delights in calling arsenals, is a gun safe. These protect the guns not only from theft but also from fire and

Miss Molly, a dog box, and a TruckVault.

even flood damage. They are expensive but so are your guns, and they provide a confident level of security against theft and misuse. The cost of a gun safe can often be recovered by the reduction in homeowner insurance premiums. The space you have for it and your budget only limit the type and quality of the safe you choose.

I have and use a gun safe. My biggest complaint about them is lack of convenience. When you get a safe fully loaded with long guns, often the only way to take one out or place one in is by completely unpacking and re-packing the safe. Otherwise, you will be constantly bumping the guns against one another, which adds to the dents, dings, and scratches. High-quality safes are available from a number of different companies, and it is just a matter of shopping for the size, model, and color that you want. A good gun safe will run several thousands of dollars, but it is a worthwhile investment.

Depending on the climate in your area, you may wish to have some type of system in the safe that controls the inside humidity. These safes are usually airtight, but moisture that gets in can still damage your guns. There are numerous types of these devices available, and, again, it is a matter of personal preference and cost as to which type you choose.

Proper maintenance, transportation, and storage of your gun will extend your enjoyment of the weapon, prolong the gun's useable life, and protect your investment. It also adds a level of confidence to know your weapons are safe and secure when you are not using them.

13 Off-Season Practice

You have probably figured out by now that I love to bird hunt. I love the excitement, the camaraderie, and the fun of going afield with my dogs and my shotguns. In my home state, I can enjoy hunting wild birds from the first of September when the dove season opens through the end of February when the quail season closes. I can enjoy bird hunting the other six months of the year also.

How? There are many different ways. Working my dogs in the field with or without live birds. Shooting various clay-target games. There are even some pest species of birds and animals that can be hunted year-round in many states. There are extended seasons on licensed and affordable hunting preserves throughout the United States. Looking at the various off-season practices available, I bet we can find at least one that will have you thinking: I need to try that!

Shotgun games are a fun social activity and a great way to hone your skills for hunting season. BROWNING ARMS

CLAY-TARGET GAMES

Before you start shooting clay-target games, you need to make a decision. Are you shooting these games to improve your field shooting or to be a competitor and finish in the money? It is unfortunate, but this is the way it is in clay-target sports today. I have had experience with several shooting sports that began as good practice and ended up as specialized competition. Back in the 1980s when I was an active participant in IPSC (International Practical Shooting Confederation), the sport developed into two classes called the "Gamesmen" and the "Martial Artists."

Unfortunately, the IPSC became so gadget- and gear-oriented that many new shooters were discouraged when they tried to compete with stock guns, practical holsters, and factory ammo. Even the Martial Artists, of which I was a member, got tired of contributing our match fees to the Gamesmen with their tricked-out competition guns. Many quit the sport of shooting completely or switched their shooting games.

Trap, skeet, and sporting clays all began as off-season clay-target games developed by hunters to practice for field shots. All have digressed into highly competitive, specialized games that require special guns and gear to be a ranking competitor. Of course, any game that gets you and your gun out breaking targets is good for your basic skills. You learn lead, follow-through, and how to compensate for varying angles and bird speeds. You are training your mental computer (brain) and your muscles to do what is needed for your load of shot to connect with the bird, either clay or feathered. This is good practice and well worth the time and money spent, even if you do not care about prizes or rankings.

I am still a Martial Artist, and although I shoot in competitions and own several guns set up just for competition, I use the same techniques and equipment that I use in the field. My competition guns often find themselves in the dove fields when the season opens, and I have even used them on waterfowl hunts. I don't use them on other upland birds because of their weight, which becomes burdensome to carry.

TRAP

Originally shot with actual pigeons being released from boxes (traps), this game is still very popular in Europe and in some areas of the United States. Pigeons make a very challenging and demanding target, and live bird shooting is a very competitive, high-dollar sport.

In the American clay-target version of this sport, a shooter shoots from one of five positions at yardages ranging from 16 through 27 yards. Five shots are fired at each of five positions on the range. The shooter starts with a pre-

American Trap Field

Point B is where the center line
of the traphouse and the center line
of the trap machine intersect.

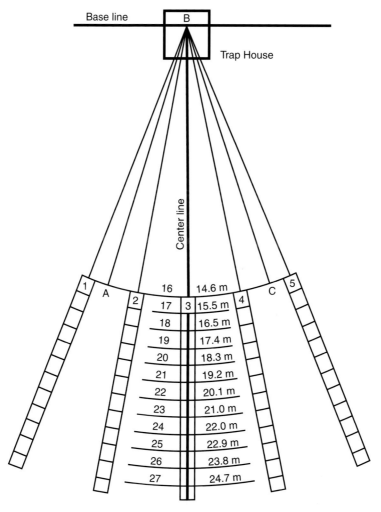

Yards (meters) from B
Diagram 1
Trapfield and firing positions

mounted gun, and when he calls for the target, it is launched from the trap house at varying angles. Most of the time the bird is broken in the 30- to 35-yard range. As the shooter becomes more proficient, he is moved back to longer yardages (handicaps) and eventually ends up shooting from the 27-yard line, where even a fast shot will be breaking birds in the 50-yard range. Breaking 100 straight birds is not unusual in American Trap, and at any match, there will be multiple shoot-offs to break the 100-bird ties.

When shot with a low (not pre-mounted) gun, trap is excellent training for the upland hunter who wants to be able to consistently hit low-flying targets at a straight-away or varying angle. Hold your gun as you would when approaching a dog on point or when following a flushing dog that is working game. The bottom of the buttstock should be at about belt level and the barrels should be pointing up at about a 45-degree angle and straight ahead. As you call for the bird, begin bringing the gun up to your shooting position. As you acquire the target, your gun should be in position and ready to shoot. Then you take the necessary lead and pull the trigger. This helps train your brain and your muscles to handle the gun and calculate the leads and speed required to connect with the target. Now shooting with a low gun will probably not put you in the money at a registered match, but you can become sur-

David Guinn's first taste of a 28 gauge.

prisingly quick and accurate. Back when I shot registered trap, I shot with a low gun and I did relatively well in my class, even in registered events.

Trap is primarily shot with a 12 gauge, but for practice, any gauge can be used. Normally loads of No. 7½ or No. 8 are used. For pattern density and performance, I would recommend you use a quality target load from any number of different manufacturers. The chokes most commonly used are Modified or Full. I have shot every gauge at trap, and believe me, it is a real challenge to shoot trap with a 28 or 410 gauge.

A few rounds of trap with your heavy hunting coat will tell you also if you need to make some modifications in your length of pull as discussed in another chapter. Many trap leagues are open all year, so a winter day at the trap range with your upland shotgun and clothing will tell you if you need to make some changes.

SKEET

Skeet began as a target game by and for hunters. Originally, one trap was used, and there were twelve positions similar to hours on the clock where birds were shot. For safety reasons, skeet developed using two traps: a high house and a low house. Shooters fire from eight positions around the field. A shooter begins a round of skeet at station one. There he shoots a high-house bird, followed by a low-house bird. While still at station one, the shooter calls for a double where the high-house and low-house birds are launched simultaneously. The shooter then moves to station two, where the same sequence is shot. Individual high and low birds are shot at stations three, four, and five. Singles and doubles are shot again at stations six and seven. Station eight is in the middle of the field, and there the shooter shoots a single from both the high and low house. After the first missed bird, the shooter can take an option shot. This totals twenty-five shells for a round of skeet.

Skeet is excellent training for the hunter. It requires rapid gun movement, and the targets are shot at angles from almost straightaway to 90 degrees. I would caution against using a pre-mounted gun if you are practicing to become a better field shot. Watch a competition skeet shoot sometime. The shooters all start with a pre-mounted gun, and since the target flight is known, they will do several practice swings before calling for the bird. There are also contortions done to get the gun in exactly the same position for each shot. Now I am not belittling competition shooters, but real birds don't give you the time to perform all these preparations.

Again, if shot without your shotgun being pre-mounted, this game is excellent practice for hunters. Although the yardage is short (the longest skeet shot is at 21 yards), the speed and flight of the bird require quick, consistent,

Skeet Field

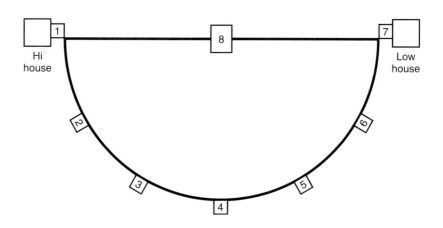

and efficient gun handling. New shooters watching a competitive skeet match will be amazed at the speed of the competitors with their pre-mounted guns. They seem to often break targets as soon as they appear. This level of performance is only achieved through years of practice and thousands upon thousands of targets.

The hunter who wishes to improve his field skills needs to forget about speed, however, and concentrate on the target. Breaking the target is what it is all about, whether you break it as it first appears or further down range. Back when I taught firearms courses in law enforcement, I used several different phrases to get this message across. One that I used was, "You can never miss fast enough." Another was that speed is fine, but accuracy is final. I *always* taught accuracy first, and then we worked on developing the speed. I used to walk up and down the line saying, "Take your time and hit, but do it quick!" In an after-action debriefing of one of my students who had just been involved in a shoot-out, he told me that as he was drawing and bringing his gun up to defend his life, he heard my voice in his mind saying that phrase.

The same applies to shotgun shooting either on clay birds or game. Each shooter needs to develop his accuracy (ability to hit), and then the speed will come as he gets smoother. Each person will develop a speed of his own. You cannot rush this. If you break targets at a certain distance, you cannot speed up your shot and break them quicker without giving up accuracy. As you practice accuracy, your speed will increase.

Competition skeet shooters know within a yard where they will break the target. I shoot skeet with a low gun, but I still know within a yard of where I will break the target. Yes, the target distance is different for me than it is for a shooter with a pre-mounted gun, but I still know that if I do everything right, I will break the target in a certain place. If I miss or break the target at another position on the field, I know not only that I have done something wrong but also exactly what I did wrong. This may include slowing or stopping my swing, lifting my head off of the stock, or concentrating on the barrel instead of the target.

Skeet allows you to shoot four different gauges: 12, 20, 28, and 410. Standard skeet loads use No. 9 shot, but skeet can be shot with target loads in 9, $8^{1}/_{2}$, 8, or even $7^{1}/_{2}$. Normally, skeet guns have very open chokes, but your Improved Cylinder or even Modified Choked field gun will work fine. For a real challenge, try shooting a round of skeet with a Full choke. You really have to be in the zone to hit the target with the small pattern of a full choke at normal skeet ranges.

Station 2 on the skeet field.

Many clubs will allow you to do some different games on a skeet field. Some of the variations my friends and I do on a regular basis are half-station skeet, dove-bucket skeet, and reverse skeet. In half-station skeet (also called off-the-pad), a regular round of skeet is shot, but it is shot from a position in between the regular shooting stations. This changes the angles and distances and adds a new level of difficulty and fun to the game.

Dove-bucket skeet began with a comment made by one of my shooting/hunting buddies a couple of years ago. We were set up at a waterhole in some low weeds, sitting on our dove buckets. If you stood up to shoot, the birds flared off or dived, making for difficult and even unsafe shots. From the sitting position, most of the birds were coming into the water. Shooting from a sitting position is different than shooting standing up and requires practice. We kicked around the idea of a way to practice using our dove buckets, and a few stations at the skeet field showed us how much fun this could be. Now we have a dove-bucket shoot a few weeks before dove season opens to raise money for our 4-H shooting programs. Very few straight twenty-fives are shot.

Reverse skeet is a standard round of skeet with two exceptions. First, it must be shot with a low gun. Second, all of the stations and birds are shot in reverse order. We start at station eight with a low-house bird and rotate around the field shooting a regular round of skeet in reverse. This challenges your mental and physical abilities to the max, because even though you are shooting the same birds, your mind wants to tell you they are different.

SPORTING CLAYS

First developed in England in the 1970s as a hunter's game, sporting clays crossed the Atlantic and was enthusiastically welcomed by American shooters. Sporting clays has probably done more for the shotgun sports than any other game. I know a number of shooters who shoot sporting clays as recreation instead of playing golf or tennis. These shooters are not hunters, but they love shooting sporting clays and have become supporters of the rights granted us by the Constitution to own and use our guns.

Any sporting clays course is challenging. The typical sporting clay course will have ten shooting stations. At each station the shooter is presented with five pairs of targets from hidden traps. These birds will be at varying angles and ranges and are either launched simultaneously or as a report pair, where the second target is launched at the shot at the first.

Not only are the presentations challenging, but this game is also shot with different clay targets. Each of these presents a different flight pattern and can make the simplest target presentation difficult. The standard clay target used in some presentations is $4\frac{1}{2}$ inches (108mm) in diameter and approximately 1 inch thick. The next clay target used in a sporting clay course is the midi target, which is $3\frac{1}{2}$ inches (90mm) in diameter and $\frac{7}{8}$ inches thick. Then there is the mini, or flying aspirin. This target is only $2\frac{3}{8}$ inches in diameter and $\frac{3}{4}$ inches thick. Although launched at the same speed as a standard target, the minis create an optical illusion of moving very fast. The eye sees a faster moving target and tells the brain to tell the muscles to speed up the shot. Most of the time this will result in a miss. Even though you know better, it is quite hard to tell your brain this target is *not* moving any faster and that the same lead that will break a standard target will also break a mini.

A sporting clays range is a great place to get together with friends and shoot your favorite hunting guns. At the 2006 Flatwater shoot, the group used two pumps, four side-by-sides, and four over-and-unders.

A rocket target is the same diameter (108mm) as a standard target but is only ³/₄ inches thick. Rocket targets present the interesting illusion that they are traveling slower than they actually are. I have seen many shooters be totally thrown off their game by a rocket target or two on a station.

Battues (pronounced baa-too) are also the same diameter as the standard target but are only ³/₈ inches thick. Commonly called flying razor blades, they can be very hard to see when flying parallel to the ground. Fortunately, their thin height causes them to turn in the air, offering a full-on shot.

The rabbit target is the same diameter and size as a standard target but has a thicker rim and center that allow it to be rolled along the ground. These targets will bounce into the air, and more than once I have shot a flying rabbit. When presented straight-on or straight-away, these can be especially difficult, for there is a tendency to over- or under-shoot the target.

When you mix these different targets into different presentations, you have a game that will definitely improve your shooting skills. Each shot is representative of a game shot, and the ranges may be from 5 to beyond 50 yards. The course designer has an almost unlimited array of presentations that are restricted only by his imagination and deviousness. Every sporting clay course I have ever shot was a challenge and a learning experience. It was also excellent practice for using my shotgun in the field.

Five-stand sporting clays is a fun game and great way to practice a variety of types of shots that you might encounter in the field. WINCHESTER

Another variation of sporting clays is five stand. In this game, the shooter fires from one of the five shooting positions (stands) set up in a row on the field. Anywhere from six to twelve traps may be utilized to present targets, and all of the different target sizes and styles will be used. In a typical five-stand course, the shooter fires at a single bird and two simultaneous pairs at each station. Five stand is very popular since it does not require the amount of space a standard sporting clay course will require. A good and challenging five-stand course can be set up on a standard skeet field with only the addition of extra traps.

Sporting clays is usually shot with a 12 gauge, but any gauge can be used. Good target loads in No. 8 or 7½ shot will break any sporting clay target. Choke choices may vary according to the presentation, but don't get into the habit of thinking that you need to change chokes and loads on every presentation. I did this when I first started shooting sporting clays and many other shooters do so, thinking it will give them an advantage. An instructor gave me a useful piece of advice. He told me you wouldn't miss a bird because of which choke or load you have in your gun. You will miss a bird when you don't handle the gun properly. Now, it is very rare that I will change chokes or loads during a course. If shooting an over-and-under, I will usually be using Improved Cylinder and Improved Modified, and if shooting a single-barrel gun, I will usually be using a Light Modified choke. I prefer 1-ounce loads in the 12 gauge and will use either No. 7½ or No. 8 shot.

No matter which game you choose to shoot, I would offer two pieces of advice. First, do not become discouraged with your scores when you first begin shooting. You are shooting these games to learn, and you learn from your mistakes. I have seen very few shooters who broke more than 50 percent of the birds their first time out. Most will be much less. Don't let this discourage you. You are there to learn how to be a better shot, and you will often require lots of spent primers and burned powder before you begin putting it all together. When you first start, you will be surprised when you hit a bird and not have a clue as to why you missed a bird. As you improve, you will know what to do right to hit the bird, and you will know what you did wrong when you miss one.

My second piece of advice is to spend the time and money to get some professional instruction. There are instructors located all over the country for all of the clay-target games. A professional instructor can recognize your bad habits and help you correct them. They can also recognize your good points and build on them. A friend of mine who attended a week-long school put it rather succinctly when he said the thousand dollars he spent on the school was worth ten thousand dollars worth of shells.

INFORMAL PRACTICE

You and a couple of buddies with a hand trap or small mounted trap can set up some challenging target presentations. Most folks using one of these will

A few boxes of shells is a small price to pay to make sure your next upland hunting isn't a bust because you can't hit the birds. WINCHESTER

primarily shoot straight-away targets and this is good training, but don't limit yourself. A little bit of ingenuity and imagination can offer some fun games. Safety should always be the first and primary concern, but some interesting target presentations can be done. Prior to each dove season, a few friends and I head out to an old gravel pit with our shotguns, ammo, a couple of cases of clay birds, and several hand traps. The shooter positions in the bottom of the pit, which is about 25 feet deep. Well back from the edge and on both sides is a thrower with a hand trap. When the shooter yells ready, one or both of the throwers toss a bird. The angles and flight patterns are very similar to doves, and since the shooter doesn't know where the bird is coming from, it is excellent training to pick up the bird and hit it. It may sound easy, but the highest score shot to date has been a twenty.

PEST SPECIES

There are a number of different pest species that can be hunted year-round with a shotgun. Check with your state game department to find out what species are considered pests or varmints in your state. Some of the species that typically can be hunted are feral pigeons, starlings, crows, rabbits, and rats. Each offers unique target opportunities, and you will often expend more rounds in a single afternoon than you will expend at wild game throughout an entire season.

Pigeons

Some of my favorite off-season days are spent shooting feral pigeons. These birds are tough and challenging targets. My friends and I have hunted them around silos, farms, grain fields, and feed lots. A pigeon has the maneuverability of a dove and surpasses a rooster pheasant in its ability to absorb lead and keep flying. I have often said that if pheasants were as hard to kill as pigeons, we would hunt pheasants with 20mm anti-aircraft guns! Although expensive, pigeons are a great training ground for the use of nontoxic shot in your favorite shotgun. Investing in a case of nontoxic shot and a couple of afternoons shooting pigeons will make you very familiar with the leads and angles required to hit with nontoxic shot, which often differs from lead. Pigeons are disease carriers for people and livestock and many farmers will welcome a reasonable request to shoot pigeons.

Starlings

Starlings are also disease carriers, especially for livestock, and are unbelievably destructive to crops and feed sources. Many dairies and feedlots will have starling problems, and if you can obtain permission, you will have a wing-shooting bonanza that will rival Mexican or South American dove shooting.

I have literally come home from an afternoon of starling shooting around a feedlot with my arms too tired to lift a gun. Four or five cases of ammo can be expended in one afternoon! Any gauge gun can be used and with any choke combination. I prefer No. 8 shot on starlings for the pattern density, but $7\frac{1}{2}$s, $8\frac{1}{2}$s, or even 9s can be used. My favorite gun for starling shooting is a 28 gauge, since it is light in recoil and doesn't beat me up when firing a thousand rounds in an afternoon.

Rabbits

Although considered a game animal in many states, others consider both cottontail and jackrabbits a pest species that may be hunted year-round. I have mentioned before that jackrabbits are tenacious and challenging targets. Their movements are unpredictable and can be very fast. They are good training for the shotgunner since proper gun movement and lead are required to connect. In some states, cottontails may be hunted all year, and a dashing, darting bunny is a tough target for even the most experienced shotgunner.

Rats

When I was a kid, many town dumps would burn trash on a regular basis. This was the time to head out with the shotgun for some rat shooting. This day and age, most town dumps are landfills that not only prohibit burning but shooting as well. Good rat shooting can still be found, however, at informal dumps and in areas where excess or damaged grain is stored. Permission must be obtained from the landowner, but the asking is well worth the challenge of these tough and tricky targets.

SHOOTING PRESERVES

The best way to train bird dogs is to get them into lots and lots of birds. The best way to become a good field shot is to shoot lots and lots of birds. In today's world, though, few dogs or gunners get enough exposure to birds during a typical season to become proficient. This is when a shooting preserve provides the necessary exposure. Most preserves are open for six or more months out of the year, and although the initial cost may seem expensive, it is worth the investment for the experience it provides. Several of my friends wonder why I spend so much time and money on out-of-state hunting trips, where the results may be uncertain, when for the same amount of money I could spend a number of days shooting birds at a local preserve. I enjoy these trips for the camaraderie of friends, the experience of the birds, and the general enjoyment of the trip away from the computer and telephone. When I have a young dog I am working, though, I will spend the time and money at a shooting preserve to get the dog into birds and to sharpen my shooting skills on actual birds instead of just on clay targets. These preserves are very valuable for the new shooter who needs to get the experience on birds just as a new pup needs to get experience on birds.

PRACTICE AT HOME

Even if you can't go shooting, you can still improve your shooting skills at home. One of the key elements to any sport is muscle memory. Golfers will hit Wiffle balls or practice on putting greens in the living room. They are training their muscles for what they need out on the course. Shotgun shooters can do the same thing. Ten minutes a day mounting and swinging your shotgun will make drastic improvements in your shooting when you do get to fire at birds.

Take an unloaded shotgun and stand in the middle of a room where you have enough space to mount and swing the gun. Focus on a point on the seam where the wall and ceiling come together. Pick a natural point about halfway along the wall. Always check to make sure that your gun is unloaded. Now, hold your shotgun with the bottom of the buttstock just at or slightly below belt level. The barrels should be pointing straight ahead at about a 45-degree

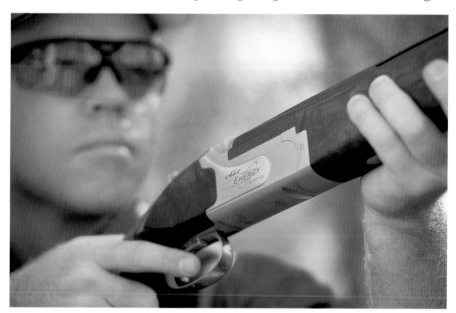

Range time is essential for training your eyes to see the target—whether it's clay or covered with feathers. WINCHESTER

angle. This is the same position you and the gun should be in when approaching a dog on point. Then bring the gun up and keep it moving along the seam from one end to the other. Pull the trigger as the gun passes the halfway point, and then keep swinging along the wall/ceiling seam. This is teaching you to properly mount the gun, to start it swinging, to concentrate on pulling the trigger at a certain point, and to keep the gun swinging after the trigger is pulled. Stopping your swing before, during, or after you pull the trigger is probably the most common mistake made by a shotgun shooter. This little exercise teaches both your muscles and your brain. My muscles got trained using this little exercise years ago. My brain is still learning.

It is a rare week during the year when I do not spend a day or two doing something that requires a shotgun. Even during the bird seasons, I may run out during an afternoon for a few rounds of skeet when my schedule prohibits a day of hunting. During the off-season, I shoot skeet, sporting clays, and five stand several times a week and usually manage a pest-bird shoot about once a month.

Yes, this requires large amounts of ammunition, which is why we will discuss reloading in the next chapter. Shooting is my recreational sport and hobby, whether it is with a shotgun, handgun, rifle, or even a BB or pellet gun. I don't play golf or tennis; I shoot. I may expend thousands of rounds of shotgun ammo during the course of a year, but I enjoy every one of them! As the old advertisement said: Try it! You'll like it!

14 Handloading for Hunting

Although done on the same equipment and with similar components, most people don't realize there is a significant difference between reloading and handloading. The two terms are often used interchangeably. There is a big difference between the two to us purists, however.

Reloading is duplicating a factory shell with the same or similar components and duplicating factory performance. Many shooters are under the impression that you cannot duplicate a factory shell with a reload. At one time this was true, but with modern components and equipment, it is easy to duplicate factory loads. Many loading manuals will often list a certain load as duplicating the factory load. Reloading is often done to save money, and in the past, it could be an excellent way to do so. Now, good quality target loads are available for just slightly more than it costs to reload a

Sure, you can save money reloading, but you can also customize loads to your guns and shooting activities—and hit more targets.
BROWNING ARMS

box of shells, so the economics for the casual shooter are not as great as they once were. Of course, when you are firing thousands and thousands of rounds a year as many competition shooters do, it is still economical to reload instead of shooting all factory ammo.

Like many other shooters, I have discovered another aspect to reloading that is seldom mentioned. This is the relaxation factor. My career in law enforcement was a series of high-stress assignments either in patrol or investigations. When I was uptight, I always enjoyed going out shooting for relaxation. When you are working a shift that ends at 3:00 in the morning, this is not possible and some nights I was just too wound up to go to sleep. On those occasions, I spent time at the bench reloading shotshells. Some nights it took only a box or two of shells to relax. Other nights I loaded a case of shells and the sun was coming up before I had wound down enough to sleep. Either way, it was a relaxing extension of my favorite sport that could be done in the convenience of my home. I usually kept a reloading press all set up on the bench, so all I had to do was organize my components and begin loading. Believe me, it is a great stress reliever and beats watching late-night television.

I am not going to list specific loads and their components in this chapter. There are numerous reloading manuals that provide all of the information you will need to duplicate factory ammo or to tailor loads to a specific need. There is one very important safety issue to bring up here before moving on. The publishers of reloading manuals have access to pressure-testing equipment, and they test thousands of combinations to obtain the information included in the manuals. Never, ever deviate from the published data using the listed components!

I have had the privilege of working with some now-available powders when they were still in the experimental stages. I still followed the data developed by the powder technicians at the powder company when developing loads. There are literally thousands of combinations of powder, primer, case, and wad that can be used in just one gauge and shot weight. The powder companies have spent thousands of man-hours testing all of the possibilities, and the data published in their manual includes the combinations that work well and are safe for pressures and velocities. I am amazed by the lackadaisical attitude of some reloaders. I have seen reloaders who use any case with their given choice of components and others who believe that all wads, primers, and even powders are interchangeable. All primers have a different ignition rate and all powders have a different burn rate. Each wad is designed for a certain type or make of case and a given load. Interchanging anything in the load data is a recipe for disaster. I have seen numerous accidents with reloads, and often when the case is investigated to the fullest, it is not the gun, the components, or the manufacturer of any of these; it is the person who assembled the shell.

One instance of substitution is a classic example. A person who had reloaded for years ran out of his favorite shotgun powders while reloading some shells for a match. The shotgun powder he was using is one of the faster burning shotgun powders, so he went to the reloading book and found the fastest burning powder for centerfire pistol cartridges. He figured that powder was powder, so he reloaded the remainder of his shotshell cases with 19 grains of pistol powder instead of the 19 grains of shotgun powder. The gun actually fired two rounds of these excessive loads before it blew up on the third round. The gun was completely destroyed, and the shooter lost his left hand, part of his arm, his right eye, and required extensive reconstructive surgery on his face. He sued the makers of the components individually and collectively, the gun manufacturer, and even the range where the accident took place. The powder company tested his normal load, and it developed 10,300 pounds per square inch (psi) of pressure. His "replacement" load developed 33,800 psi of pressure. When it was proven in court that it was his negligence and not the fault of any of the defendants, he lost the case. Pardon my cynicism, but every once in a while the American justice system does work!

How can a handloader improve on the factory ammunition available? In some instances, you cannot. If you are shooting a given load with a certain velocity, shot weight, and shot size that is readily available, it is seldom that a handload will surpass a factory load in performance. For example, if you are shooting a 12 gauge with a 1,200 fps load made up of $1^1/_8$ ounces of No. $7^1/_2$ shot, you will find that many factory target loads will perform well in your gun. One brand may perform slightly better than another, so you need to test various ones. This is a favorite target load and is also an excellent dove and quail load. The only reason to reload this load is to save money over factory ammo.

Let's say, however, that you would like this load in some different shot sizes. Maybe No. 6 shot for sharptail grouse or in No. 7 shot for western quail. This is when being a handloader pays off. You can take any load combinations available and custom tailor it for your gun and your hunting. By the way, those are my favorite loads for grouse and western quail when I am carrying a 12 gauge! I have mentioned before my preference for No. 5 shot for pheasant. For years, even in 12-gauge loadings, No. 5 was hard to find in factory loads. If I wanted to shoot No. 5 in a 16 or 20 gauge, these shells weren't even made. As a result, I handloaded all of the shells for my different gauges. By handloading, I could use plated shot (which was not available in factory loads) and load to the velocity and shot weight that I wanted to use. I could also reload equivalent target loads for off-season practice.

One year was very wet with a lot of rainfall, and the early-season cover in our quail country was as thick as I had sever seen it. Even on a covey rise, it was more like grouse hunting where you shoot through the vegetation and hope to connect with the bird since there are no openings through which to shoot. I had loaded some No. 9 shot for starling control in 12-, 16-, and 20-gauge shells. These worked very well in the thickets on quail.

We had already tried No. 9 skeet loads, but these had not increased our bird-to-shell ratio. The loads I had handloaded had heavier shot charges and were at a higher velocity. They were just what we needed.

When you shoot as much 16- and 28-gauge ammunition as I do, you do a lot of handloading of specific components to tailor shells to different birds and situations. Probably 90 percent of the shells I use for hunting in either gauge are handloads. If you have never reloaded or handloaded, there is a mystery about it that frightens some people. Many is the time I have heard shooters say they would like to reload their own shells, but they are scared they would do something wrong. Yes, this should be a concern, but if you do some research before you ever load your first shell and follow listed recipes, it is not a problem.

There are some things you need to do before you ever reload your first shell or even before you buy the equipment. The very first thing to do is read! Read reloading manuals from the various powder manufacturers. Read a good informational book on reloading shotshells. There are several good ones out there, and I have not only read them, but I buy the updated ones for the information they contain. I often use these as reference books when I am researching a new handload; they are well worth the investment.

After you have read everything you can get your hands on, then you have to make some decisions. The first is to decide why are you going to reload. Are you going to do it to save money? To tailor loads? As a way to spend additional time in an activity related to shooting? All of these are good reasons, but you need to decide which is your primary goal. Next, you need to decide which gauge and load you are going to start with and use most often. Many new loaders will decide to go whole hog and load all of the different gauges they shoot, so they invest a large amount of money in presses, components, and all of the accessories needed. They are often overwhelmed by all of this and end up frustrated.

You should decide on one load and one gauge to start with. Another important point to bring up here is your selection of the cases to be used. Many new loaders want to use the cases they have acquired. If these are high-quality target cases made by Winchester, Federal, or Remington, then you are set because these are the cases you will use the most often. If you have a large quantity of promotional or seasonal load cases made by different manufacturers, take a piece of advice. Throw them in the trash and buy all of one brand of once-fired target cases to start. You will expend less time, money, and frustration by doing this than trying to reload the promotional cases. Most of them are made out of thinner plastic, and since they will vary from manufacturer to manufacturer, you will need many more components than if you stick with one brand of target cases. These thinner cases are also real pains to get proper crimps on, and the thin plastic will often bulge somewhere on the case during the crimping stage, making the shell unusable.

Your next decision is what type of press to buy. Shotshell loading presses are made by a number of different companies and they all make fine products. Shotshell presses come in two basic styles: single-stage and progressive. With a single-stage press, an individual shell is taken through all of the various stations. It is resized, deprimed, and primed; the powder and shot are added; and then usually two stages of crimping occur. The first stage starts the crimp, and the second stage does the final crimping of the shell. Each of these functions requires a pull of the handle by the person operating the machine.

With a progressive press, there is a shell at each of the stations, and one pull of the handle will perform each respective function on a shell. Either the machine or the person operating the machine then rotates the shells to the next station. All the operator has to do is add the wad, feed empty cases into the machine, and remove loaded cases from the machine. Some models even do this for you. Others have electric or hydraulic pumps operated by a foot pedal or switch so the operator does not even need to pull the handle. Progressive loaders are very fast, and they can turn out a large number of shells in a short amount of time. The drawback is that they are more complicated, and when you do have a glitch while reloading, it

MEC Sizemaster single-stage reloading press.
MEC

will require more time to correct and get operating properly again. In my experience, progressive machines also require much more time in setting up and timing to get them running smoothly and operating properly.

My recommendation to someone just getting started is to buy a single-stage machine and learn the basics of reloading. Later on, you may desire to go to a progressive machine. I own and use both. When I want to turn out a large amount of shells of a particular load for any reason, I set up my progressive machine in that gauge and go to town. I can easily and comfortably do a case of shells (250 rounds) in an hour. When I want to load a box or two of shells, or experiment with a new load on the pattern board and the chronograph, I will do this on a single-stage machine. During a year, I load more ammo on progressive machines, but much of the ammo I use in the field is loaded on my single-stage machines.

After you decide which single-stage machine you wish to purchase, there are several other things that are needed. First and foremost is a good reloading scale. I have both electronic and mechanical styles and use both. For a first scale, my recommendation would be a mechanical one. A scale is important because the various bushing charts are good recommendations of the powder charges; they are not totally accurate. Many things can affect the weight of the powder, and a bushing may be above or below the listed and required amount. Usually bushings run light, so adjustments need to be made upward to get the required powder charge. A scale is required to find out what charge your machine is throwing with a particular brand and lot number of powder. Most of the reloaders on the market have shot bars, which

MEC 9000GN progressive reloading press.
MEC

throw a certain weight of shot and have an opening for a powder bushing. Some, however, have bushings for both powder and shot. Use of a scale will help you to get your loads to the exact specifications you need.

Many things can affect the amount of powder or shot thrown. I have said before that I live in West Texas in a very dry climate. We average around 14 inches of rain a year. A good friend of mine lives in an area that averages over 60 inches of rain a year. One day we got to talking about favorite 12-gauge practice loads and discovered that we both loaded a $1\frac{1}{8}$- or 1-ounce load with $19\frac{1}{2}$ grains of Green Dot powder. In further discussion, we discovered that I was using a bushing two sizes larger than the listed one to get the desired weight on my machine. He was using a bushing one size smaller than the one listed. Now the variations in the machines and the bushings would account for some of this difference, but the difference in humidity in the areas where we live also accounted for a large part. In his high-humidity area, charges ran heavier than in my area of low humidity. There are also adjustable charge bars, which are fully adjustable for both shot and powder weights. These are a good investment, especially if you are going to be custom-tailoring loads.

Your next investment will be in components. Again, I would offer the advice to keep it simple. Start with one case, powder, and primer combination. This will also usually only require one wad, even for different weights of shot. Again, I would caution that you should *never* substitute components. You are now ready to begin loading. You will find it an enjoyable and exciting experience that enhances your shooting and enables you to shoot more. Not only will you shoot more, which will improve your skills, but you will also find there is a satisfaction and special feeling when you start taking game with shells you have loaded yourself. You have become another part of the entire hunting process, and this is always rewarding.

Another logical step from reloading is to pattern test and chronograph your loads. The first chronograph I owned was a large, bulky affair that required several hours to set up and fine tune. It cost me $700 used. Now, chronographs are self-contained units that can be set up on a standard camera tripod in less than a minute. The costs are less than $200 and many now can be directly downloaded to your computer. The effects of velocity are not as stringent with shotshells as they are with metallic cartridges, but a chronograph is still a worthy and useable tool.

More important than a chronograph, however, is a way to check the patterns of your guns and loads. Now I have mentioned patterning and pattern boards quite a bit. Many shooters claim that since the pattern board is two-dimensional, it is not a relative representation of the three-dimensional actions of the shot load and shot string. I have never found a load that performed poorly in the two dimensions of the pattern board that improved dramatically in three dimensions. Using hard or plated shot in a shot cup that completely encloses the shot charge will often shorten the shot string and provide an even, tight, and complete pattern. With soft shot and an inadequate shot cup, I don't care how much you try; this load will perform poorly in either dimension. There is currently a computer-assisted pattern board that will measure the total amount of time required for a shot string to strike a pattern and will print this information out in an easily understood formula. One of these costs in the area of $30,000 and not many are in use by the general public (or even impoverished gun writers).

So what do you need to pattern test your gun and loads? The materials required are very simple. You need some large sheets of paper, a target frame to which to attach them, and a place to shoot them. It is that simple. For years, I used a 50-yard pistol range at our police academy for my pattern testing. I bought large rolls of butcher paper for about $30 a roll. This paper was 36 inches in width, and I cut it into 36-inch squares for my pattern paper. This gave me about eighty-four pieces from one 250-foot roll at a cost of about $0.35 per sheet.

One target will not give you a good indication of your load. I have fired as few as three and as many as ten shots to develop a database. Now I usually fire five shots of a given load to get the data I need. I have portable stands that enable me to set up ten targets at the same time, so I can do two sets without having to change paper.

The standard distance for patterning is at 40 yards. This is a good place to start with any load, as it gives you a reference point using published data for percentages. You can then test the loads at the distances where you normally take your game. Again, your pattern at 40 yards is an indicator of how well the load/gun/choke combination will perform at other yardage. Most of my pheasants are taken at or around 30 yards. I test my pheasant loads in 5-yard increments from 20 to 50 yards to give me the knowledge and confidence I want when taking shots at longer or shorter ranges.

A favorite 28-gauge woodcock load barely meets Cylinder percentages on the paper at 40 yards. This load is tested from 5 yards out to 25 yards since I cannot recall ever having a shot at a woodcock past 25 yards. At 10 yards out of the Skeet tube, this load gives me a pattern almost 12 inches in diameter. This helps even a guy like me connect with a woodcock. A friend of mine had a favorite 20 gauge, and when he was introduced to grouse and woodcock hunting, he thought this gun would be perfect. We tested his favorite quail load prior to his trip to the Northeast, and it is good that we did. At 10 yards, he had a tight concentration of shot out of his Improved Cylinder barrel that measured barely 6 inches in diameter. Switching to a seasonal promotional load enabled him to have an effective load at the ranges he encountered woodcock and grouse. He was soon addicted to grouse and woodcock hunting, and we spent quite a bit of time the next year working on different loads in different shot weights and sizes for his new passion. These included special spreader loads that allowed us to use hard and plated shot but still have open and even patterns. This was a classic example of handloading giving someone the shells he needed for the game he was hunting. Without this testing and handloading, he would have been very limited in his choice of factory ammunition.

Beginning reloaders should always test their first efforts at the range—don't wait until the middle of a hunting trip to discover problems.
WINCHESTER

Not many people like to count the pellet holes in paper, but that is the essence of pattern testing. A 30-inch diameter circle is drawn around the densest part of the pattern. An additional 20-inch circle can be drawn in the center, or the circle can be divided into quadrants. Both make the counting process a little quicker and easier and both will tell you if your load is evenly distributed. I have used all three methods and still do. I use the simple 30-inch circle on my first testing of a load. If the load shows promise, I use both the quadrant and the center circle on subsequent testing. After counting the pellet holes, you need to divide by the total number of pellets in the shell to get your percentage. This same formula can be used to determine the percentage of the shot charge in each quadrant or the center core. You can use published charts to determine the number of pellets or you can individually count the pellets in a given load or charge weight. Although very, very time consuming, counting pellets from factory ammo can be extremely informative. You need to cut the shell apart, which gives you an idea of the type of wad used and the inside construction of the case. It also tells you the quality and type of shot used. I have dissected hundreds of loads and counted thousands of individual pellets. Last year I did a "shotshell round-up" for a magazine article. I had twelve cases of loads from various companies to test and use. Although some of these were from off-brand companies, I was impressed that every maker used high-quality wadding and uniform, round, and hard shot in their target loads. I have also dissected loads marketed as premium loads and that carry an accompanying high price only to find out they contained out-of-round shot of various sizes and questionable hardness. Again, one shell does not give you an average, so I usually dissect three to five shells and count the pellets.

After years of testing loads, guns, and chokes, I have discovered the only unchangeable fact is that you should never expect any given results. I have had premium loads that did not perform well and loads I thought would perform poorly that performed very well. I have also discovered that 0.05 inches of choke restriction often means little since the variation from shot to shot will be greater than the amount expected from the restriction. Again, this can only be determined by pattern testing at different ranges and with different combinations of choke, load, and gun.

When I taught hunter education classes for the Colorado Division of Wildlife, my co-instructor was a good friend and hunting partner. Colorado was an either/or state, where you hunted big game with either a bow or a gun. You could not do both. Don was an enthusiastic bowhunter and often talked about the aesthetics of the hunt when hunting with his bow. This was a major part of the enjoyment of the hunt for him. Much of the satisfaction for my rifle hunting came from spending hours at the reloading and shooting benches tailoring the most accurate and powerful load in the cartridge and gun I was using. I felt a great sense of accomplishment when I was able to take a deer or elk with one well-placed round from a cartridge I had handloaded. I still experience the same sense of accomplishment when I take a game bird with a custom-tailored handload for the gun/choke/gauge combination I am using. It adds another aspect of enjoyment to the sport. This is a fun, informational, and exciting addition to shooting, whether you call it reloading, handloading, or "rolling your own."

15 Beyond the Basics

When you have been chasing upland birds and game as long as I have, you learn there is a lot of gear available for the upland hunter. You also learn that not all of the stuff works the way the ads say it should, and after a couple of times in the field, the article is regulated to a corner of the garage and not used again. There are also the things that work better than you thought they would, and here I would offer a sage piece of advice from the late Gene Hill: "When you find something that works very well or fits just right, buy at least two more because they will either quit making it or change it."

You may be wondering what all this has to do with upland shotguns. There will be lots of times when you are out in the field in inclement weather. Wearing clothing and boots that keep you comfortable will allow you to enjoy the hunt. You may be cold and wet, but you won't be cold, wet, and miserable or hot, sweaty, and miserable. Also, some of these items, such as boots, can add to your enjoyment and your comfort, which will affect your hunt as much as your gunning skills. Years of government service wearing mandated clothing gave me lots of experience being miserable under all weather conditions. When I'm out there by choice, I dress to be warm, dry, and comfortable.

CLOTHING

What you wear for hunting is definitely a personal choice. Some hunters prefer full hunting coats. Some prefer sleeveless vests while others (myself included) wear a strap-style vest. Some favor chaps while others use faced hunting jeans or pants. Gloves are a personal choice and depend on the temperature and area you hunt. Boots are another very personal choice dictated by terrain, moisture, and individual comfort. In this chapter, I'll discuss what I wear and what I don't wear and why.

Boots

Let's start from the ground up with boots. Boots come in three basic styles. There are the lace-up boots made of leather, nylon, or a combination of the two. These come in varying heights, weights, and styles and with or without insulation. There are three criteria I use to choose a boot: comfort, protection, and weight.

An upland hunter does a lot of walking in varied terrain. The desert quail or chukar hunter may have different requirements for a boot than the fellow who spends most of his time in grouse cover and woodcock hollows. Both will do a lot of walking, though, and the fit and comfort of the boot will make a big difference by the end of the day. This was made painfully clear to me on a pheasant hunt this year. I had bought a new pair of boots and had worn them enough during the off-season that they were broken-in and comfortable. I had not worn them for eight or ten hours of steady walking, however, which I did on the first two days of the hunt. These boots were a half-size larger than my normal shoe size, and I hadn't had a problem wearing them with one pair of medium-weight socks during the breaking-in period. There was enough slip with those socks, however, that after two days of heavy walking, I had very painful blisters the size of quarters on each heel. Thicker socks and heel pads got me through the hunt, but every step was painful for the next two weeks or so until the blisters healed.

Leather boots are a must for almost all of my upland hunting. The nylon and soft ones are nice, comfortable, and lightweight, but they do not stop cactus spines. Since Spanish Dagger, Cholla, and Prickly Pear are just some of the cactus I encounter on a regular basis, I need a boot that will stop these and some of the other lovely plants I run across in the West and Southwest.

Now I know there will be a physicist or mathematician reading this that will disagree with me, but the lighter your boots the better. Back when I was in my twenties, I wore my favorite pair of Corcoran jump boots as my hunting boots also. Hey, I trained, ran, and humped many a mile of boonies with those on my feet and I loved them. Sometime around my late thirties, though, I discovered that there were lighter boots out there and that I wasn't as tired at the end of the day when I wore the lighter boots. I think it has something to do with the earth's gravity getting stronger. There was another theory advanced by my hunting buddies, but it was too bizarre to even consider. Now that I am in my fifties, the lighter the boot the better. My current love affair is with a pair of lightweight kangaroo-leather boots that weigh less than some of my sneakers. The leather is tough and turns away all of the nasties, and they are available with a number of different sole and heel designs that work in any terrain. I prefer a relatively lightweight tread for most of my hunting, but when hunting in the shale hills of Arizona, I like the heavy tread

Some of the author's favorite boot styles for a hard day in the field.

of a Vibram-style sole and heel. I have several pairs of these and I love them. I figure that if I am wearing a boot that weighs 2 pounds per pair, I have lifted 2,640 pounds of weight with each foot when I have gone a mile. If my boots weigh 4 pounds, I have lifted an additional 2,640 pounds of weight each mile.

I have a metabolism that requires I wear uninsulated boots. Gore-Tex-lined uninsulated boots work fine for all of my upland hunting. Even when hunting in wet conditions or snow I wear these, although on occasion I will wear a leather/rubber "Bean"-style boots in very wet conditions. Other folks need an insulated boot no matter what the conditions. The best way to find what works for you is to try both styles and see which is most comfortable.

The rubber/leather Bean-style boot is an old stand-by for hunters and has been for over a hundred years. Available in a number of heights and with or without insulation, the only criticism I have had with these boots over the years is that they do not have a very aggressive sole and heel, which is needed when hunting in snow-covered rocky terrain. When I lived in Colorado, I took a couple of toboggan runs down steep slopes when wearing this style of boot. Fortunately, I wasn't injured, but I did have a few scary and sometimes hilarious moments.

Some folks prefer knee-high all-rubber boots. These are great for swampy conditions, but my feet sweat too much in them. One year on a Kansas pheasant trip, we had mist and rain the first two days of the hunt. The fields were a muddy mess. A companion was wearing some knee-high rubber boots and was almost becoming obnoxious talking about how well the boots were keep-

Guns Carry Options in the Field

A good gun carry position in the field.

A good one-handed field carry.

A good, safe—yet ready—gun carry.

A weak hand one-handed carry.

ing his feet dry. The second night the temperature dropped well into the teens and stayed there for the next three days. Muddy fields became skating rinks and the wet vegetation was covered in a quarter-inch layer of ice. My friend discovered that the mild tread on the boots made them very tricky on ice and that ice particles breaking off and going into the boot from the top soon melted and had his pants soaking wet. Since the boots were uninsulated, he was soon cold, wet, and miserable. These were the only boots he had along, so part of the afternoon was spent driving several hundred miles (round trip) to a town where he could buy a pair of regular hunting boots. I usually pack three pairs of boots along on a hunt that will be for several days or more. I typically take two pairs of my Gore-Tex leather boots and one pair of the Bean-style boots. In over twenty years, these have served me well in all kinds of weather, terrain, and covers.

Pants

It is one of those strange quirks in life, but my father hated blue jeans and never owned a pair in his life that I can remember. I, on the other hand, wear blue jeans every day of the year. I wear jeans all of the time when hunting and either wear regular jeans with chaps over them or hunting jeans with a nylon facing on them. In some of my Arizona quail covers, I wear both and still get stuck! A word of advice about jeans; they're made of cotton, which is part of the reason they are so comfortable. Cotton, however, has almost no insulating capability, either wet or dry. When wet, cotton may actually steal your body heat instead of keeping it in. If you are going to be hunting in wet conditions, even heavy dew, you may not want to be wearing jeans. When they get wet, you will lose body heat unless you have on insulated underwear (not cotton). Even if the temperature is going to be in the 50s, you will have to have some insulating clothing or you may become hypothermic. When I know I'm going to be hunting in wet grass or wet conditions, I wear a pair of lightweight polypropylene long johns under my jeans. Even when wet, these will still keep you warm. These same warnings apply to even regular hunting pants, as they will usually be primarily made of cotton also.

Shirts

Shirts are a personal choice, but again, there are some recommendations I can make. While many of the newer fabrics can be very soft and very warm, some of these are made for stationary or slow-moving hunters that avoid the thick stuff. When you take some of these newer fabrics through the briars and the brambles, a new shirt becomes an old shirt in one outing. If you are wearing a coat, you can wear any style or weight of shirt under it. Since I seldom wear a coat and prefer to dress in layers, the shirt is usually my top layer. Several manufacturers make good shirts for brush busting. These will have reinforced or nylon sleeves to protect your arms from the worst of the thorns or thickets. Even in warm weather, I will usually wear a long-sleeve shirt. If you try to wear a short-sleeve shirt in the mesquite and cat claw of the Southwest and West, your arms will look like you have been branding cats by hand.

Here's an old tip I picked up from a veteran trapshooter about shirts: if your shirt has a two-button cuff, button the inside button on your strong arm. On your weak arm, button the outside button. This will keep the shirt from binding in the sleeves while swinging your gun. It doesn't sound like it would make a big difference, but you will be amazed at how much it does. Try it.

Coats

Many hunters prefer a full hunting-style coat that may be long (finger-tip-length) or short (waist-length). I have the same problem with hunting coats that I have with suit coats and dress-uniform coats. When I get a size that fits me in the shoulders

Ty Green, the author's Iowa hunting buddy, prefers a full coat.

and is loose enough to swing a gun, the sleeves stop about 4 inches past my hands and there is so much extra material around the waist that I could make another coat with the excess. This excess material is needed to carry game in the game pocket inside the coat. A couple of pheasants in a game bag will put a weight on your shoulders and a strain on your swing and follow-through. The same problems are found with the sleeveless vests also. If the vest or coat isn't loose enough for this, it may actually prevent you from even getting your gun up.

Several years ago a friend of mine bought a high-dollar coat made under a licensing contract with a well-known gunmaker. My friend is tall and thin, and he thought that one size larger than his normal coat size would work well. It did in the store. Out in the field, we discovered the entry into the game pouch was so small that the only way to get a pheasant in it was to take the coat completely off and work the bird into the game pocket. Then, when he put the coat back on, he found that the pheasant in the game pocket put so much strain on the shoulders of his now-too-tight coat that he couldn't even bring his gun up. He still has the coat, but now he calls it his conservation coat because when he is wearing it, he is limited to six quail or ten doves. Any more than that and the coat starts to bind.

Danny Swoap prefers to wear a sleeveless vest over layered clothing.

Vests

For years I wore a sleeveless-style vest, and I still have a couple in the closet that I wear on occasion. The problem I found with these is that you often have the same binding that occurs with a coat and the shell loops seldom hold the shells securely. The pockets seldom have any type of closure system, which makes them impractical for carrying gear such as cameras, transmitters, phones, walkie-talkies, etc. After switching to a strap-style vest, a friend of mine calls these sleeveless vests No. 6 vests. They are like No. 6 shot; they may not be the best for your hunting situation, but millions of them are sold every year.

My preference is a strap-style vest. There are several advantages to this type of vest. First is that the straps do not bind your arms and shoulder while swinging a gun. Many of these vests have also included a waist belt that assists in bearing the load, which takes more strain off the shoulders and helps with gun mobility. During the course of a season, I may hunt in temperatures from below zero to 80 degrees. With the strap-style vest, I can dress appropriately and don the vest over my other clothing. This way I can keep my vest organized, and I know which pocket everything is in and don't have to be like a woman switching purses when going from coat to vest and back to coat. I have even gotten to the point where I have a different vest for each gauge, so that I don't even have to switch when changing guns.

A number of different companies make these strap-style vests. I
have used almost all of them and
my favorites are the Bird'n'Lite
Upland Strap Vest made by Pella
and the Open Prairie made by Orvis.
Cabela's also offers their Ultimate
strap vest, which I have used and
recommend. All of these vests have
large enough game bags to carry
two or more pheasants. Even more
important, the game bags are accessible with entries that don't require
you to lay your gun down and take
the vest off to place a bird in it.

What I really like about this
style of vests is the extra pockets. I
can carry shells in the shell pockets
and other gear in the other pockets.
I usually have a camera, water, and
some other items in my pockets, and
they can be carried so I do not have
to reach around them while trying
to get shells to reload! With the Velcro or spring steel closures, I can
carry shells loose in the shell pockets
and not worry about them falling
out when crossing fences or doing
the other contortions you sometimes
need to do in the field. Since most
also have shell loops inside the

*A Cabela's strap vest, an A.H. Fox 16 gauge,
and a successful pheasant hunt.*

pockets, I can carry different loads. I will often carry my pheasant shells loose
in the pocket and a few rounds of No. $7\frac{1}{2}$ or No. 8 shot for quail in the shell
loops. Since I often hunt areas where several species can be found, I do this
quite often.

Hats

I have mentioned before my internal furnace that keeps me very warm. It is
well into winter before I quit wearing a mesh-style ball cap or a mesh-style
hunting hat. In wet weather, I prefer a crush-style hat that will keep rain off my
glasses and still keep my head relatively dry.

Safety Gear

Whatever style of vest, coat, or hat you wear, please have it in blaze orange. There is no reason to be wearing full camouflage while upland bird hunting, but I see hunters doing it every year. As I am writing this, there is still a buzz in the news media about Vice President Dick Cheney accidentally shooting a hunting partner while quail hunting. Having been involved in hunter education, I know how just one incident like this gives stockpiles of ammunition to the anti-gun and anti-hunting factions. Be visible; wear orange!

There are several other safety articles that should *always* be worn. First is a good pair of shooting glasses. I'm not talking about the sunglasses you got at the drugstore, but a good pair of glasses that will protect your eyes. I have worn prescription glasses for almost fifty years. I spend the extra money to buy shatterproof safety lenses and have several different tints for different light and cover conditions. I have never had to test these against shot pellets, but they have saved my eyes from numerous branches, briars, and even tree limbs over the years.

Another expensive but essential item of gear is a good set of electronic ear protectors or earplugs. I have a total hearing loss of almost 50 percent and have over a 60-percent loss in my left ear. There are hearing protectors on the market today that cut out the damaging noise of gunfire but increase your hearing at normal levels. I have to wear these just to be able to hear at even a reduced normal level in the field. They enable me to hear bird flushes and calls that I cannot hear with my gunfire-damaged ears. They also saved me from being bitten by a rattlesnake on several occasions since I cannot hear a snake with my normal hearing.

Even one shot fired from a shotgun or any firearm can damage your hearing. These are expensive, costing from about $150 for the muff type up to almost $1,000 dollars for the custom made-in-your-ear models. They are well worth the price to protect your hearing. Hearing loss is gradual, and you don't notice it is gone until it is too late. At that point, nothing can be done to improve it. Even with the advancements in hearing-aid technology over the last few years, there is still not a hearing aid out there that will restore the damage in the frequency range that gunfire affects. Please purchase and wear hearing protection, even while hunting.

Gloves

Another essential item for me is a good pair of shooting gloves. I started wearing shooting gloves years ago as a street cop and got very used to wearing them while hunting. They protect my hands from our entire local fauna with all of its stickers and thorns and also give me better control of the gun. I usually use a high-quality shooter's glove on both hands. There is a great glove

A pair of quality shooting gloves, such as these from GripsWell, will protect your hands from the elements and improve gun handling in the field. GRIPSWELL

for shotgunners and other shooters called the GripSwell. With a built-in padded grip swell on the strong hand, they are made in both right- and left-hand models. The control you achieve with these is absolutely amazing. As your gun is coming up, you instantly know if your hand is properly positioned for good grip and trigger control. These gloves give you built-in muscle memory. They also reduce the shock of the gun firing and recoil fatigue in the wrist. Shoot a hundred rounds on the skeet field with these on and then fifty rounds without them and you will see what I mean.

How important are gloves? Last year on the second day of dove season, I had taken my gloves off back at the truck before I checked my Brittanies for stickers and thorns. While running my hands along one of the dogs, I encountered a little sand burr. It jammed just under my nail on the index (trigger) finger of my right hand. I didn't get the entire spine out and it swelled up and got infected, making me shoot with an awkward middle-finger trigger pull for several weeks. I also had to type with one less finger, which really slowed down my already pitiful words-per-minute rate. It is six months later, and I still have an area of scar tissue where that tiny sand burr spine was! The gloves I use are thin enough, even in the insulated styles, that I can manipulate the safety and load and unload my gun safely. Some heavier gloves can create problems with your gun. They may be too thick to manipulate the safety or even fit in the trigger guard. I was hunting with a friend in very cold weather who was using a double-trigger side-by-side. He was wearing thick insulated gloves. His first rooster of the day was hit at about 20 yards with 2 ½ ounces of No. 5 shot because when he pulled the front trigger, his thick glove also tripped the rear trigger, causing the gun to double. We had three different dogs busy retrieving pieces of that bird!

OTHER GEAR

There are some other items that I consider essential. They may not improve your shooting, but they will be worth the effort. First is a good pocket camera. I carry a small one in my vest, and it has enabled me to record my daughter's first pheasant, many first points and retrieves by my dogs and the dogs of companions, and numerous other photo opportunities that have presented themselves. There are hundreds of cameras to choose from in various formats and styles; just don't forget to bring yours along. You will be surprised at how often you use it.

Have you ever looked at an invention and thought: "Why didn't I think of that?" Several years ago, Jeff, my hunting buddy, found a great little tool known as the T-Post Stepper. This wonderful invention enables you to easily cross any barbwire fence supported by T-posts. I always have one in the pocket of my upland vest since I am as graceful crossing fences as a pig on ice skates. These also make great gifts to farmers for being allowed to hunt on their land.

Jeff McVay demonstrates how well the T-Post Stepper works.

A good topographic map of the area you are hunting is a worthwhile investment. You can use it to mark areas of interest and combine it with a compass or a GPS unit to save yourself a lot of wandering. A GPS unit can be a lifesaver when hunting in unfamiliar terrain. There are many different styles and types on the market. Get one that fits your needs and your budget.

Upland hunters seldom think about carrying a first aid kit, but it can be a very important piece of equipment for you, your hunting companions, and your dogs. I have used mine to stop the bleeding on deep cuts on people and dogs and to wrap a sprained ankle or even to brace a broken leg. As an old EMT, I carry a homemade kit that I can use on either a person or a dog. I have more extensive kits that include suture materials back in my vehicle. Several companies make first aid kits for both people and dogs. Check out the different ones available and get one that matches your level of expertise. I hunt with a couple of vets and surgeons on a regular basis. The vets actually have more experience in emergency medicine than the surgeons do. It has a lot to do with the areas that I hunt, but two other essential pieces of gear I carry are good surgical forceps and tweezers. These are great for removing cactus spines, stickers, and mesquite thorns from myself, my hunting companions, and the dogs.

Of course, if you take any type of prescription medication, you should carry some with you. You should also make your hunting companions aware of any severe medical conditions and what to do if you experience an attack. I have several hunting friends who have heart conditions and carry medication with them all of the time. They also make sure their companions know how to administer the drugs in an emergency. I have severe anaphylactic reaction to insect stings and carry an anaphylactic kit in my vest and another in my truck. When hunting in hot weather when insect stings are possible, I make sure my companions know where the kits are since I have a less than five-minute window between a wasp sting and death.

Years of experience have taught me that these items are as essential to my hunting as my dogs, guns, and shells. They can add to the enjoyment, safety, and experience of your hunt.

16 Passing on the Heritage

The wildlife of today is not ours to do with as we please. The original stock was given to us in trust for the benefit both of the present and the future. We must render an accounting of this trust to those who come after us.

—Theodore Roosevelt, 1900

In today's fluid and affluent society, hunters have both the means and ability to take game of different types and in different locations. Hunters can travel throughout the United States and many other countries. There are hunts available today that were only accessible to the very wealthy just a generation ago.

As a kid growing up in the 1950s and 1960s, I remember the trips that my uncles would take to South Dakota from our home in Indiana. These trips were as exotic to a youngster as a trip to Africa would have been. While I was a teenager, my understanding father took me on bird hunting trips throughout the United States. As an adult, even on a police officer's salary, I have been able to hunt in different states and areas for game that I thought I would never even see, yet alone be able to hunt. I have been fortunate to take every type of

Heading out in the field with a favorite over-and-under and a trusted Brittany—a legacy that all hunters should work to pass on to future generations. BERETTA U.S.A.

game bird available in the continental United States with the one exception of California or valley quail.

I have not ventured to Canada or Alaska for ptarmigan, but a chance encounter during a pheasant-hunting trip will soon be correcting that. Chatting with another hunter while cleaning our day's limits in Iowa brought about an offer to visit him in Alaska for a combination ptarmigan-fishing trip. He is an officer in the U.S. Army and has been stationed there for the last ten years. Now, I may have to get some advice about what type of fishing tackle to take, but I know that I will have the right gun and loads for these birds.

I was fortunate to grow up where and when I did. Although I grew up in a city, there were numerous opportunities for me to go hunting. My parents had relatives that lived on farms, and for a number of years, we lived on the last street in the city limits. Acres of farmland with a variety of game were just a short walk away. In those days, a kid could walk down the street carrying a shotgun accompanied by his dog and not have a SWAT team responding to his location. I think you had to be twelve before you needed a hunting license, and if there was a requirement for an adult to be present, I never knew about it. Many were the days I came home from school and grabbed a shotgun. Accompanied by Pearlie, our mostly-rat-terrier mutt, I took off for the croplands, creeks, and woods just a mile or so away.

I was also fortunate that my father, uncles, and grandfather took me along on hunting trips with their friends. It was a great experience for a kid to be welcomed into a man's world of hunting. There weren't the requirements for hunter education in those days, but my mentors, especially my father, made sure I knew and obeyed all of the firearms safety rules and procedures.

It happened almost fifty years ago, but I still vividly remember one incident. I was six and was allowed to carry an unloaded single shot .22 while tagging along with my father, uncle, and older brother on an upland hunt. I let the muzzle of the unloaded .22 point at my brother while I was walking along. My father's reaction was swift and immediate. It was also, in my opinion, cruel and unusual punishment. The .22 was immediately taken away, and I was walked back to the car where the .22 was locked in the trunk. I was left to stand (I couldn't sit for obvious reasons) outside the car and ponder my actions for the next hour or so. I was also not allowed to carry a gun for the rest of the day.

I was taught other things besides gun handling and safety. Men who lived on and with the land taught me about the land and the animals. I was taught the tracks, signs, and habits of birds and animals. They introduced me to the unique love relationship between a hunting man and the dogs with which he shares his hunts. I was taught respect for the game, the landowner, all adults, and the land itself. I learned the reason for laws is that people often don't know how to behave and be respectful because they have never learned or they have forgotten how. During a thirty-year career in law enforcement, I learned how true that was! I was also taught that a man's word is unbreakable and that a handshake seals an agreement much better than a team of lawyers and a lengthy contract will ever do.

Among my friends and hunting companions are several that grew up in the same era and type of environment that I did. There are others who were not exposed to hunting until they were adults. Without exception, I have found that my friends who were taught to hunt as youngsters are more ethical and less likely to have to think about doing something they know is wrong. The others have a less-defined set of ethics and definition of right and wrong.

Jim and Garret Irwin after a successful Texas pheasant hunt.

As an adult, I have been active as a hunter education instructor and have also had the opportunity to expose many young and not-so-young people to hunting and shooting for the first time. It is very hard to teach a lifetime of learned lessons in a ten-hour class or a few hunting trips. I try very hard to do so since this is the heritage I was given, and I want to pass it on.

There is no quicker way to alienate new shooters, either young or old, than to give them too much gun too early. I live in a city that has a large university and many of my students are college-aged young ladies who want to learn how to shoot. Too often I hear from them that their one experience with a shotgun was a boyfriend, father, or brother giving them a 12 gauge with a heavy field load. With no ear or eye protection and very minimal instruction, they take one shot and are immediately turned off. For some reason, the males involved think this is funny, when, in fact, it is really quite tragic. They have taken a potential supporter of our sports and turned her against guns by reinforcing many of her fears and suspicions.

I prefer to introduce a new person to shooting on a skeet field with no one else around. I like to have no more than two students, since this enables me to work with both of them individually and to give them a chance to watch the other while I am teaching techniques and gun handling. I prefer to use a gas-operated semi-auto shotgun to help reduce the felt recoil. The shooter will only be firing one round at a time, and a semi-auto is the simplest for them to operate. Many instructors prefer a 20 gauge, but I have found that many 20s have too much felt recoil for beginning shooters, especially women and youngsters. I prefer to use a 28 gauge or a 12 gauge with very light loads. My personal skeet-practice loads use only $7/8$ ounces of shot at 1,200 fps velocity. These are very pleasant to shoot and make a great training round. Mine are reloads, but several makers offer these loads in factory-loaded ammunition.

Before the first round of ammo is ever fired, we spend time on safety and gun handling. I let the new shooter get used to the weight and balance of the gun and get comfortable with handling it. Many people have been raised in an environment that has caused them to be scared of guns, and giving them the chance to handle and become familiar with one helps to over come this phobia. I stress that a gun is only a piece of machinery and is no more dangerous than any other piece of machinery, but it does command respect and awareness just as driving a car does.

Some new shooters take to this immediately and become comfortable with the gun quickly. Others need more time to overcome their fears. It is important for the instructor to realize this and to encourage the students to talk about their feelings while they are handling the guns. During this time, they are also being told of the safety rules of handling a weapon and are gently reminded if they violate one of these. The instructor should always remember that the student's frame of mind affects how well they listen and perform. I have had students who never fired a shot at their first session because they needed more time to just become comfortable with the gun and to overcome their fears. While they are getting comfortable handling guns, I also introduce them to the clay targets that we will be using as targets. I show them how easily one breaks and discuss the shot charge and how the pellets strike the target.

Only when students feel that they are ready do we go out onto the skeet field. I start new shooters at station seven shooting low-house targets. Eye and ear protection is mandatory. I show the students how to stand, and then throw several targets for them to track with an unloaded gun. I usually have the student stand to one side and watch the gun while I shoot a target. I have them

Training a new shooter—a young lady learns shotgun skills on the skeet field.

watch the gun to see how little it recoils and to get them used to the muzzle blast. I then have them stand behind me and watch the gun in relation to the target. It is very embarrassing when the instructor misses a target at this point, but it does happen. I usually use this as a point of encouragement to the new shooter. They shouldn't worry about missing a target since all of us do so at one time or another. If you can pull off acting like you missed on purpose, all the better.

I do something else that is rather unusual. On the guns I use for training, I remove the front sight for the first few lessons. This enables the student to focus only on the target and removes a distraction of trying to aim at the target. Later, after the student becomes more confident, the front sight is introduced and the concept of the barrel in relation to the target at different ranges and angles is discussed. Interestingly, about half of the students discover that they can shoot better without a front sight and continue to shoot without one.

One shell is loaded into the student's gun, and he or she shoots the low-house station seven target. After the student has hit this target four or five times, I demonstrate a high-house target and have them track it with an unloaded gun. When they tell me they are ready to try a shot, the gun is loaded and they try for the high-house target. Most new shooters hit this target the first time.

By this point, they have been concentrating on the target, and most don't even realize when the gun has gone off. The light recoil and the attention paid to the target have overcome their fear of the gun and they start having fun.

After they have hit the incoming high-house target a few times, we move to station one. I start them here with the low-house target since this is an incoming target very similar to the high-house station seven target they have just shot. After they have hit it a few times, we switch to the high-house station one target.

By the time they have shot this target a few times, we have usually gone through a box of shells. At this point, we call it a day. I have found that students usually aren't recoil shy. Often, however, they have been using some muscles in a different way, and if they become fatigued and start missing, the shooting ceases to be fun. This is a key point: shooting should be fun and exciting to the new shooter, either young or old.

The next time out I take the new shooter around the skeet field, throwing single targets at each station until they start hitting on a regular basis. This does not take as long as many would think. The last two young ladies I taught to shoot were breaking birds at each station, and when we shot a regular round of skeet, they broke thirteen and fifteen, respectively. Of course, by this time, they are usually hooked and wanting to know when they can come shooting again.

Introducing a new shooter to live birds is very similar to introducing a bird dog pup to live birds. You need lots and lots of birds. Unfortunately, there aren't many places available where you can go and introduce the new shooter to lots and lots of wild birds. So, you do the same thing that a dog trainer does with a new pup; you go to a preserve. There are hunting preserves throughout the United States. Many are multi-purpose locations that offer clay-target games in addition to hunting planted birds. This is a great way to introduce a new shooter. He or she can spend a day doing a lot of shooting on both clay and feathered birds.

Sometimes you take Dad hunting—David Guinn Sr. and Jr. after a full day of pheasant hunting.

Most preserves offer quail, pheasant, and chukar, and you can use your dogs or have a guide and dogs available. Although I get to hunt wild birds for six months of the year, I spend a couple of days each year at a preserve. I use the planted birds for tune-up training on my dogs and since I am working as dog handler, I try to include a new shooter or two as my companions for the day. The nice thing about preserve birds is that the shooter can usually use a lighter gun and loads than are used for wild birds.

I would recommend starting the new shooter on chukar partridges. The pen-raised chukars will hold tight and flush close, giving the new shooter a close shot. When combined with a gun with light loads and an open choke, the new shooter does not even notice the recoil. After a morning of chukars, take them out into the pheasant field and let them shoot a few roosters. At most preserves, this will cost about $200 per gun for the day. This may seem like a lot, but it is money well spent. The new shooter gets to use their skills on live birds and in a

Sometimes Mom is the hunter—Drue and Caitlin Farmer with Caitlin's first pigeon.

relatively easy environment where they don't get tired or discouraged tromping empty field after empty field. Just as with a bird dog pup, the new shooter is exposed to more birds in one day on a preserve than in several weeks of hunting wild birds.

Some may wonder why I keep comparing new shooters to bird dog pups. The comparison is valid and simple. The more birds I can get in front of a pup's nose the more I can keep the pup interested in birds and work on its skills. The same is true with the new shooter. The more birds I can get a new shooter into the more interested they will be in bird hunting and the better their skills will be. A young friend of mine gave a day of hunting at a preserve to his girlfriend for a birthday present. At first she was not very happy with his gift choice, but after spending a day shooting live and clay birds, she now gushes about how it was the best birthday present he had ever given her.

Her Christmas present that year was a new shotgun. The Christmas present she bought for her boyfriend was also a new shotgun. Now one of the things they enjoy doing together is clay- and live-bird shooting. She went from tolerating his shooting and hunting to being an active participant in his favorite sports. I think she was as excited about the new shotgun as she was about the engagement ring she also got for Christmas.

This is exactly the kind of enthusiasm we need to cultivate in a new generation of shooters. The more new people we can get active in our sport the more our sport will become accepted among the general public and defeat the media focus on the negative side of gun use. The various sporting-clay games have been great for our chosen sports. Many people who just a few years ago were indifferent towards guns are now active participants in the shooting sports.

I know if you have read this far in the book that I am preaching to the choir, but we need to get more and more people involved in the shooting sports. So when you take your new shotgun out to the clays range to practice, ask a non-shooting friend along. I have made many shooting and hunting buddies by doing this over the years.

I was fortunate in having a father, grandfather, and uncles who loved hunting and shooting sports enough to pass on the heritage to me. We should all appreciate this and take advantage of every opportunity to pass the heritage on to others.

"How's that look, Grandpa?" The author's grandson, Lance, after he arranged the shells during a photo shoot.

Manufacturers

GUNS

Austin & Halleck
15556 Shadow Creek Road
Maple Grove, MN 55311
763-494-9844
www.austinhalleck.com
    Austin Halleck makes a modern black-powder muzzleloading upland shotgun.

Benelli USA
17603 Indian Head Highway
Accokeek, MD 20607
301-283-6981
www.benelliusa.com
    Benelli manufacturers a line of pump and semi-auto shotguns.

Beretta USA
17601 Beretta Dr.
Accokeek, MD 20607
800-636-3420
www.berettausa.com
    Beretta manufactures a line of semi-auto, over-and-under, and side-by-side shotguns.

Browning Arms Co.
One Browning Place
Morgan, UT 84050
800-333-3288
www.browning.com
    Browning manufacturers semi-auto, pump, and over-and-under shotguns.

Charles Daly
P.O. Box 6625
Harrisburg, PA 17112
866-325-9486
www.charlesdaly.com
    Charles Daly imports a line of semi-auto, pump, over-and-under, and side-by-side shotguns.

CZ-USA
P.O. Box 17103
Kansas City, KS 66117
800-955-4486
www.cz-usa.com
    CZ-USA imports the Huglu line of shotguns with semi-auto, pump, over-and-under, and side-by-side models available.

Franchi
    Franchi guns can be viewed on the Benelli USA website.

Maverick Arms
    Maverick shotguns are made by Mossberg.

The Marlin Firearms Co.
100 Kenna Dr.
P.O. Box 248
North Haven, CT 06473
203-239-5621
www.marlinfirearms.com
    Marlin imports the L. C. Smith line of side-by-side and over-and-under shotguns.

O. F. Mossberg & Sons, Inc.
7 Grasso Ave.
North Haven, CT 06473
203-230-5300
www.mossberg.com
    Mossberg makes a complete line of pump, semi-auto, and over-and-under shotguns.

Remington Arms Co.
P.O. Box 700
870 Remington Dr.
Madison, NC 27025
800-243-9700
www.remington.com
    Remington manufactures pump, semi-auto, and over-and-under shotguns. They also import the Spartan line of side-by-side and over-and-under shotguns.

Rizzini USA
P.O. Box 199
Harpswell, ME 04079
866-833-5276
www.rizziniusa.com
    Rizzini USA imports a line of over-and-under and side-by-side shotguns.

Savage Arms
118 Mountain Road
Suffield, CT 06078
866-312-4120
www.savagearms.com
    Savage is importing a line of over-and-unders in 12, 20, 28, and 410 gauges.

SKB Shotguns
4325 S. 120th St.
Omaha, NE 68137
402-330-4492
www.skbshotguns.com
    SKB makes a line of over-and-under shotguns.

Sturm Ruger & Co.
200 Ruger Rd.
Prescott, AZ 86301
928-541-8820
www.ruger.com
    Ruger makes the Red Label line of over-and-under shotguns and the Gold Label side-by-side shotgun.

Traditions Firearms
P.O. Box 776
1375 Boston Post Rd.
Old Saybrook, CT 06475
860-388-4656
www.traditionsfirearms.com
    Traditions imports a complete line of affordable shotguns.

TriStar Sporting Arms LTD
1814 Linn St.
N. Kansas City, MO 64116
816-421-1400
www.tristarsportingarms.com
    TriStar imports an extensive line of over-and-under, side-by-side, and semi-auto shotguns.

Verona Shotguns
B.C. Outdoors
P.O. Box 62508
12801 US 95 South
Boulder City, NV 89005
702-294-0025
www.pmcammo.com
    Verona makes a large line of affordable shotguns.

Weatherby
3100 El Camino Real
Atascadero, CA 93422
805-466-1767
www.weatherby.com
    Weatherby makes a line of over-and-under and side-by-side shotguns.

Winchester/U.S. Repeating Arms
275 Winchester Ave.
Morgan, UT 85050
800-333-3504
www.winchesterguns.com
   Winchester makes pump, semi-auto, and over-and-under shotguns.

AMMUNITION

ARMUSA Performance
227 Bridge Crest Blvd.
Houston, TX 77082
281-381-7773
www.armusa-performance.com
   ARMUSA has a full line of hunting and target ammunition, including shells for guns with $2\frac{1}{2}$-inch chambers.

B&P
1241 Ellis St.
Bensenville, IL 60106
630-350-1116
www.bandpusa.com
   B&P offers a complete line of hunting, target, and nontoxic ammunition.

Bismuth Cartridge Co.
7155 Valjean Ave.
Van Nuys, CA 91406
800-759-3333
www.bismuth-notox.com
   Bismuth offers an extensive line of nontoxic ammunition.

Estate Cartridge Co.
900 Ehlen Dr.
Anoka, MN 55303
800-322-2342
www.estatecartridge.com
   Estate offers a full line of target and hunting ammunition loaded with either lead or steel. Estate is now owned by Federal.

Federal Premium Ammunition
900 Ehlen Dr.
Anoka, MN 55303
800-322-2342
www.federalpremium.com
   Federal is one of the "Big Three" shotgun ammunition manufacturers in the United States. They offer a complete line of target, hunting, and premium ammunition.

Fiocchi of America, Inc.
6930 Fremont Rd.
Ozark, MO 65721
417-725-4118
www.fiochiusa.com
   Fiocchi offers a full line of lead and steel ammunition for target shooting and hunting.

Hevi-Shot (Environ Metal Inc.)
P.O. Box 834
1307 Clark Mill Road
Sweet Home, OR 97386
www.hevishot.com
   Hevi-Shot offers a superior line of nontoxic ammunition for hunting.

Kent Cartridge Co.
P.O. Box 849
727 Hite Rd
Kearneysville, WV 25430
888-311-5368
www.kentgamebore.com
   Kent offers a complete line of shotshells with both American and English loadings.

Olympia USA
3619 Cantrell Industrial Highway # 100
Acworth, GA 30101
770-966-0600
www.olympia-cartidges.com
   Olympia USA specializes in target loads but also offers a selection of hunting loads.

PMC Ammunition
P.O. Box 62508
12801 US 95 South
Boulder City, NV 89005
702-294-0025
www.pmcammo.com
PMC offers a complete line of target and hunting ammunition.

Polywad Shotgun Shell
P.O. Box 7916
Macon, GA 31209
800-998-0669
www.polywad-shotgun-shells.com
Polywad offers some unique custom ammunition not available from other companies.

Remington Arms Company, Inc.
P.O. Box 700
870 Remington Drive
Madison , NC 27025
800-243-9700
www.remington.com
Remington is one of the largest makers of shotgun ammunition in the world.

Rio Ammunition
2650 Fountainview #207
Houston, TX 77057
www.rioammo.com
Rio offers a complete line of target and hunting ammunition.

Winchester Ammunition
427 North Shamrock
East Alton, IL 62024
www.winchester.com
Winchester is famous for their AA and Super-X product lines.

Wolf Performance Ammunition
1225 North Lance Lane
Anaheim, CA 92806
888-757-WOLF (9653)
www.wolfammo.com
Wolf offers high-quality, reasonably priced target and hunting ammunition.

CHOKES AND CHOKE TUBES

Ballistic Specialties
P.O. Box 2401
100 Industrial Dr.
Batesville, AR 72501
www.angleport.com
Ballistic Specialties offers a full line of chokes and barrel modifications.

Briley
1230 Lumpkin
Houston, TX 77043
800-331-5718
www.Briley.com
Briley offers choke tubes, tube sets, and a full line of barrel modifications.

Carlson's Choke Tubes
P.O. Box 162
Atwood, KS 67730
785-626-3700
www.choketube.com
Carlson's offers a full line of replacement choke tubes and also installation services.

Colonial Arms, Inc.
P.O. Box 636
1109 C Singleton Dr.
Selma, AL 36702
www.colonialarms.com
Colonial Arms offers a full line of replacement tubes and installation services.

Patternmaster
6431 North Taos Rd.
Scott City, KS 67871
620-872-3022
www.patternmaster.com
Patternmaster offers aftermarket choke tubes.

Seminole Chokes and Gunworks
Mitchell Machine & Manufacturing Inc.
3049 US # 1
Mims, FL 32754
www.seminolegun.com
    Seminole offers a full line of choke
tubes, tube sets, and gauge reducers.

Teague Precision Chokes
Edinburghway
Leafiled Industrial Estate
Corsham, Wiltshire
SN13 9XZ United Kingdom
    Teague makes a line of aftermarket
chokes.

Trulock Chokes
P.O. Box 530
113 Drayton St.
Whigham, GA 39897
800-293-9402
    Trulock Chokes offers an extensive line
of aftermarket chokes for a number of different guns.

MISCELLANEOUS
Here are the names and addresses of some
of the makers of products mentioned in the
book.

Lobo Products, LLC
2800 Coltrane Place, Suite 3
Edmond, OK 73034
800-719-2856
www.tpoststepper.com
    The maker of the T-Post Stepper. The
best way there is to cross a barbed-wire
fence.

Pella Outdoor Clothing
Pella Products, Inc.
835 Broadway / P.O. Box 324
Pella, IA 50219
800-832-6225
www.pellaproducts.com
    Makers of the Bird'n'Lite vests and
jackets.

Orvis
888-235-9763
www.orvis.com
    Makers of fine upland hunting cloth-
ing and gear.

Kick Eez
417-649-2100
www.kickeez.net
    Makers of the Kick Eez line of recoil
pads.

Sims Vibration Laboratory
877-257-2761
www.limbsaver.com
    Makers of the Limbsaver line of recoil
pads.

    There are many other companies out
there that make fine products related to
hunting and shooting. I would suggest you
pick up a copy of *Black's Wing & Clay* at
your local bookstore or from Black's Sporting Directories, 200 Croft Place, Suite 1,
Birmingham, AL 35242, phone: 1-800-260-
7323. I use this excellent reference book all
of the time, and it is a worthy addition to
any hunter or shooter's library.
    Good hunting!

Index